THE QUINTESSENCE OF CAPITALISM

THE QUINTESSENCE
OF CAPITALISM

A STUDY OF THE HISTORY
AND PSYCHOLOGY OF THE
MODERN BUSINESS MAN

By WERNER SOMBART

TRANSLATED AND EDITED BY
M. EPSTEIN

NEW YORK
Howard Fertig
1967

First published in 1915

Howard Fertig, Inc. edition 1967

Published by special arrangement with
E. P. Dutton & Co., Inc. (New York) and
Ernest Benn Limited (London)

Library of Congress Catalog Card Number: 67-13645

PRINTED IN THE UNITED STATES OF AMERICA
BY NOBLE OFFSET PRINTERS, INC.

CONTENTS

BOOK I

THE DEVELOPMENT OF THE CAPITALIST SPIRIT

SECTION I

THE SPIRIT OF ENTERPRISE

6 *CONTENTS*

SECTION IV

THE BOURGEOIS—PAST AND PRESENT

BOOK II

×THE ORIGINS OF THE CAPITALIST SPIRIT

SECTION I

THE BIOLOGICAL FOUNDATIONS

SECTION II

MORAL FORCES

TRANSLATOR'S INTRODUCTION

THIS is the Book of the Modern Business Man. Never before has an attempt been made to describe him in detail or to discover when he was born. Recent novels, such as Mr. H. G. Wells's *Wife of Sir Isaac Harman*, have depicted his activities and suggested the mental traits that governed them. Certain well-known caricatures have no doubt succeeded in giving his supposed outward appearance a measure of permanence. But a balanced and scientific analysis we have not hitherto had until the author of this book gave us the results of his researches into history and psychology.

The book is no dull treatise.* It presents a living picture, the work of a scholar who is also a literary man and æsthete, whose nature (to use his own terminology) is a seigniorial one (see p. 205), who is a dreamer and an artist, "many coloured in all he says and does."

The history of the modern business man is interesting enough. He is a comparative newcomer in modern life. A moment's thought will show that economic activities through the ages, while springing from one unchangeable need—human wants—have not always had the same end. Man goeth forth unto his work—in order to produce what he requires. In a broad way this statement sums up the economic history of mankind. But only in a broad way. Economic history plainly shows that the

* [See the review of the original by the present writer in the *Economic Journal* for September 1914, p. 403.]

thing was done variously in different ages, and differently among different peoples even in one and the same age. The mediæval craftsman, for example, went about his business in a different way from the modern American captain of industry. Their ideals were dissimilar, so was their outlook, despite the fact that both produced in order to satisfy human wants. What is apparent here is equally manifest if we look at life as a whole. Though human nature is human nature, the same to-day and for ever, though the fundamentals of life have always remained constant—birth and death, love and hate, honour and treason, truth and falsehood, hunger and thirst, riches and poverty—yet the panorama of human life has taken on manifold aspects in successive ages. To account for these varying results we speak of a distinctive spirit in each. The mediæval spirit, for example, was nothing like that of modern times. So in man's efforts to satisfy his wants. A different spirit actuated him at different periods. It may be difficult to realize this all at once. It may seem, for instance, that profit-making, in which the great majority of business men to-day is engaged, is surely as old as the hills. In a measure this is true. But it must be remembered that differences in degree may be so great as to be virtually differences in kind. After all, the diversity between a giant and a dwarf, between heat and cold, between age and youth, between a thickly-peopled and a sparse settlement, between large and small towns, between " forte " and " piano," is merely one of degree. Yet will anyone assert that these things are the same ?

In every age, therefore, human activities that had reference to wealth were directed, first, by certain ideals, that is to say, certain desires of the mind ; and, secondly, by certain given external circumstances. The latter may be compared to the body, the former to the soul. Now the expressions of the soul that are brought to bear on the everyday business of life are all included when we speak of some economic spirit—say, the capitalist spirit.

This book will consider the different economic spirits that were influential at various periods of European history, and inquire into the origins of the capitalist spirit which practically alone sways our economic activities to-day. It will show that during the history of Europe, from the appearance of the Germans, Slavs, and Celts to our own time, the economic outlook has changed root and branch. Capitalism has succeeded that for which no good term is available ; let us call it pre-capitalism. This modern capitalist spirit, beginning in the early Middle Ages, was something new in the history of Europe. But it does not follow that a similar economic spirit may not have been operative in the ancient world, nor yet that this spirit, if it existed, was not one of the contributory forces that produced modern capitalism. Be that as it may, this book will provide a clear and interesting analysis of an expression which is to-day perhaps more used and less understood than any other—capitalism.

A few notes have been appended in the hope that they may help to a better understanding of the book. These, as all other additions by the Translator, are in square brackets.

It only remains for me to express my best thanks to my wife for many valuable suggestions in the final revision of the work.

M. E.

London, *June* 1, 1915.

CHAPTER I

THE PRE-CAPITALIST ECONOMIC OUTLOOK

THE pre-capitalist man was a natural man, man as God made him, man who did not stand on his head or run on all fours (as is the case to-day in economic activities). The pre-capitalist man stood firmly on his two legs, by the aid of which alone he moved about. His economic outlook is therefore not difficult to ascertain ; it springs quite easily from human nature.

In that outlook man is the centre of all effort and all care ; man is the " meteyard of all things "—*mensura omnium rerum homo.* Consequently all economic activities take thought only of man's needs.[1] This principle is fundamental. Economic activities provide such commodities as will satisfy man's natural wants. The amount of commodities produced must equal the amount required for consumption ; a man's expenditure must balance his income. Indeed, the expenditure determines the income. An economic order of this kind may be properly termed an " expenditure system " ; and all pre-capitalist and pre-middle-class economies were " expenditure systems " in this use of the term.

Now man's needs were not settled by the mere caprice of the individual. Their measure and quality grew up in the process of time for each social group separately, and gradually became customary. Hence the idea of a sufficient livelihood for each class in accordance with its needs became the governing conception of all pre-capitalist economic activities. What experience had slowly evolved as needful, that received the approval of legal and moral authority, and came to be regarded as the norm. One of the fundamental teachings in the system of Thomas Aquinas was this conception of a sufficient livelihood. The relation between man and the world's goods requires, according to St. Thomas, some limiting influence, some canon or rule ; and it is to be found in his needs according to his station in life.[2] Consequently, every station or condition had its own standards, both of quality and of quantity. Broadly speaking, two groups soon appeared in the pre-capitalist system : the lords and the common people ; the rich and the poor ; the nobility and the peasants ; craftsmen and traders ; those who lived an untrammelled, independent life, doing no useful work, and those who earned their bread in the sweat of their brow.

And what was the lordly way of life ? To enjoy abundance and to employ others to work for you ; to spend your days in warlike undertakings and hunting in the wilds, and your nights in the revelry of a merry dicing throng or in the arms of beauteous ladies ; to build castles and churches ; to show off your fineries at tournaments or jousts ; to indulge in luxuries whether your means allowed or not. Expenditure always exceeded income, and therefore the latter had to be constantly increased. So the steward had perforce to augment the dues paid by the villagers, and the bailiff to raise the rents ; or else recourse was had (as we shall see presently) to other than economic methods in order to cover the deficit. In any case, your lordling despised gold ; he turned his nose up at filthy lucre, just as he regarded all economic activities as low and coarse. As Aquinas has it : *usus pecuniæ est in emissione ipsius.*[3]

Such was the life of the lords temporal ; such, too, for a considerable period, that of the lords spiritual. A picture which may be taken as typical of the lives of all the wealthy in the pre-capitalist age is the description by L. B. Alberti of the seigniorial existence of the clergy in Florence in the 14th century. " The clergy," he says, "desire to surpass all others in splendour and ostentation ; they wish to possess a great number of fine horses beautifully groomed, wish to appear in public with a large band of retainers ; from day to day their idleness grows apace and their conduct more impudently immoral. Although Fate has provided them with ample fortunes they are yet discontented with their lot, and without thought of economy or thrift, all their energies are devoted to discovering new means of gratifying their lusts. Their incomes are always too small for them ; their expenses are constantly on the increase. Thus they are ever on the alert to make good the deficit." 4

Is it not obvious that living on such lines as these must inevitably lead to ruin ? Indeed, history shows that numbers of families of ancient lineage in all lands have suffered economic shipwreck on account of their riotous living.

So much, then, for the one kind of life. What of the other, the life of the great mass of the people ? For these throughout the pre-capitalist age it was a dire necessity, seeing that the family incomes were never very large, to balance spending and earnings, wants and that which satisfied them. Of course, here too the norm of the wants was that of the social class, and was fixed by tradition. Consequently the idea of a sufficiency for existence slowly became paramount in all pre-capitalist economic legislation and organization.

For the origin of this idea we must turn to the youthful races who were cradled in the primeval forests of

Europe. They held that to each peasant family should be given just so much manorial land, so much plough land, so much of the common woods and pastures as would suffice to maintain it. The village communities of the Germanic tribes were the units incorporating this means of production ; but the conception was to be found also among the Celts and Slavs. In actual practice it meant that the quality and quantity of the economic activities of the individual household were determined by the quality and quantity of its needs. In a word, the whole object of economic activities was merely to satisfy certain given needs ; these activities were (in the terminology I have adopted) subject to the principle of a sufficiency for existence.

The peasant's conception of providing for his livelihood slowly crept into handicrafts, commerce, and intercourse, and ruled men's outlooks so long as these were organized as callings or mysteries. It was merely the organization of the village community applied to trade and industry ; the ideal of the village community and that of the gild were one and the same. Compare the two, and the similarity is striking. Both start out with the conception of limited and well-defined wants to be satisfied, and consequently can prescribe how much work may be done ; both direct their attention to a sufficiency for existence. The dominating thought of every craftsman was that his craft should provide him with sustenance in accordance with the needs of his station. He would work only so much as would yield him his living, for, like the manual labourer of Jena of whom Goethe speaks, he " had the healthy instinct not to produce more than was necessary to lead a jolly life." 5

What a sufficiency for existence was differed, and could not but differ, between individual and individual, between calling and calling, between the peasant and the craftsman. What was the peasant's ideal ? To establish himself as owner of his holding, and so himself provide for his own needs. But the craftsman was dependent on the sale of what he made, on the utilization of his services by others. The peasant must have a sufficiently large holding, the craftsman a sufficiently large clientele. But the underlying idea in both cases was the same. In a word, economic activities in the pre-capitalist period were regulated solely in accordance with the principle of a sufficiency for existence ; and peasant and crafts man looked to their economic activities to provide them with their livelihood and nothing more.

To understand the spirit that actuated the economic activities of the peasant and the craftsman, it is needful only to picture to ourselves what manner of men they were that did all the necessary work—directing, organizing, and carrying out—either by themselves or with the help of a few assistants. Were they other than simple, average folk, with strong passions and strong feelings, but with little intellectual development ? Small wonder that unclear thinking, no very distinctive mental energy, and weak intellectual discipline are all found among the people of those days, not only in the countryside, but also in the towns, which for centuries and more continued to be large organic villages. We meet the same folk with their limited intellectual outlook in other spheres too. As one writer cleverly remarked of the growth of law in the Middle Ages, " We notice in all the old laws a certain lack of mental nimbleness, due to the fact that they were formulated by men unused to clear thinking." [6] It is the same in the economic world. Take as an instance exact measurements. There was small comprehension of these ; and the handling of figures was very primitive. This applies even to traders. But, as a matter of fact, little stress was laid on the need of being exact.   To be exact, to make calculations balance, is something modern.   In all previous ages numerical statements were always only approximate.   Any one who is at all acquainted with calculations in the Middle Ages knows that if you check the columns the general thing is to find the totals quite incorrect.   Mistakes in arithmetic were common occurrences.7   So was careless usage of figures in calculating prices.8   But then to think of numbers, to retain them in the memory even for a brief minute, was difficult enough for the people of those days.   In that respect they were like children of to-day.

All these errors are clearly seen in the so-called book-keeping of the Middle Ages.   If you look through the books of a Tölner, a Viko von Geldersen, a Wittenborg, or an Ott Ruhland, you will find it exceedingly difficult to believe that the writers were great merchants in their generation.   All their calculations amount to this : they just note down the sums paid and received, without any attempt at order, much like the small country trader does to-day.   These documents can hardly be called "books"; they are merely rough jottings, taking the place of the knots in the kerchief made by the peasant going to market.   There is no conception of exact statement, nor any effort to make clear how much is owed or owing.   "Item, a box of gloves—but I do not know how much they were."   Or, "Item, one owes me 19 gulden . . . but his name I have forgotten."

If the quantitative aspect of commodities was thus neglected, the qualitative aspect was laid stress on.   In modern phrase, not values in exchange were made but only values in use.

As for work itself, for the peasant and the craftsman alike it was lonely, patient effort.   Man lost himself in his work.   He lived in it, as the artist does ; he loved it so, that he would much rather not have parted with his handiwork. When the dappled cow was led from the stables to the shambles, the old peasant woman's eyes were wet ; the potter strove hard not to be tempted by the trader's offers for his pipe. But if it had to be sold, then the commodity was to be worthy of its maker. The peasant, like the craftsman, had put something of himself into his product ; and in its making the rules of art were obeyed. Can we not understand, therefore, that the craft ideal looked with scorn on scamped work, and on the substitution of bad for good materials?

Moreover, economic activities moved at a slow pace, and every excuse was welcomed to cease from them. An occasion for holiday-making was seized upon with avidity, for men's attitude to work was like that of the schoolboy to his school : he goes because he must. There is not one sign of love for economic activities. Throughout the whole pre-capitalist period highdays and holydays were very numerous. A writer,9 dealing with the Bavarian mining industry in the 16th century, shows that, in one case, out of a total of 203 days only 123 were working days ; in another, out of 161 days 99 were working days ; in a third, out of 287 days 193 were working days.

In addition to this, work itself was slow. There was no occasion to finish a commodity in a short time or produce a great deal in any given space. Speed was regulated by two considerations. The first was the length of time needful to produce good and reliable commodities ; the second was the elementary require-ments of the worker himself. The work of production in the Middle Ages was a work for living, human beings, whose lives were devoted to it. Hence the laws govern-ing it were thoroughly natural, comparable to the growth of a tree or the singing of a bird. Here, as in all things relating to production, the rule was *mensura omnium rerum homo.*

Empiricism or, as it has recently been called, Traditionalism governed economic activities of the type described. Economic life was arranged traditionally; that is to say, as you were taught, as it was handed down from past generations, as you were accustomed to. In any rule or decision you did not look to the future, and ask what its result might be, or what purpose it would serve, but only to the past, to the models, to the accepted usages and experiences. Man in his natural state is always a traditionalist in this sense; and every civilization was in its earliest stages dominated by tradition because of reasons rooted in human nature and traceable ultimately to the strong tendency in the soul of man to remain stationary. From our very birth, possibly even before, we are forced into a certain groove by our environment; we accept unquestioningly all the teaching and instruction, the actions and feelings and prejudices of parents and teachers. " The less developed a human being is, the more subject is he to the power of example, tradition, authority, and suggestion." [10]

The influence of tradition is helped by habit, which inclines man to do that which he has already done, and therefore knows how to do. This likewise tends to keep him in the old grooves. Habit has been well defined [11] as will-power or desire engendered by experience. Ideas that were originally indifferent or unpleasant become pleasant by mere association and fusion with ideas that were originally pleasing. Experience is practice, and practice produces habit. Practice, at first difficult, become easy by repetition, and makes uncertain actions certain, trains particular organs and energy centres. Thus, man in his activities is more and more inclined to repeat what has become easy; in other words, to abide by what he has learned, unconcerned with, nay, hostile to, anything new. In a word, he becomes traditionalistic.

Another point must not be lost sight of. The individual is a member of a group, and in striving to be a worthy unit in the whole pays special attention to the needs of the group. Consequently the individual will care little for what is new, but will do all he can to perfect the old. Thus, manifold influences forced man into the ruts of existing civilization, and gave his mind a certain direction. "Spontaneity, initiative, independence, weak enough in all conscience, are further weakened in accordance with the rule that capacities and powers can develop only if they be exercised, and cease if neglected." [12]

All these characteristics of the economic activities of the pre-capitalist age, as indeed of the whole life of that age, were rooted in the fundamental conception of a stationary society. The highest ideal of those days, as manifested in the final form of the wonderful system of Aquinas, is the individual, introspective soul, endeavouring to become more and more perfect. All the demands of life, as all its forms, were so arranged as to aid that ideal. Hence the rigid system of dividing up men into callings and estates, all regarded as of equal worth for the entire social organism, all providing rules and regulations for the individual, by the help of which he might direct his life aright. Hence, too, the guiding principles of economic life—sufficiency for livelihood and traditionalism, both static principles. Life in the pre-capitalist age was characterized by assured restfulness. To show how this restfulness became unrest and restlessness, how from its static state society became dynamic, is our next business.

The spirit that was responsible for the change, that

shattered the old world into ruins, was the spirit of capitalism (so called from the system in which it has its being). It is the spirit of our time; the spirit which moves every American dollar-king and every aviator; the spirit that rules our life and directs the fate of the universe. It is the purpose of this book to follow up this spirit from its earliest appearance down to the present day, and even beyond.

Our task will be twofold. First we must trace the origin and growth of the capitalist spirit. That is done in the first book. There we dissect the whole into its component parts, and we shall turn our attention chiefly to two, the spirit of enterprise and the bourgeois spirit, which when united generated the capitalist spirit. Each of these is in its turn a complex of contributory forces. The spirit of enterprise is a synthesis of the greed of gold, the desire for adventure, the love of exploration, to mention but a few elements. The bourgeois spirit is composed of calculation, careful policy, reasonableness, and economy. We may say that in the fabric of the capitalist spirit the bourgeois spirit is the cotton warp, and the spirit of enterprise the silken woof. Secondly, we shall have to consider in systematic form the causes and circumstances that made possible the rise and growth of the capitalist spirit. This we do in the second book. The first book shows how the capitalist spirit arose; the second, why it arose.

BOOK I

THE DEVELOPMENT OF THE CAPITALIST SPIRIT

SECTION I

THE SPIRIT OF ENTERPRISE

CHAPTER II

THE GREED OF GOLD

If not the whole of European history, then surely at least the history of the capitalist spirit, must begin with the struggle between Gods and men for the possession of that accursed thing, gold.

The Völuspá relates how all conflict and crime came into the world through the union of the primeval Kingdom of Water, wherein dwelt the Wanes, and the Kingdom of Light, inhabited by the Anses ; and that gold was the cause of it all. For the yellow metal belonged to the Water Realm, but the dwellers in the Realm of Light obtained possession of it by the aid of the dwarfs who lived in the deep caverns of the Earth, enjoying the reputation of gold-thieves and goldsmiths. Gold is the symbol of the earth, which glitters in the light with its yellow fruits and seeds, the objects of all envy and strife ; but the place also of sin and atonement. Indeed, gold is the symbol of pomp and power, two things all men covet.[13] The striving for gold is put by the Edda in the forefront of human history.

The Saga but reflects reality. Everything points to an early appearance of a desire for gold and its possession among the European peoples in their prime, certainly at least among the upper classes. The origins of the desire, to be sure, are lost in dim antiquity ; but we are justified in assuming that the stages of growth were the same as in the case of other peoples. The first stage was that of the pleasure of adornment, which the precious metals with their glitter engender. Next came the pleasure of much adornment. Then the desire to possess the glittering things ; then the joy of possession ; and finally, the delight of owning much gold, no matter in what form.

We thus reach the epoch of treasure-hoarding, through which the Germanic tribes were passing when we first learn of their attitude to gold and silver. Treasure-hoarding is so important a fact in the history of European peoples that we shall dwell at some length upon it. Readers are recommended to turn to one or two pen-pictures of Gustav Freytag's,* who has so vividly portrayed the early Middle Ages.[14]   He tells us that when the Germanic races first broke in upon the Roman Empire, they had then no money economy. When, therefore, they first saw gold it attracted them. They desired, however, not golden coins, but ornaments and vessels of gold. For the warrior these were objects of pride and glory. For his overlord they meant even more. His largess was sure to be praised at the minstrel's board, and he would lack no following. Therefore to the overlord treasures spelt power. Accordingly, among the nomadic peoples the princely families sought to lay up a store of gold. About the year 568, Leuvigild, King of the Visigoths, exhibited his treasure as he sat on his throne in royal robes ; he was the first to do

---

* [Gustav Freytag, 1816–95, German novelist. Between 1859 and 1867 he published five volumes of *Pictures of the German Past*, a most valuable work on popular lines, illustrating the history and manners of the early Germans.]

so, for his predecessors had neither throne nor royal apparel. But from his day onwards the bulwarks of kingly power were realm, people, and treasure.

In ancient times the last-named consisted of gold and silver ornaments and utensils, such as chains and bracelets, drinking horns, ewers, and the like. It was not until much later that coins began to be collected, especially if they were large in size ; and later still, gold in bars was valued too. Most of these things were gifts on great occasions, such as a royal visit or a treaty ; others were obtained as tribute from subjugated peoples ; others, again, were the spoils of predatory expeditions or the income from domains.

Not merely kings, but whoever was able to do so, gathered treasure. For baby princes treasure hoards were started at their birth ; and we are told that when, in 584, the two-year-old son of Fredegunde died, his treasures of gold and silver, jewels and silk raiment, filled four wagons. Kings' daughters likewise received a store of treasure as their dowries, and it frequently came to pass that, for the sake of the spoil, they were attacked on their journey to their new homes. Often enough these bridal gifts were raised by so-called free contributions, but in many instances the kings were exorbitant in their demands. What the kings did, the lesser nobles imitated ; and sometimes the lesser nobles were so many sponges for the kings to squeeze dry.

Cathedrals and monasteries were like the secular nobility in this respect. They, too, accumulated treasure ; they possessed silver cups, and flagons, and Bibles bound in gold and studded with gems.

What Freytag depicts as a characteristic of the earliest Middle Ages continued right through the mediæval period. As a matter of fact, the accumulation of treasure was not unknown in the Ancient World ; nor has it yet completely disappeared from among primitive races.   In any event it gave birth to the love of money.

As for the Middle Ages themselves, we come across large quantities of silver in the 10th and 11th centuries, from Silesia in the east to the shores of the Baltic in the west.   Not only was silver in bars found, but also clipped coins, which would seem to show that what was valued in those days was the metal.[15]   About the same period we read of the existence in Germany,[15A] in France,[16] even in Italy,[17] of the treasure chambers of the wealthy, filled with gold and silver vessels.   In some countries, such as Spain, the habit of treasure collecting continued until right into the modern period.   When the Duke of Frias died, he left 600,000 scudi in cash.   This was placed in three boxes, destined for the dowry of each of his three daughters.   Even in the 16th and 17th centuries it was still usual in Spain for people to stuff their houses with all manner of gold and silver ornaments.   To weigh the gold and silver vessels of the Duke of Alberquerque after his death, and to make an inventory of them, took no less than six weeks.   Among other things he possessed 1,400 dozen plates, 50 large and 100 small dishes, and 40 silver ladders for reaching up to the sideboards.   The Duke of Alba, who was not considered wealthy, left no less than 600 dozen plates and 800 silver dishes.[18]   So widespread was the fashion in Spain of laying up treasure, that Philip III, in 1600, had to issue an ordinance requisitioning all the gold and silver vessels in the land in order to have them melted down and coined.[19]

This peculiar mental state of the Spaniards in relation to gold, in the 16th century, was an anachronism ; in the rest of Europe the general attitude with regard to the precious metals had advanced far beyond the period of treasure gathering, which closed in the 12th century.

From that time on, people indeed continued to value the precious metals, but their form was now different. Before it was the precious metals in the lump that were desired ; now it was the precious metals in the form of money ; that is to say, in their commonest form—in their aspect as a medium of exchange.

The greed of gold was succeeded by the love for money. Curiously enough, it would seem that the desire of gain, or, as it began to be termed, *lucri rabies*, first became most marked (if we exempt the Jews) among the clergy. Anyhow, we have references dating from quite early times to the shameful greed of the clerics. As early as the 9th century there were frequent complaints at the Councils concerning the usury of the clergy ; [20] and it is a well-known fact that money was a mighty influence in ecclesiastical appointments all through the Middle Ages. Alberti, usually a calm observer, would make it appear that the pecuniary greed of the clergy of his time was a universal phenomenon. Of Pope John XXII he says on one occasion, "He had his faults, and above all that which, as everybody knows, is found in all our clerics— he was avaricious even to venality." [21]

When Alberti wrote this, the love of money was no longer limited to the Jews and the clergy (if indeed it ever was a characteristic of these two classes alone). It had seized upon pretty nearly all sections of the population. The line of demarcation was probably the 13th century ; at least, for the more advanced countries, Germany, France, and Italy. I say probably, for obviously it is impossible to date exactly tendencies or movements of this sort. At any rate, in the 13th century, more particularly for Germany, we find an accumulation of complaints that the love of money had become a general evil. [22] The poets of the time were full of it, among them Walter von der Vögelweide ; but the bitterest reproaches came from the preachers of morality, such as the anonymous author of the *Carmina Burana*,[23] or the popular orator, Berthold of Regensburg.[24]

About the same time, Dante was thundering his denunciations against the greed of the nobles and the middle classes of the Italian cities, which must have been unbridled in the 13th century. " They think too much of gain ; indeed, it may almost be said of them, their desire for worldly possessions is like a consuming fire within them." So we read in the *Description of Florence*,[25] of the year 1339. Another writer of the period is Beato Dominici,[25A] who complains that " money is much beloved of high and low, of the laity and the clergy, of rich and poor, of monks and prelates ; in fact, everything is subject to money—*pecuniæ obediunt omnia*. The cursed gold-hunger leads the crazy souls to all manner of evil ; it dims the intellect, blots out the conscience, weakens the memory, misguides the will, knows no friendship, loves no relation, has no fear of God nor shame before man."

It was the same in Florence as early as the 14th century. Descriptions and reflections such as those in the family records preserved by Alberti would tend to demonstrate that a strongly-marked worship of mammon breathed through the life of the city on the Arno. Riches is praised as a good thing, necessary to all civiliza-tion ; profit-hunting was regarded as a general and ordinary activity of the population. " All think of gain and riches " ; " my every thought is occupied with business " ; " unto riches almost everyone aspires." [26]

Fifteenth and sixteenth century voices sing the same song. Not a place in Western Europe but gold was in a position of pre-eminence there. *Pecuniæ obediunt omnia* is the lament of Erasmus, and Hans Sachs mourns that *Gelt ist auff erden der irdisch gott* [Money is the god

of the earth]. We need only add Colon's eloquent praise
of the excellencies of money, in his famous letter to
Queen Isabella.[27]

Besides these expressions of opinion there is much
evidence of the increasing influence of money and of the
cash nexus in the whole of life. Offices under the
crown were purchasable ; the nobility married into city
families ; the policy of states was to obtain large supplies
of bullion (mercantile system) ; the ways and means of
money-making (to be treated in the next chapter) became
more numerous and cunning.

In the 17th century, which we are apt to picture
to ourselves as dismal and solemn, the love of money
grew apace. Jeremiads still continued ; they came from
Italy,[28] from Germany,[29] from Holland. In the last-
named country there appeared, towards the end of the
17th century, a little book, quickly translated into
German, which, despite or rather because of its satire, is a
source of much illumination on the general acquisitiveness
current in the society of the day. As I have never come
across a reference to this important publication I shall say
a word or two about its lively contents. The title of the
German translation runs as follows : *Das Lob der Geld-
sucht. Satyre. Aus dem Holländischen des Herrn von
Deckers. . . . Bei Benjamin Schillen in Hamburg und
F. Groschuff in Leipzig zu finden. Im Jahre* 1703.
[In praise of money getting. A satire. Translated from
the Dutch of Mr. von Decker. . . . To be obtained at
Benjamin Schillen's in Hamburg and F. Groschuff's in
Leipzig. 1703.] The motto of the book? *Quid
rides ? Mutato nomine de te fabula narratur.*

The author appears to have been a man of the world
with an eye for the weaknesses of his age. His book
may be put in the same category as Mandeville's *Fables
of the Bees,* though it cannot compare with the latter for

point and wit. I have only seen the translation, and it is as likely as not that there is no Dutch original at all, although the translator in some cases gives the original text. The story is in rhymed verses, numbering no less than 4,113. Money-getting is personified, and tells its life-story. Caution was its father, and its mother Superfluity. Then follows a laudation of gold, " appraised more than the arts, more than health, yea, more than life itself." Nor is this high approval in anywise undeserved. For the love of money is one of the founders of human society ; it arranges marriages, produces treaties, sets up states and cities, provides honour and renown, gives joy and pleasure, advances the sciences and arts, stimulates commerce, alchemy, and medicine. And does not money-getting give an impetus to philosophy, painting, the drama, the printer's craft ? Nor yet the printer's craft only ; the art of war is likewise sustained by money-getting ; and the discovery of new lands too, as Madame Isabella and King Ferdinand, no less than Columbus, found out. Finally, love of money aids in obtaining everlasting salvation ; money-love is not heretical, but good Lutheran ; nay, money-love is herself a Goddess.

What the Dutch experienced about the year 1634, the English and the French went through for the first time in the early decades of the 18th century—a feverish, greedy money madness, which since then has reappeared from time to time, though its onslaughts may have become less elemental. But so widespread has been its influence that the greed for gold may legitimately be regarded as constitutional in the soul of modern men and women. I shall refer in due course, in connection with the rise of speculation, to the ravages of the fever, as exemplified in Holland by the tulip madness, in France by the Law swindles, and in England by the bubble companies. For the moment we turn to the ways and means which human ingenuity discovered, whereby to obtain possession of gold, the object of universal desire. In our consideration of this problem it will be necessary to discriminate between those methods which contributed to the growth of the capitalist economic outlook and those which soon died away, dropping like a useless branch from the tree-trunk.

CHAPTER III

WAYS AND MEANS OF MONEY-GETTING

It would be childish to imagine that the greed of gold
and the love of money had so direct and immediate an
influence on economic life that the capitalist spirit and
capitalist enterprise came into being almost at once. The
genesis of modern capitalism cannot be traced so speedily.
It took time. In all probability the increasing acquisitiveness made little actual difference in economic life.
People sought to obtain possession of gold and of coin in
all sorts of ways, but none of them had anything to
do with economic activities. Indeed, many a time and
oft their economic activities were neglected in the pursuit
of the golden will-o'-the-wisp. It never once entered the
head of the simple peasant or shoemaker, nor necessarily
that of the merchant, that he could amass riches and accumulate treasures by his ordinary everyday avocations.
Even Alberti, who had no little commercial experience
and who may be said to have been dominated by the capitalist spirit, gives a list of no less than four ways, in
addition to wholesale trading, by which to acquire
money.[30] They are these : to seek for treasure-trove ;
to ingratiate yourself with rich folk with a view of
becoming their legatee—a course of conduct affected,
says Alberti, by not a few ; usury ; and to let out
pastures or horses and the like.

Advice of this kind sounds curious enough to modern

ears ; but no less so than that of a 17th-century writer [31] who mentions three roads to wealth : the royal service, soldiering, and alchemy. Yet strange as this may appear to-day, it was actually what acute observers saw in their own time. As a matter of fact, all the methods enumerated above were resorted to, and were, indeed, of far greater significance in the minds of those who were bent on the acquisition of riches than industry or commerce or agriculture. Nor were they the only ones. As however we are here principally concerned with those that aided the rise of a capitalist economic order, I will briefly mention those that had no such influence, reserving for fuller consideration the capitalistically important ones.

1. First on the list I place official careers, which were looked upon with favour as a means of attaining to riches, because of the opportunity they offered for small embezzlements, bribes, and such-like additional sources of income. I shall have occasion in a subsequent chapter to deal a little more fully with details on this point.

2. Closely akin to the first-named method was the purchase of appointments, which was in reality a species of investment. You paid down a lump sum and obtained in return the right to receive the dues and levies of the office. Often enough, however, the expected returns did not repay the original sum expended.

3. A third way was to become some rich man's retainer, a form of service met with frequently in the 17th and 18th centuries, and one that brought great wealth to quite poor folk.

4. Finally I would include the loans made to states, which began to be numerous from the 17th century onwards.

All these methods of earning money contributed nothing to the development of the capitalist spirit ; on the contrary, they were stumbling-blocks in its path.

It is for the same reason that I omit any reference to the old-fashioned *haute finance*, as we know it in England and France in the 17th and 18th centuries. The participants were very wealthy folk, most of them of middle-class origin, who made money as tax-farmers or money-lenders to the state, and represented, as it were, grease spots on the soup surface. These men were far removed from economic activities. They were the *fermiers généraux, partisans* or *traitans* of France, where they were nicknamed *Turcarets*, from a character in one of Le Sage's comedies of the year 1709, wherein is described the social advance of a former lackey named Turcaret, " le financier dont l'esprit et l'education ne sont pas à la hauteur de sa fortune " ; they were the stock-holders, or the moneyed interest of England, where, about the middle of the 18th century, it was said that there were no less than 17,000 of them.

But in the other methods of acquiring riches we shall find the seeds of capitalist enterprise. These, therefore, demand a somewhat ampler consideration, and for the sake of clearness we shall arrange them under four heads, according as (1) force was the dominant factor in them, or (2) magic, or (3) scheming and invention, or (4) money.

1. Acquisition by Force.

I am not here thinking of all manner of unlawful pressure exercised by the authorities for the purpose of obtaining taxes and dues, but rather of highway robbery, a form of economic activity much beloved and practised for centuries by knights and barons everywhere. This was no mere occasional adventure on the part of the gentry in the Middle Ages and beyond, but a social institution, and it was known in France, Germany, and England, as a good deal of contemporary evidence would show. " In those days," writes Zorn in his Worms Chronicle (14th century), "it was a common thing in Germany, and more especially in the Rhineland, for the strong to bag what they could from the weak ; the knights and esquires, when they met, fought and killed each other, and were the terror of those whose business took them through the highways and byways of the land." This may be paralleled by the advice of one poet [32] to young noblemen as to how they should earn their living. Let them prowl about the forest, and lie in wait for the burgher with his well-lined purse. As a matter of fact, is it not well known that highway robbery as a trade was learned in the same way as weaving or shoemaking ? It is the same story in France. " Les seigneurs ne laissent pas d'aller à la proie," says Jacques de Vitry.

In Italy and England the robber knights turned their attention, not to the king's highway, but to the sea. Their activities, however, were mostly organized enterprises, and we shall have something to say about them elsewhere.

2. ACQUISITION BY MAGIC.

Very different was the utilization of magic for the attainment of riches. Belief in spirits and demons was necessary, and faith in the possibility of getting into touch with them, of making them subservient to the desires of man. A vivid imagination, which but too often was the child of a mind diseased, soon discovered propitious times and places for this superhuman intercourse. Men wanted gold, and two ways were possible for its attainment : they had either to find it or to make it. So we must deal in turn with searches for treasure-trove and with alchemy.

The first was known in very early times. " From the

barbarian invasions to the present day the Germanic peoples have always included the finding of treasure-trove among their secret desires ; during fifteen centuries we meet with the same formulæ and superstitions." 33   It must be confessed that in those early periods attempts to dig up hidden treasure were not by any means foolish. Everybody knows that large quantities of coin and gold and silver ornaments and jewellery were often hidden in the earth, especially when war ravaged the land.   Many were the magic formulæ which should indicate the wished-for spot ; and the night was more propitious for the expeditions than the light of day.   People with little love for work and little diligence, but with strong passions, constant readiness to turn to something new, persistent manias, and unlimited gullibility, dug for treasure again and again throughout their lives.   Later, when in the great days a rumour spread throughout the land that an abundance of gold and silver had been discovered in new countries, it was the same type of person that left wife and child to follow the will-o'-the-wisp that beckoned, the while their bench was covered with dust, their shop became a wilderness, or their ploughshare stuck useless in the furrow.   The mediæval records abound in information as to the magnetic influence of this digging craze ; the fever for gold-shovelling broke out constantly afresh, and what happened in Klondike at the end of the last century, or in California in the eighteen–fifties, must also have come about at Rammelsberg in the 13th century, in Freiburg in the 14th, in the Inntal in the 15th, in Peru in the 16th, and in Brazil in the 17th.   Possibly we are calmer in the 20th century.   Fairy tales of wondrous golden princes, or of the Sun's golden palace, no longer attract the gold-digger ; but the inwardness of our present-day efforts differs in no wise from those of long ago.

Gold-digging may be good, but gold-making is surely

better. To this end men gave themselves up to the magic arts and practised alchemy, not as a common every-day affair, but as a species of divine service, over which hung a cloud of mystery. In its earliest stages alchemy may have had attractions for various reasons ; but there is no doubt that in the process of time the great goal of this pseudo-science was the making of gold.34 This certainly holds good from the 15th century onward ; every Tom, Dick, and Harry sought his fortune 35 by attempting to master the craft, to the great disgust of the specialists. 36 The fever reached its height in the 16th century, when all classes of the population were seized with it. Lout and lord alike believed devoutly in the truth of alchemy, and the longing to get rich quickly drove both to its practice. You could find laboratories in the palace and the cottage, in the poor craftsman's dwelling no less than in the wealthy burgher's comfort-able home, where for long years men sought for the philosopher's stone. Even the monasteries were not immune from the epidemic ; not one of them but had a furnace for gold-making. 37

Many of the professional alchemists, as is known, won for themselves high positions at royal courts, and profited by them all they could. These court alchemists, who were also, in many cases, astrologers royal, were quite common in the 16th and 17th centuries, from Cornelius Agrippa, the "magician" of Cologne, to the mercury quacks of Venice, who became notorious at the court of Vienna.38 John Joachim Becher mentions a long list of them : "among the alchemists of these days who are looked upon as public swindlers and charlatans may be noted Rochefort, Marsini, Croneman, Marsali, Gasner, Gasman, to say nothing of Jacobi de la Porte, who professes to dig for treasures with the aid of the ' claviculam Salomonis.' "

These royal specialists were near cousins of another curious type, which in those ages of twilight began to play a rôle of some importance. I refer to the " projectors," who were, as it were, the connecting link between the witches' kitchen and the board-rooms of modern banks.

3. ACQUISITION BY SCHEMING AND INVENTION.

In a study of mine 39 on the part played by technical knowledge in the early capitalist age, I showed how the period of the Renaissance abounded in inventive geniuses, how, in consequence, there was a shower of technical inventions in those days, to which all classes contributed. But the sphere of technical science was not the only one affected by the flights of human imagination ; pretty well all activities were influenced, and in some cases reforms were suggested, notably in public finance. Here, however, these things do not specially concern us. What we have to note is the fact that, for centuries, there were scores of people whose calling it was to live by their wits. Scheming, as we may term it, became a business ; the man with ideas was ready to sell them to whomsoever chose to pay his price. These professional gentry set about winning the interest of princes and nobles and the wealthy generally in their schemes and projects. Wherever the influential folk forgathered — in Parliament, at courts—there you were certain to meet the project-mongers. But you found them in the market-place too, offering their ideas for sale.

There can be no doubt as to the importance of this phenomenon in economic history, and as it has to my knowledge received but little attention hitherto, I propose saying a word or two about its characteristics and extent.

Project-mongers are met with as early as the 16th

century—at the courts of the Spanish kings. Ranke [40] has something to say of one of these adventurers, Benevento, by name, who demanded a mere 5 per cent. of the profits which should accrue when his plans had been carried out. The Emperor Ferdinand had dealings with him ; so had Philip of Spain. It was in the 17th century, however, that the tribe became most prominent, and for its appearance in England we have the evidence of Daniel Defoe, whose *Essay on Projects* was published in 1697. " About the year 1680," he tells us, " began the art and mystery of projecting to creep into the world." He calls his time " the Projecting Age," and this is how he describes the projectors [pp. 31–35]. They are men who—

being masters of more cunning than their neighbours, turn their thought to private methods of trick and cheat, a modern way of thieving . . . by which honest men are gulled with fair pretences to part from their money. . . .

Others yet, urged by the same necessity, turn their thoughts to honest invention, founded upon the platform of ingenuity and integrity.

These two last sorts are those we call projectors ; and as there are always more geese than swans, the number of the latter are very inconsiderable in comparison of the former ; and as the greater number dominates the less, the just contempt we have of the former sort bespatters the other. . . .

A mere projector then is a contemptible thing, driven by his own desperate fortune to such a strait that he must be delivered by a miracle or starve. And when he has beat his brain for some such miracle in vain, he finds no remedy but to paint up some bauble or other, as players make puppets talk big, to show like a strange thing, and then cry it up for a new invention, gets a patent for it, divides it into shares and they must be sold. Ways and means are not wanting to swell the new whim to a vast magnitude ; thousands and hundreds of thousands are the least of his discourse, and sometimes millions ; till the ambitions of some honest coxcomb is wheedled to part with his money for it, and then *nascitur ridiculus mus.*

Defoe is of opinion that the French were not so fertile

in projections as the English. He was mistaken. If
anything, they were far superior, and France may be
termed the classical land of projecting. From about the
middle, or the close, of the 17th century until well into
the 18th, the same tendencies manifested themselves there
as in England ; the only difference being that in France,
as we should expect from the temper of its people,
the schemes were more brilliant and dramatic. Some
authorities would even assign to the beginning of the
17th century that feverish inventive activity which was
speedily to enrich its authors.41 These were called
donneurs d'avis or *brasseurs d'affaires*.42

In the 17th century these gentry crowded the streets
in Paris. You could meet them in the Place du Change
as early as 10 a.m., jabbering away without intermission.
Most of them knew what hunger was ; and if they had
no greatcoats, they possessed boundless faith. Whenever you came across them they offered some marvellous
suggestion for your consideration. They lurked about
the antechambers of the great, frequented the offices of
state officials, and had secret meetings with the fair ladies
of society. Their To-day was always pitiful : so much
the more promising and brilliant was their To-morrow, for
should they not then rake in their hoped-for millions ? A
certain amount of understanding cannot be denied them,
but their imagination was more powerful than their
judgment. So it came about that, more often than not,
their ideas were childish, or curious, or grotesque, or
utterly impossible. Nevertheless, they were able to
prove to you, almost mathematically, that the results
they promised were assured. For their advice (*avis*),
which was the flash of the moment, they received a fee,
the *droit d'avis*. Some, it must be confessed, like Tonti,
the inventor of Tontine, made some very useful suggestions which brought them opulence ; others wasted their

energy or were exploited by those with less brain-power but more worldly wisdom, or by those who had greater influence and knew how to get at money. Their true nature has been described as being restless, watchful, penetrating, greedy, and acquisitive. In their ranks you might have found misunderstood inventive geniuses ; Don Quixotes of all degrees ; feverish minds of delicate texture ; bankrupts with their scarecrow hats ; Bohemian stragglers, who had once been respectable and were anxious to be so again ; and bold adventurers of more than average intelligence, who dined in the lowest chop-house if their expected loot was not forthcoming, and who ended their days either in the gutter or as financial magnates.

That the type must have been pretty numerous in the France of that period is evident from the part assigned to the projector by Molière in his *Facheux*. He is there made to appear as a recognized element in Parisian society. The descriptions of Paris at the end of the 18th century make it quite clear that the scheming projector had not disappeared even then.43

Other lands, too, were acquainted with the type. We may mention Austria as an instance. About the middle of the 18th century a certain Caratto was a prominent scheme-monger at the court of Vienna, and on the 25th of January, 1765, he provided the authorities with a scheme concerning the profitableness of certain commercial ventures. He has been " carrying on the business of projecting for more than forty years," we read ; 44 " his suggestions are good and attractive, but the results he promises are exaggerated."

Finally, we need only mention Cagliostro for a definite conception of what projecting was. It is true that in this notorious character there was a strong admixture of the adventurer and the swindler. Nevertheless, the root of the matter was the same. Cagliostro, who was known the world over, and welcomed in all the capitals and at half the courts of Europe, was, when all is said, a true projector, his end to make money easily (chiefly by the aid of fair ladies), his means to interest the great and the wealthy in his bold, unheard-of schemes, the while he sold elixirs of life, universal panaceas, and beauty lotions.

What was the position of these schemers and projectors in the genesis of the capitalist spirit? It is not difficult to see. Were they not the ancestors of men like Law, Pereire, Lesseps, Strousberg, Saccard, and a host of lesser company-promoters who are so prominent in these days? What the projectors lacked was a definite sphere of activity. They were not yet undertakers; they stood without; they were not in business. But theirs were the ideas that were to generate capitalism, a consummation which came about so soon as the ideas were united with enterprise. How that happened we shall see later. For the present, we have yet one more method of money-making to consider.

4. Acquisition by Money.

The mere possession of money placed its owner in an advantageous position. No need of robbery for him, nor yet recourse to magic. With the aid of money he could get more, in various ways. If he were of a cold, calculating nature, there was money-lending; and if he were hot-blooded and careless, there were games of chance. In any event, he had no occasion to associate himself with others for common action; he could sit at home in cloistered ease, the sole pilot of his fortune.

The tremendous influence of money-lending throughout the Middle Ages and down to our day has already been fully set forth in my *Modern Capitalism*. There is therefore all the less reason for me to go into it again here. I would only like to say, in passing, that the rôle of money-lending in moulding the capitalist spirit was a double one. In the first place, it produced in the minds of those who engaged in it professionally certain special tendencies of great importance in the growth of the capitalist spirit ; and secondly, it was one of the starting-points of capitalist enterprise.

No less significant has been the contribution of Hazard in the history of the capitalist spirit ; that is to say, leaving out games of dice and cards, which rather tended away from it. The same may be added about lotteries,[45] which, since the end of the 17th century, have become universal. But stock-exchange gambles, which first gathered strength some time in the 17th century, and became fully developed in the 18th, certainly did contribute to the expansion of capitalism. Not that stock-exchange activities were, as has been often assumed, a direct expression of the capitalist spirit. As a matter of fact, those activities are no more of a really economic character than card-playing or lotteries. It was their indirect influence, however, that was considerable.

Let us acquaint ourselves with the psychology of stock-exchange gambling. Nothing will serve our purpose so well as an abridged sketch of the tulip mania, prevalent in the Netherlands.[46] This manifested in their pristine purity all the characteristics which marked the later ages of speculation.

In 1534 Busbeck, the famous scientist, introduced the tulip from Adrianople into Western Europe. For some unaccountable reason the flower, about the year 1630, enjoyed a tremendous popularity in Holland. Everybody wanted to own tulip bulbs. And before long the mere pleasure of possession gave way to the desire to obtain profit out of them by advantageous sales. What more natural than that this should produce an organized speculative business, upon which all classes of the population seized ?   An old book, published in Amsterdam, and entitled *De opkomst en ondergang van Flora*, relates how knights and squires, merchants and craftsmen, sailors and peasants, peat-diggers and chimney-sweeps, men-servants and maids all were afflicted with the same craze—tulips.   In every town you would find some public-house serving as the exchange, where high and low, rich and poor, forgathered to deal in tulips.   So much did the nuisance spread, that in 1634, according to John Francis, not an important city in the Netherlands but its legitimate trade was threatened by the speculation engendered by the tulip traffic.   There was temptation for the greed of the rich and the need of the poor, and the price of a flower rose far above its weight in gold. As in all such cases, the bubble burst and brought devastation and wild panic in its train.   Many were utterly ruined ;   only a very few made a fortune.   But the point to notice is that in 1634 tulips were in as much demand as railway shares in 1844.   It was the same kind of speculation.   Deals were closed for the delivery of certain sorts of tulip bulbs ;   and if, as in one instance, two specimens only were available, some one had to sell his all, lock, stock, and barrel—land and houses, horses and oxen—in order to pay the difference.   Contracts were signed, and many thousand gulden paid for tulips that neither the middlemen, the buyers, nor the sellers had ever set eyes upon.   For a while, of course, as we should expect, everybody did well, and nobody lost money. Poor people became rich.   Rich and poor alike were tulip dealers.   The legal profession made fortunes ;   and the Dutchman, sober-souled though he was, began to dream of a golden age.   Everybody's head appeared to be turned.   People of the most varying occupations changed their possessions into ready cash, and houses and machinery were offered at ridiculous prices. The whole country gave itself up to the deceitful hope that the passion for tulips would endure for ever. When the news spread that in other lands, too, the fever had caught on, men's imaginations ran away with them ; and they believed that the wealth of the universe would be concentrated on the shores of the Zuyder Zee, and that poverty in Holland would be but a traveller's tale. The prices that were paid for tulip bulbs prove how earnestly such things were credited. Estates valued at 2,500 florins were given away in return for one special kind of bulb, 2,000 florins were offered for a second species, and a brand-new carriage and pair, with harness, for a third. The records of the town of Alkmar show that in 1637, 120 tulip bulbs were publicly sold for the benefit of the city orphanage, and fetched 90,000 florins.

In 1637 the pendulum began to swing back. Confidence disappeared ; contracts were broken ; bankruptcies were the order of the day. The visions of wealth beyond the dreams of avarice vanished like a mist, and those who a week ago rejoiced in the possession of a few tulips in the expectation that they would bring certain fortune, looked sadly at the miserable onion-like bulbs, which were inherently of no value whatever, and for which nobody would now offer a farthing.

This tulip speculation is interesting from many points of view. To begin with, because it was the first swindle of its kind on anything like a large scale ; secondly, because of the commodity that all men desired. Later on it would seem that securities alone were the objects of speculation, as was the case shortly after the tulip craze in the two greatest speculation epidemics that had afflicted mankind until then—the foundation of Law's bank in France, and the South Sea Company in England (1719–21).

But to understand the inwardness of these speculation manias we must leave securities out of account. For what is a security? It sets forth the right to a portion of the profit of some particular enterprise. Now at first sight it may seem that the hoped-for profits influence the price of the security. This in reality is not so; the expected profits are but another bait to attract attention to the security. What is at the root of the whole process is an instinctive hazard. Consider for a moment, that in a rising market the price of shares is out of all proportion to the profits expected. Let me give an illustration. On the 30th September, 1719, the statutory meeting of Law's bank took place. Before that a dividend of 12 per cent. on the nominal capital had been promised. That worked out at $\frac{1}{2}$ per cent. on the real capital. Law was afraid that, if this became known, his whole edifice would collapse like a pack of cards. So he promised 40 per cent., which was equivalent to $1\frac{2}{3}$ per cent. on the real capital. Did the public see through the trick? On the contrary, after the general meeting, the price of the shares began to rise, until eight days later it reached the highest point ever attained—18,000 florins. The truth is that in such cases it is a question of crowd psychology: men are seized by a fever, an intoxication, a longing desire which silences any reasonable consideration. By a process of reflex suggestion, some object or other (the classical case is that of the tulip) is assigned a fabulous value, and so its price tends to rise upwards with all rapidity. High prices are thus the bait which the passion for speculation seizes. This latter in its turn then becomes so strong that it dominates all the factors in the situation.

The speculative passion as seen on the Stock Exchange, however, whether it appears in the high temperature of a rising market, or the low temperature of everyday deal-

ing, has inherently as much to do with the development
of the capitalist spirit as a quiet game of bridge or poker.
In reality, economic activities, inspired by the spirit of
capitalism, are rather deadened by this sort of gambling.
Is it not now generally admitted that in periods when
speculation is rife, trade and commerce tend to decline,
because those who should be engaged in them neglect
their business, wasting their time in public-houses on the
look out for news of stocks and shares, or entering into
speculative transactions ?

If this is so, how does stock-exchange speculation come
into contact with the capitalist spirit? The answer is
twofold. To begin with, stock-exchange hazards eventually developed into the enterprise of the capitalist
undertaker. The gaming passion and the pleasure of
winning naturally turned to such emprises as were
capitalist in their character. As a matter of fact, every
modern capitalist undertaking (as we shall see in due
course) has in it a goodly dash of the gamester's energy
and passion. In the next place, the progress of stock-
exchange activities has exercised and developed just those
habits of mind that were needful for the growth of the
capitalist spirit. Think of projecting, which, when the
7th century closed, was known all over Europe. And
did not projecting create the habit of company forming ?
It could not, however, have done this by itself ; it had to
co-operate with stock-exchange activities. The latter
provided the necessary channels for the realization of the
schemes ; it also prepared men's minds for the reception
of the baits held out by the projectors.

That the two were necessarily interwoven we learn
from Daniel Defoe, one of the cleverest observers of the
period, whose testimony is exceedingly valuable. He
is speaking of the period, about the end of the 17th
century, when Dutch Jews were very influential

on the London Stock Exchange.47 This is what he
says :—

> But here began the forming of publick joint stocks which . . .
> begot a new trade, which we call by a new name, stock-jobbing, which
> was at first only the simple occasional transferring of interest and
> shares from one to another, as persons alienated their estates. But by
> the industry of the exchange-brokers, who got the business into their
> hands, it became a trade ; and one perhaps managed with the greatest
> intrigue, artifice, and trick, that ever anything that appeared with a
> face of honesty could be handled with. For while the brokers held
> the box, they made the whole exchange the gamesters, and raised and
> lowered the prices of stock as they pleased, and always had both
> buyers and sellers who stood ready innocently to commit their money
> to the mercy of their mercenary tongues. This upstart of a trade
> having tasted the sweetness of success which generally attends a novel
> proposal, introduces the illegitimate wandering object I speak of
> [projects], as a proper engine to find work for the brokers. Thus,
> stock-jobbing nursed projecting, and projecting in turn has very dili-
> gently pimped for its foster-parent, till both are arrived to be public
> grievances ; and indeed are now almost grown scandalous.48

But with this we have already touched upon capitalist
undertaking, which is the subject of the next chapters.
The various methods of making money, which we have
considered up to this point, had nothing of undertaking
in them. But in process of time the love of money
united with enterprise, and the capitalist spirit was the
result.

CHAPTER IV

THE SPIRIT OF UNDERTAKING[48A]

UNDERTAKING in its broadest conception means the realization of a well considered plan, for the carrying out of which it is needful to have the continued co-operation of many individuals under the guidance of a single will.

The plan must be well defined. Hence sudden instinctive actions are excluded. You don't talk of an " undertaking " when a few tramps quickly resolve there and then to set upon and rob a passing traveller. On the other hand, it is distinctly an " undertaking " when a gang of desperadoes calmly decide on a burglary on a certain day, and resolve to meet to do the job.

Item, the plan must needs be realized. It is not enough merely to conceive the idea, or even to decide upon its realization. The action must be consummated.

Item, it must be a plan, " for the carrying out of which it is needful to have the continued co-operation of many individuals." Your plan may be ever so well considered, but if only a single person carries it out, it is not an " undertaking." Accordingly, every artistic effort and every handicraft production is thus excluded from the conception.

And the plan must be carried out under the guidance of a single will, which may be embodied in more than one person. If a number of friends plan to take a walk, that is not an " undertaking." But an African expedition, or a Cook's tour, undoubtedly is.

Note that the possibilities of undertaking are coextensive with all human activities, and are not by any means limited to those only that have reference to wealth. Undertaking in the economic sense is merely a subdivision of undertaking as a whole ; and capitalist undertaking is a branch of undertaking in the economic sense.

And how shall we describe the spirit of enterprise ? It is the resultant of the combination of all the qualities of the soul necessary for the successful consummation of an undertaking. These qualities may be divided, on the one hand, according to the different functions an undertaker has to carry out; and on the other, according to their importance, which varies with the varying work of the undertaker. But in every case, the successful undertaker must be a trinity composed of (1) conqueror, (2) organizer, and (3) trader.

1. The Conqueror.

What are the psychological qualities necessary for carrying out an enterprise ? I should say they are three in number. (1) To make plans is one. Which is to say, that you must have ideas. The undertaker must thus possess a certain measure of intellectual freedom. (2) The will to carry out the plan—the will to do. The inventor does not possess this characteristic. For him the discovery or invention suffices. But the undertaker must needs reproduce the invention, must duplicate and multiply it. His one thought is the realization of his plan. What he needs above all is intellectual energy. (3) But he must also have the capacity to carry his scheme through. In other words, he must possess diligent application, turning from his goal neither to the right nor to the left. Your true undertaker, who is a conqueror, will have sufficient determination and strength to break down any obstacle that stands in his way. But he must be a conquerer also in his ability to take high risks, and to stake his all in order to achieve greatly. In this he is akin to the gambler.

Sum it all up, and what is his mental outfit? Intellectual elasticity, mental energy, and intensity and constancy of will.

2. THE ORGANIZER.

Seeing that the work on which an undertaker is engaged always requires other people to work with him and be subservient to his will, it follows that the undertaker must above all be a successful organizer. And organizing means so to dovetail the work of many persons as to produce the most efficient results ; so to dispose of human beings and commodities as to effect the desired creation of utilities. Now, obviously, this requires a complex of qualities for its achievement. For one thing, your successful organizer must have the knack of taking exact stock of people, that is, he must be able to pick out of a crowd just those individuals that are going to serve his purpose. For another, he must have the capacity of letting others do his work, putting each one in the place best suited for him, in order to obtain the maximum possible result, and also of getting the most from each. Thirdly, and lastly, it is the organizer's business to see to it that the co-operating individual units form a productive whole, that the complex relationships are properly co-related. As Clausewitz says of the ideal military commander, what he needs is to gather his forces in the right place, and to have them ready at the right time.

3. THE TRADER.

But organizing ability does not complete the under-taker's outfit. His contact with human beings calls for much besides. In the first place, he must obtain the services of his employees. Next, he must by peaceful means influence masses of people whom he does not know, so to shape their conduct that he will derive benefits from it. That is precisely what is done by the leader of an expedition, who obtains leave to pass through a strange territory, or gets provisions for his party ; or by a capitalist undertaker who disposes of his goods ; or by a statesman who arranges a commercial treaty. In all these cases negotiation is necessary, and negotiation means to confer with another, and, by making the best of your own case and demonstrating the weakness of his, get him to adopt what you propose. Negotiation is but an intellectual sparring match.

Thus, the undertaker must be a skilful negotiator and dealer ; and a dealer in the broadest economic sense is a trader.[49] Trading, then, means negotiating concerning the buying and selling of commodities, shares, capital, or businesses. The rag-and-bone man at the backdoor, hig-gling with cook for a rabbit-skin ; the old-clo' dealer who spends his eloquence for hours together in order to get the country yokel to buy a pair of his trousers ; a Rothschild conferring with an agent of some South American Republic in order to arrange for the floating of a large loan ; the representative of the Standard Oil Trust obtaining special freight rates from all the railways in the States ; Carnegie and his associates discussing with J. Pierpont Morgan a plan for the taking over by the latter of the Carnegie Works, at a price that ran into thousands of millions, and of which the historian of the United States Steel Corporation remarks, " it was the most masterly piece of diplomacy in the history of American industry " ;—all these are instances of trading. The difference between them is merely quantitative ; the thing is the same in each case. For the essence of all modern trading is negotiating, though not necessarily face to face. It may even be achieved impersonally, as when a shop-keeper resorts to all manner of tricks in order to try and induce the public to buy his wares. What else is advertising ?

In every case, the end in view is to convince buyer or seller of the advantage of the contract. And when the populace is convinced, and hastens in crowds to some particular shop, the shopkeeper's ideal has been realized. To arouse interest, to win confidence, to stir up the desire to purchase—such is the goal of the successful trader. How he reaches it is immaterial, so long as he does reach it by any method except the appeal to force. He must make the other party eager to complete the bargain. The trader must work by suggestion ; and one of the most effective suggestions is to convey to the mind the vital importance of closing with the deal at once. " ' It looks like snow, boys,' said the Finns, for they had Aander (a kind of snow-shoe) to sell." So we read in the Magnus Barford Saga (1006 A.D.), and the story summarizes all trading, and is an instance of one of the earliest advertisements—that weapon of every modern trader, who no longer dwells in a strongly fortified house, as did his predecessors in Genoa in the days of Benjamin of Tudela ; nor does he use cannon to force the natives of some newly discovered territory to trade with him, as did the East India merchants in the 17th century (of whom more anon).

That every enterprise may be affected by unforeseen circumstances goes without saying. Hence the undertaker must be capable of accommodating himself to changing conditions, must keep his nerve, must be able to do the right thing at the right time. *Coup d'œil* Frederick the Great called the quality, which he regarded as an essential in his generals (and a general, remember, is also an undertaker in the broad sense) ; and its realization is assured by determination.

If you wish for an instance of a classical undertaker, turn to Dr. Faustus :—

> What I have thought I hasten to fulfil ;
> The master's bidding, that alone has might.
> Up vassals, from your lairs ! Give me to scan
> The glad fulfilment of my daring plan.
> Up, to your tools. Ply shovel, pick, and spade !
> Straight must the work be done, so long delayed.
> Stern discipline and toil intense
> Shall have the amplest recompense.
> *And that a mighty work completed stands,*
> *One mind suffices for a thousand hands.**

There you have the essence of all undertaking.

---

* [Goethe's *Faust*, Part II, Act 5, Scene 3 (towards the end). The translation is by Sir Theodore Martin, save the two last lines, which are from the version of Bayard Taylor, who seems to have got nearer the original than Sir Theodore.]

CHAPTER V

THE BEGINNINGS OF UNDERTAKING

SUCH, then, is the spirit of undertaking. When did it first manifest itself? What were the earliest undertakings?

To my mind, there were four distinct forms of undertaking in European history, and each was not without influence on the future. They were (1) Martial undertakings; (2) The Manorial System; (3) The State; and (4) The Church.

Clearly, we cannot in this book consider each of these organizations in all its complexity, nor can we attempt to write their history. These aspects, in so far as they are necessary for a complete understanding of economic development, will, I hope, be dealt with in the revised edition of my *Modern Capitalism*. What is desirable here is to note the connection between the four organized forms above mentioned and the idea of undertaking. To that I shall briefly address the reader's attention.

1. MARTIAL UNDERTAKINGS.

These were no doubt the first kind of undertakings, and no doubt, too, the other three mentioned were possible only when this, the first, had been carried out.

What is a martial undertaking? When a leader (or it may be a small group of leaders) decides upon a plan of campaign, which he carries out with the aid of a number of fighting men chosen and led by himself, we may speak of a martial undertaking. It was not a martial undertaking, therefore, when the Germanic tribes united for defence against the Roman onslaughts. On the other hand, it certainly was when a band of them marched out on a raiding expedition, especially when they crossed the sea. This last must have been schemed and planned, must have been the result of a process of reasoning in the mind of a leader. Recall the expedition of Beowulf for the rescuing of Rodgar.* There we have an excellent instance of martial undertaking, even though it be free from the desire for spoil. Observe that the heroic age is about to dawn. In other words, that men with the spirit of enterprise and undertaking in them have arisen, standing head and shoulders above the great indolent mass, and that they were able to force their will upon the rest. This is essential, for in every undertaking we needs must have the contrast between leader and followers, between the director and his myrmidons, between subject and object, between mind and body.

Martial undertakings retained their true character so long as there was this personal element in them, and the most perfect form of the martial undertaker is found in the leader of hireling soldiers, so well known in the later Middle Ages. It is not the fact that soldiering becomes a profession that is pertinent (that only gives this sort of undertaking a capitalist touch) ; it is that the leader is all-powerful. These generals are described by one authority [49A] as wicked and cruel, but, he adds, "in the process of time many a one developed his capacities to a very high degree, so that he won his soldiers' admiration. The first armies of modern history were held together

* [Cf. W. Morris and A. J. Wyatt's translation of the Beowulf, p. 12.]

solely by the personal influence of their leaders. One of the best instances is that of Francesco Sforza. His popularity among his men was general, and he knew how to utilize it to the full."

One other characteristic of these trained-band leaders stamped them as true undertakers : they bore the risk of the enterprise, and had to provide all that was necessary for a military campaign—the men and their equipment, the daily commissariat, and suitable accommodation.

It is not difficult to realize that the qualities of the good general are those needed by the successful undertaker. To see how closely akin the two are, turn to the fascinating chapter in Clausewitz which is headed " The Military Genius." 50

2. THE MANORIAL SYSTEM.

It is pretty generally admitted now that the manorial system was common to all European peoples throughout the Middle Ages, and that its influence on the development of each was enormous. Everywhere the system in its organization presents the same picture—whether you look at the monastic institutions (say, Bobbio or Farsa), or the domains of the Patriarch of Grado or the Archbishop of Ravenna, or the benefices of Worcester or Peterborough. The reasons for this similarity need not be considered here ; suffice it to say that Roman tradition, the levelling influence of the Church, and the general trend of things, must all have contributed to bring about this result. As a matter of fact, tendencies towards the manorial system seemed to be manifest among the Germanic races in the time of Tacitus.

What manner of organization was the manorial system ? It was an economic order by which the wealthy class, who were the landowners, had their wants supplied, chiefly if not entirely in kind, through the labour of others. Accordingly, the chief point of interest to us is the necessity there was of organizing a large number of workers for a common purpose. That made the manorial system an undertaking. The guiding principle of this undertaking was to produce just so much as was necessary for consumption, and no more.

For the realization of this end there was not a sufficient supply of free labourers. Consequently, enforced labour had to be employed. The peasants were *adscriptii terræ*, bound to the soil ; and service dues or payments in kind were exacted from them. So it came about that the organism became a sort of mosaic of varying relationships between landowner and land-tiller. But the details need not detain us. The root of the matter is this : in the manorial system a group of people was organized for regular work in accordance with a pre-arranged plan, under the direction of some one individual. In the course of centuries an artificial organization was thus created, which could be utilized now for this end, now for that; and not necessarily for production sufficient to satisfy wants. Its spirit helped the growth of the capitalist spirit.

The manors then were undertakings (often on a great scale), in the midst of a world which was innocent of the undertaking spirit. They thus contained the seeds of future growth.

3. THE STATE.

May it not be said that the modern state is an undertaking for peace and war alike ? Not indeed every state ; but undoubtedly the state that was evolved when the Middle Ages passed away. Its true nature may be perceived from the spirit that gave it birth. What was that spirit ?

Recall that the centralized, absolute states of Europe about the beginning of the 16th century were organisms in which a very large number of people—that is to say, larger than the inhabitants of a mere city or even a country district—were subject to the will of one man, the ruler or his representative, for his own interests.

The logical consequences of such an organization are not difficult to see. In the first place, in order to make the people serve the interests of the monarch, a scheme was necessary for their government, and often enough this had vital effects on the lives of the subjects. The scheme provided for the accumulation of forces, regulated what actions were permissible and what forbidden, organized a governing machine of vast proportions, the influence of which was exceedingly extensive. Moreover, the scheme served as a model for smaller organizations.

In the second place, the whole life of the subject was circumscribed by the interests of the state. The state interfered with his private affairs, and so got the average citizen accustomed to the idea of undertaking. By constantly striking at the stone, the state, as it were, produced sparks which gradually formed into a flame. How the spirit of enterprise must have been nurtured by the needs of the state for centuries and centuries! How much of it must have run over and seized upon the individual!

The idea of the modern state, I imagine, was born in the Italian tyrannies of the 13th and 14th centuries. Both rational planning and "over-government" were fully developed in them. "The conscious valuation of all possible influences, whereof princes beyond the borders of Italy had not the faintest notion, and an absolutism which was almost boundless in power, produced in the Italian states special types of men and organization."

States such as these may surely be classed as private undertakings of the rulers. The prince in each case took up the reins of government, much like an adventurous undertaker ; fully aware that every moment he is running the danger of riding to a fall ; and therefore on the lookout for the proper instruments and methods that are to serve his end. In a word, he was an organizer on a very large scale, and success came to him because of his daring, his skill, determination, and tenacity.[51]

From the Italian tyrannies these ideas passed into the larger states of Europe, and continued there so long as they remained absolute monarchies.

4. THE CHURCH.

I include the Church in my list because, next to the state, it was the largest organization of human beings. Moreover, it was characterized, as are all undertakings, by rational planning ; and history shows that many a skilful undertaker sprang from among its leaders. And no wonder, seeing how much organizing talent was called for in its midst. The establishment of a monastery or the carving out of a bishopric called, in effect, for the same activity as the founding of a cotton-spinning business or the organization of a banking concern.

CHAPTER VI

FUNDAMENTAL TYPES OF CAPITALIST
UNDERTAKINGS

THIS chapter is to tell the tale of the extraordinary unions into which the greed of gold and the spirit of enterprise entered, and it will unfold the history of their offspring, the spirit of capitalist undertaking. We shall hear that the unions were of exceeding great variety, so that the resultant types of capitalist undertakers were perforce of a tremendously varying character. All former attempts at the reconstruction of the genesis of Capitalism, it appears to me, have not laid nearly sufficient stress on this particular point.

To understand the spirit that pervades all capitalist economies, we must strip them of their mechanical devices, their outer trappings, as it were. And these devices have always been the same, from the earliest dawn of capitalism down to this very day. A large sum of money is necessary for the production of marketable commodities ; we call it capital. Some one has to provide this money ; has to advance it, as it used to be called ; perchance to enable a weaver to buy his raw material, perchance to provide the wherewithal to install a new pump in a mine ; or, indeed, for any and every industrial or commercial purpose. The money with which banks worked was from a very early period provided by deposits ; the capital for commercial and shipping companies was forthcoming either by the underwriting of stock or through partnership contributions.   Or, it might have been, that an individual had sufficient spare cash of his own with which to start a capitalist concern.   But the different ways of collecting the capital had no influence on the spirit of the enterprise itself.   The men who financed the scheme did not determine its spirit ; that was done by the man who utilized the capital.   More often than not the former were a very mixed multitude.

An instance or two must suffice.   When the Peruzzi and Bardi became bankrupt (in the 14th century) the clergy alone were creditors to the extent of 550,000 florins.   About the year 1328 the Scali and Amieri could not meet their liabilities, and more than 400,000 florins were lost—"everybody in Florence who had any money was affected," writes Villani.[52]   Again, we read of Ambrosius Höchstetter (towards the close of the 15th century) how "princes, earls, and knights, burghers, peasants, menservants, and maids all deposited their money with him, and he paid them five per centum. Even many a farmer's lad, who had no more than 10 florins, invested those in his concern. . . . Thus for a long time he was paying interest on a million gulden. With this he bought up stocks of wares and increased prices all round."[53]

From the 15th century onward the mining industry especially was maintained by moneys that flowed in from all manner of social groups from the four quarters of the globe.   In the mining works at Goslar, between 1478 and 1487, contracts for gallery extensions were made with Johannes Thurzo, citizen and senator of Cracow, and with burghers of Nuremburg, Chemnitz, and Leipzig.[54]   This same Thurzo had also invested some of his money in Hungarian mines, and a number of his fellow-citizens joined him.[55]   In the 17th and 18th centuries the Dutch creditors of the Austrian court

were the financiers of the Schmölnitz and other copper
mines.[56] Foreign noblemen and merchants were financially interested in the quicksilver mines of Idria ; [57]
the same applies to the salt-mines of Wieliczka in the
16th century,[57A] the mines in the Schlackenthal,[58] and
the tin works of Cornwall.[59] Again, we hear of an
archbishop who advanced money to enable the mining of
gold to be continued in the Province of Salzburg ; [60] or
of iron dealers who provided the wherewithal for the
further extension of the iron foundries of Carinthia ; [61] or
of the King of Bohemia who opened a fund to assist
mining in Joachimstal.[62]

The same story is heard in the textile industries, where
the money was advanced now by journeymen grown
wealthy, now by rich traders or "wholesalers" ["clothiers"],
as they were called.[63] Nor must it be forgotten that
people from the upper classes, at a time when stocks
and shares were not very numerous, put their money
into commercial concerns much more than they do to-
day.[64] When the Compagnie des Indes orientales [the
French East India Company] was founded in 1664, its
capital was to a large extent subscribed outside the rank
of the merchant class.[65] Or, take the case of the
Compagnie de l'Orient. The principal shareholder was
the Duc de la Melleraye.[66]

Let me now return to my point. I was saying that we
should not discover the spirit of the earliest capitalist
undertakings by referring to the people who provided the
necessary capital. As well attempt to characterize modern
capitalist enterprises by considering the social origins of
the shareholders of the various companies.

In order to find out their true spirit we must go to their
very heart ; in other words, to those who gave them form
and shape. It is true that we may thus stumble across
the financiers, but in that case it will be the financiers

who are at the same time organizers, creative artists in undertaking ; and it is in this capacity that they will count for the spirit of enterprise.

To facilitate our search let us commence with the three earliest kinds of undertakings (treated in the previous chapter), and observe how gradually they were filled with the spirit of capitalism. In other words, we shall discover that these undertakings, which as such were not at first concerned with money, were gradually utilized for the purpose of money-making. Three types were evolved, corresponding to the three forms dealt with in the fifth chapter. These were (1) the Freebooter, (2) the Landlord, and (3) the Civil Servant. [Three other types will then be considered : (4) the Speculator, (5) the Trader, and (6) the Craftsman.]

1. THE FREEBOOTER.

A military expedition is not in itself necessarily an undertaking for monetary profit, despite the fact that money generally is its strongest motive force. It is true that in the ancient world the wars of the Phœnicians, the Carthaginians and the Romans for the conquest of Spain were primarily enterprises for the possession of its stores of gold. It is equally true of the wars of the Middle Ages for the possession of Bohemia, and in the modern period of history of the wars against Spain.[67] But we feel somehow that it would be a mistake to see in these enterprises very early instances of capitalist undertakings.

There are other military undertakings, however, which appear in a different light. These, ostensibly and from the first, aimed at providing profit ; apart from this they had no meaning. Think of the maritime adventures. What else were they but undertakings in which military skill and organization were utilized for the pursuit of gain ?

Piracy as an institution already existed in the Italian seaports in the Middle Ages. Amalfi, Genoa, Pisa, Venice, all alike were centres of organized sea-robbery (often enough combined with highway robbery). All these cities drew a very large proportion of their wealth from this source, and their piratical expeditions were the first forms of capitalist undertaking. Of Genoa, for instance, we are told [68] that " the real corsairs were difficult to distinguish from the burghers who took part in the raids and battles for their own profit under the supervision of the state. As a matter of fact, the two classes were but two types of the same species. That is why it is not easy to explain the different shades of meaning in the terms *cursales, prædones* and *pyrate*. Moreover, the term *corsar*, which is a technical expression in the Genoese documents, had nothing blameworthy or discreditable about it. . . . Nor was there anything dishonorable in the calling itself, in the *pyraticam artem exercens*. The fitting out of pirate vessels, or participation in the same, could only take place with the consent of the government. . . . Indeed, any one who did so without the necessary official authority could not sue for the return of his capital."

Or again : " Many an Italian merchant who had a claim against a Greek and could not get his money . . . became a corsair in order to make good his loss. It would seem that not a few traders of Genoa or Pisa devoted themselves to piracy in Greek waters. The wretched state of the Byzantine navy made it possible to carry on this calling on a very large scale." [69] For the most part the corsairs came in flotillas, such as, for example, that of 1194, which was composed of five ships from Pisa, and robbed round about Abydos.

In the first centuries of the modern period in history all the Powers of Western Europe condoned the practice of organized sea-robbery as a calling. The constant wars of the 16th and 17th centuries gave it an impetus ; besides, the capture of enemy vessels in those days played a very important rôle in maritime law. But capturing legitimate prizes developed before long into piracy pure and simple. The privateer became a pirate, and the pirate was frequently taken into the service of the state. In France, in the 16th century, we learn that " the lesser nobility, chiefly the Protestants, continually supplied from among its ranks that dauntless army of corsairs who, from time to time, avenged on Spanish and Portuguese trade the butcheries of Fort Coligny and La Caroline." [69A] In the 17th century French corsairing had reached a high state of development. Of its extent and condition there is ample information in the two reports [70] on the *capitaines corsaires*, made for Colbert, when he formed the plan of joining the Dunkirk pirate ships into a fleet, under the command of Jean Bart, for the service of the crown. The reports deal with 33 captains commanding 15 frigates and 12 large barques. Of French origin also were the notorious buccaneers or filibusters who plied their nefarious trade in the waters of the Spanish colonies, round Jamaica and Haiti. [71]

But the classical instances of sea-robbery in the 16th and 17th centuries were to be found in England and the New England States in America. About the middle of the 16th century the coasts of England and Scotland fairly swarmed with those maritime highwaymen, the privateers. According to a report of Sir Thomas Chaloner, there were no less than 400 of these lawless adventurers in the Channel during the summer of 1563, and they captured between six and seven hundred French prizes in the course of a few months.[72]   In this connection, it is interesting to recall what Erasmus wrote in his *Naufragium* concerning the dangers of corsairing in these waters. English historians trace the sudden outburst of piracy to the Marian persecutions, as a result of which many members of the best families took to sea-robbery, and continued in it even after the accession of Elizabeth, having been joined by unemployed fishermen. " Almost every gentleman on the West coast participated in the business," we are told by Campbell, whose judgment is, as a rule, very cautious. His expression is the right one ; for an organized business it was. The ships were fitted out by wealthy folk, who were termed gentlemen adventurers ; often enough they were but the agents of others who advanced the necessary cash at a high rate of interest. Even the highest nobility did not scorn to be associated with these concerns. The Earl of Bothwell [73] in the days of Mary Queen of Scots, and the Earl of Derby and other royalists [74] in the Stuart period, are cases in point.

The American colonies became apt pupils of the mother country. The extent of sea-robbery, especially in the state of New York, would appear to have been incredible, except that evidence of it is supported by numerous reliable witnesses. According to the testimony of James Logan, Secretary of State in Pennsylvania, no less than 1,500 pirates cruised along the shores of Carolina alone in the year 1717 ; and of the total, 800 had their base in New Providence.[75] In the 17th century almost every colony had some connection with sea-robbery in one form or another.[76]

One species of the business was the voyages of discovery which had become so numerous since the 15th century. It is true that in the majority of cases all sorts of non-material motives were responsible for the enterprises—science, religion, glory, or pure adventure ; yet the strongest, and often enough the only moving influence was the desire for gain. In reality these voyages were nothing more than well-organized raiding expeditions to plunder lands beyond the sea ; more especially after the reports of Columbus, that on his voyages of discovery he had come across veritable gold-dust. El Dorado henceforth became the avowed or implied goal of all the expeditions.[77] Digging for treasure and gold-making, these superstitions were now united to a third—the search for a new land where gold could be gathered in spadefulls.[78]

What manner of men led these expeditions? They were strong, healthy adventurers, sure of victory, brutal and greedy, conquering all before them. Common as they were in those days, they have more and more ceased to exist in our own. These attractive, ruthless sea-dogs, who abounded more especially in England in the 16th century, were made of the same stuff as the leaders of hired bands in Italy of the type of Francesco Sforza and Cæsar Borgia, only they were more intent on the acquisition of gold and goods. They were thus more akin to the capitalist undertaker than their Italian predecessors. They were men who combined within themselves an adventurous imagination with great energy in action ; who were full of romance and yet possessed a keen eye for realities ; who commanded a fleet of buccaneers one day and held high offices of state the next ; who with itching palm dug for treasure to-day, and to-morrow began writing a universal history ; who, though their joy of life was hot and passionate and their love of pomp and luxury intense, were yet nevertheless able to bear for months together all the privations of a sea-voyage with an uncertain goal. They were men with the greatest capacity for organizing, and yet full of childish superstition. And they were the forerunners of the capitalist undertakers of to-day. Their names ? History has recorded them in plenty. The place of honour must

be given to Sir Walter Raleigh, " great Raleigh," as he
has been termed,[79] whose motto might well be applied to
the whole group—*Tam Marti quam Mercurio* (To Mars
and Mammon equally subject). Next to him may be
named Sir Francis Drake, the "noble pirate," as
Hentzner, who saw his ships in 1598, called him ; Sir
Martin Frobisher, who combined the spirit of a filibuster
with that of a scholar ; Sir Richard Grenville, of whom
John Smith in his *History of Virginia* speaks as " the
valiant " ; Cavendish, who came home with the " richest
prize that ever was brought at any time into England." [80]
There were many others, as readers of Hakluyt's third
volume of *Voyages* are aware.

It may be asked, what is my reason for bringing these
conquerors and robbers into connection with capitalism ?
The answer is simple enough. Not so much because they
themselves were a sort of capitalist undertaker, but
principally because the spirit within them was identical
with that in all trade and colony planting right down to
the middle of the 18th century. The two were equally
expeditions of adventure and conquest. Adventurer,
Sea-robber, and Merchant (a man was a merchant when
his argosies crossed the ocean) are but three impercep-
tible stages in development.

Benjamin of Tudela tells us [81] of the citizens of Genoa,
that "each of them has a tower in his house ; if civil war
breaks out, the battlements of these towers are the scenes
of conflict. They are masters of the sea ; they build
them ships, called galleys, and roam for plunder in the
most distant parts, bringing the spoil back to Genoa.
With Pisa they live in continual enmity." To whom is
he referring ? Does he mean the sea-robbers or the
" royal merchants " ? Obviously both are implicated.
Or, again, take the Levant trade. What was it for the
most part but strife and war ? Any one who wanted to

carve out a position for himself in a foreign land had to be a fighter, or be able to call in a fighter's aid, and be supported by the organized power of the state.[81A]   Shipping merchants in England in the 16th and 17th centuries are as good an instance as any.[82]   Consider the Hawkins, especially John and William.   Their careers were very chequered.   Now they were discoverers, now in the service of the state ; one day they were sea-robbers, the next they were captains of merchant vessels doing legitimate trade.   John Hawkins, "a wonderful hater of the Spaniards" (as his contemporaries called him), was as famous as a doughty champion against Spain as he was as a trader.   It is pretty much the same tale with others of this type, such as the Middletons.   Their "traffic" consisted of fighting with the East African natives, of being taken captive by them, and of negotiating with them.

Traffickers of this sort were not unknown in Germany. The Welser expedition to Venezuela[83] was a case in point.   At first sight it is not clear whether it was a voyage of discovery, or a colonial plantation, or merely a raiding enterprise or a commercial undertaking.   Who shall say ?   And what of Ulrich Krafft, who made voyages for the Manlichs ?   His adventurous career reads like a fairy-tale.[84]   Was he a trader, or just an adventurer ?   We should have to say that he was both.

It is the same story in France, where the word *armateur* means a shipper as well as a pirate.   And why ?   The reason is clear.   The men who in the 16th century sent their argosies from Dieppe, Havre, Rouen, or La Rochelle to Africa and America were shippers and pirates in one.[84A]

It is not until we come to the great trading and colonial companies that we see how much of that early commerce was freebooting, pure and simple.

The Italian trading companies of the Middle Ages

already showed signs of this. The Maone of Genoa were the best known among them. The most famous Maona, that of Chios, was established in 1347, and for two centuries owned the *dominium utile* not only of that island, but also of Phocea, Samos, Nicæa, and some others. Truth to tell, it was nothing more than a privileged and consolidated robber band. Its origin is interesting. A fleet of private merchantmen took Chios. When the armada returned to Genoa, the owners demanded 203,000 lire from the government as compensation for their trouble. But as the government was not in a position to pay, this debt was converted, on February 26, 1347, into the Compera or Maona of Chios. That island, and its neighbour Phocea, were handed over to the creditors as security.[85]

The great trading companies of the 16th and 17th centuries were not unlike their Genoese forerunners. They may be described as semi-warlike, conquering undertakings, to whom sovereignty rights, backed by the forces of the state, had been granted. Put it a little differently, and you may call them permanently organized bands of freebooters. Sea-robbery in the old style was, until well into the 17th century, a most important branch of the business of these companies. Take as an instance the Dutch West India Company. Between 1623 and 1636 it fitted out no less than 800 ships at a total cost of $4\frac{1}{2}$ million lire. But the outlay was more than recovered by the prize ships which it took, 540 in number, with goods to the value of 6 million lire. To this sum must be added another 3 million lire seized from the Portuguese.[86] It was a common thing to find in the balance-sheets of these trading companies the item " Privateering profits (or losses) " !

As for trade with native races, was that aught else but thinly veneered thieving ? Forced trading is the proper term to apply to all barter between uncivilized peoples and Europeans in those days. You can see its true nature in the state of mind which it produced in the natives—either despair or fierce anger, according to the temper of the race. The inhabitants of the Molucca Islands themselves destroyed the spice-trees, which they looked upon as the cause of their cruel sufferings. But their vengeance was not always aimed at the trees of the field ; often enough it burst on the heads of their oppressors, who had to shelter behind their citadels. " If the gates of the forts were not carefully closed at night, it might well be that the Indians with whom ' peaceful traffic' had been carried on in the day would break in, and murder the traders." This is a cameo picture from among the records of the Hudson Bay Company ; [87] it may be taken as typical for the beginnings of all colonial trade. The warlike preparations which all the companies found it necessary to make only go to support this view. And these preparations, which were intended to assist trade, were by no means insignificant. Those of the Italians in the Levant set the pace. Giovanni Bembo's account of the Venetian " factories" in Tana tells of fortifications and towers, castles and drawbridges, and similar evidence of strong defences.[88] Almost identical were the pictures of the settlements of the commercial companies in the 16th and 17th centuries. Thus, we are told of the Dutch " factory " in Bengal, " It looks more like a castle, surrounded as it is by deep moats full of water, high walls and bastions bristling with cannon." [89] As for the military strength of the English colonies during the 18th century, we have a series of reports [90] of the year 1734, which show that Jamaica had 6 forts and 3,000 men, out of a total of 7,644 white inhabitants ; Barbadoes 21 forts, 26 batteries of 463 cannon, and 4,812 militia out of a total of 18,295 white inhabitants ; the

Leeward Islands, 3,772 militia out of a total of 10,262 white men.

The warlike and freebooting spirit, which characterized all maritime trade in those days, was also in the men who stood at the head of the great trading enterprises. A goodly number of them were noblemen, who thus found an outlet for their military ardour, which the army at home was not sufficiently able to utilize. It was not until much later that the English East India Company adopted a resolution " not to employ any gentleman in any place of charge or commandment in the said voyage. . . . They wished to sort their business with men of their own quality." [91]

Even the Dutch companies could not escape this tendency. Their leaders likewise were heroes and adventurers. If we were to arrange a portrait gallery of the Governor-Generals of the Dutch East India Company,[92] we should find that most of them had the appearance, especially those of the 17th century, not of linen-drapers but of hard, enterprising, military commanders. Curiously enough, the military touch was general in Holland at the time.[93]

To carry on great trade, then, meant to fit out ships and arm them, engage the services of fighting men, conquer new lands, have dealings with the natives with a gun in one hand and a sword in the other, rob them of their possessions, carry back the spoil in the ships to the motherland and sell it there at auction to the highest bidder. Besides all this, it meant seizing by force as legitimate prize as many ships of foreigners as opportunity allowed. Are we not justified, therefore, in saying that the spirit of all trade and colonial undertakings (in so far as the latter had not for their object the plantation of new colonies) was the spirit of freebooting and privateering ? Let me once again quote Goethe's lines,

which sum up epigrammatically the inwardness of my
thesis :—

> War, traffic, and piracy
> Are an indivisible trinity.

Capitalism is a complex of many contributory spirits,
and it is one of the principal aims of this book to establish this view.   We have examined the plant that sprang
from the warlike root.   We now turn to another.

2. THE LANDLORD.

There is nothing in landlordism that is inherently
capitalistic, any more than there is in warlike undertakings.   The manorial system, as such, does not aim at
gain ; for a very long period it remained an economic
organization for the satisfying of wants, no more and
no less.

But in the process of time a change set in.   The
domestic economy of the landlord was narrowed, and,
side by side with it, there sprang up an economic order
bent on profit, which slowly but surely became capitalistic
in its nature.   What happened was that the overlord
organized the labour at his disposal for the purpose of
getting gain.   The land was his and he became a corn-
grower ; the treasures of the earth—its minerals and
metals—were his also ; he claimed the ownership of
woodlands and meadows ; and he disposed of the labour
of the human beings on his estates.   He combined all
these factors in production, and the result was varying
forms of capitalist undertakings, all of them filled with
the spirit of their master-mind, and therefore all of them
semi-feudal in their nature.

Semi-feudal ?   I mean that all these undertakings had
not yet thrown off the character of enterprises for the production of just so much wealth as would satisfy the wants

of the community. One reason for this was their limited scope. They were bounded by the property of the landlord. This has been recognized as a check on the free expansion of capitalist undertakings. Thus, we are told of the Silesian mines at the beginning of the 19th century, "The landlord owns the iron ore ; he mines annually no more than will use up his surplus timber, which he cannot utilize in any other profitable way." [94]

These undertakings were semi-feudal also in the means they chose for their end. The conception still prevailed in them that the power of the state was the almighty influence that was to be looked to for one's interests, whether for the disposal of men or commodities ; or an indirect influence which aided in a sale or a bargain—say, the granting of a concession, privilege, or monopoly. This gave birth to an important sub-species of undertaking, partly capitalistic, partly feudal. Influential members of the nobility associated themselves with the moneyed sections of the middle classes, or with impoverished inventors, for the purpose of common gain. The lordling provided the necessary privileges or liberties, the other partner the money or the brains. Partnerships of this sort abounded in scores, both in France and England, throughout the 17th and 18th centuries.[95]

But the undertakings of the landlords, and of the nobility and gentry generally, played a more important rôle in the early capitalist age than has been commonly assumed. Their influence in the development of capitalist undertaking cannot of course be exactly demonstrated, lacking as we do any statistical information on the point. But a general notion of their influence is undoubtedly possible, if we glance at some of the cases of capitalist enterprise in which the nobility took part.

Let us begin with capitalist farming, which certainly in its earliest forms was carried on by the landed interests.

From the 16th to the 18th centuries, England [96] and Germany [97] both have numerous instances.

But industry was by no means neglected. Mining was a favourite undertaking in which the nobility engaged. They not merely received the royalties from others ; they participated in the industries themselves. As royalty-receivers they do not interest us in this place ; what we are concerned with is their activity as undertakers ; and it is surprising to find how extended that was. A comprehensive consideration of this strongly marked aspect of capitalist enterprise is undoubtedly a desideratum. Here we can touch on but a few examples.

In England, in the 15th century, we have information of the Bishop of Durham's forge at Bedburn, in Weardale. This appears to have been organized on a capitalist basis ; certainly the number of employees seems great.[98] In 1616, a courtier entered into an agreement with the pen-makers' company to supply them with wire, which, seemingly, he produced on his estates.[99] Again, in 1627, Lord Dacre received a patent granting him the monopoly of steel production, according to new methods.[100] Or, to take yet another instance. From the 16th century landlords set up tin-works on their estates, the so-called clash mills, for the preparation of the tin from their own mines.[101] In 1690 a number of lords and gentlemen helped in the foundation of the Mine Adventurers' Company.[102] It was the same with the earliest enterprises for coal-mining ; many a nobleman was interested in this industry likewise, and the conditions of labour in English, and especially in Scottish, mines in the 18th century smacked of feudalism.[102A]

If we turn from this country to France, the same phenomenon may be observed. The mines in the province of Nevers, one of the centres of the industry, were owned by the local landed gentry until well into the 18th century. Villemenant was in the hands of the Arnault de Langes; their neighbour, the Seigneur de Bizy, conducted on his estate not only mining operations, but smelting as well. All these establishments passed in the 18th century into the possession of the rich Paris banker Masson.[103] In the Franche-Comté likewise there were numerous mines, all owned by the ancient nobility.[104]

Of the manufacture of iron the same story may be told. The landowners participated in iron-making. The cases were numerous, and we need only mention two. Seigneur F. E. de Blumenstein erected an ironworks near his castle, in 1715;[105] and the Duc de Choiseul about the same time was manufacturing steel.[106-7] But it was the coal industry that specially interested the French nobility.[108] Henry II had granted the sole right to exploit coal-mines to François de la Rocque, Seigneur de Roberval; it passed from him to Claude Grizon de Guillien, Seigneur de St. Julien, and another nobleman. At a later date Louis XIV granted a monopoly of 40 years' duration to the Duke of Montauzier for the sole working of all coal-mines in France, excepting only those of Nevers. In the following reign, the Regent issued a similar privilege to a company which included, among others, the names of Jean Gobelin and Sieur de Joncquier. But the nobility possessed not only the right of working mines; the actual work was carried out under their direction. Thus, in Louis XIV's reign, the Duc de Noailles opened a mine in the Duchy of Bournonville; the Duc d'Aumont another; the Count d'Uzès a third;[109] and the Duc de la Meilleraye a fourth.[110] Instances of this kind, where the nobility obtained monopolies to work coal, either on their own estates or elsewhere, became more and more abundant in the second half of the 18th century.

The same tale comes from Germany and Austria. In both these countries the earliest mining undertakings were

conducted by the nobility. In a document entitled
"Masters and Establishments on the Imperial Estate of
St. Kathrein" (the mercury-mines of Idria) for the period
1520–26, we come across an exceptionally large number
of names of noblemen, e.g. Gabriel Count Ortenburg,
Bernard von Cles, the Lord Cardinal-Bishop of Trent, to
name but three. The lists of the years 1536, 1557,
1559 and 1574 [111] bear the same character.

Gradually the names of traders crept in too. But it
must be remembered that, often enough, even though no
nobleman was mentioned in connection with the undertakings, these were still dominated by the feudal spirit,
and the influence of the landlord made itself felt in a
thousand ways.[112]

The iron industry in Germany had likewise to thank
the nobility for its capitalist spirit. Count Stolberg
became famous in the 16th century for his interest in ironworks; Count Wolfgang established the foundry of
Koenigshof, made Ilseburg a centre for iron-casting, and
erected the first brass-works there. His neighbour,
Count Julius von Braunschweig-Lüneburg, was a strong
competitor. In the case of another iron-foundry, that of
Gitteld, in the Harz Mountains, the income and expenditure accounts from 1573 to 1848 are extant, and from
these it is evident how strongly marked was the influence
of the nobility here also.[113] The same was true of the
iron industry in Styria; [114] and as for the Silesian mines,
have they not remained in the hands of the local
landowners down to this very day?

Finally, let me instance Sweden, where iron-mining
was a subsidiary industry of agriculture. The lords of
the land employed miners as well as their agricultural
labourers on the work. And to-day, when mining and
agriculture are independent industries, the old conditions
still continue in Dannemora.[115]

So much for mining. In the textile trades the influence of the noble families was no less marked. The most competent historian of the woollen industry in England sums up the position there by saying that the great sheep farmers were very often cloth-weavers, using the wool they themselves grew.[116] Silk-making likewise was in their hands. Thus, in 1689, we find "a grant to Walter, Lord Ashton, of the keeping of the garden, mulberry-trees, and silkworms near St. James in the county of Middlesex."[117] Again it was the same in France. There also the landowners had spinning-wheels on their estates for wool or silk.[118] In the 18th century the Marquis de Coulaincourt erected a factory for muslin and silk veilings; the Marquis de Louvencourt one for linen; the Duchesse de Choiseul-Gouffier a cotton-spinning establishment, and so forth.[119] Indeed, the number of noblemen engaged in the textile industry in France in the 18th century was very large indeed.[120]

Bohemia serves as an excellent instance of the influence of the aristocracy on industrial development in the 18th century. Fired by the example of Duke Josef Kinsky, a number of them established factories on their estates. By 1762 Kinsky was able to report to the Empress the "joyful news" that many a nobleman in Bohemia, including among others Count Waldstein, Prince Lobkowitz and Earl Bolza, was inclined to aid the growth of manufactures on his lands.[121] "But the majority of these nobles' establishments," such was the view of a man of the people, "lacked the necessary energy and vitality. Things changed, however, with the appearance of John Josef Leitenberger (1730–1802), the son of a small Bohemian master dyer."[122]

Another industry much favoured by the nobility and gentry was glass-making, probably because it provided such excellent opportunities for the utilization of the abundant supplies of timber on the estates. In France the nobility practically held a monopoly of glass-blowing, hence the term *verriers gentilshommes*.[123] Commoners might erect glass factories only by special permission, or they were allowed to participate in the existing establishments. What applied to France held good equally for other countries also.

Finally, the manufacture of porcelain, corn and paper mills, and such industries as gave opportunities for burning peat, must also be mentioned.[124] In a word, there are many points in the economic history of Europe where the landed gentry may be seen contributing to the development of capitalism. We are justified in regarding the landlord, therefore, as a type of an early capitalist undertaker. And our conviction of this can only be strengthened as we remember that capitalism in colonial foundations was for the most part of a feudal nature. The Italians in their settlements in the Levant established an economic order modelled on the feudal system. In many cases the change was merely a change of masters; the Turkish landlord was replaced by a "Frank." As for the towns, they were expropriated just like the country districts; the Italian conquerors divided the craftsmen among themselves like so many serfs. The whole structure rested on enslaved labour.

The Spaniards and Portuguese did exactly the same in their treatment of the American Indians. The newcomers regarded themselves as feudal landlords, with sway over the inhabitants. The Spaniard spoke of *Encomiendas* and *repartiementos*; the Portuguese of *Kapitanien* and *Sesmarias*. Labour, at first on a feudal basis, later developed into slavery. The mine-owners and planters who worked their possessions in a capitalist spirit were feudal lords of the old type.[125]

The same may be asserted of the earliest undertakers

in the Southern States of the American Union. We need only call to mind Lord Delaware, the principal participant in the Virginia Company of London, established in 1606 ; or Lord Baltimore, the " founder " of Maryland, whose desire for profits is no longer doubted ; or of the eight landowners, among whom we find the Duke of Albemarle, the Earl of Clarendon, Sir William Berkeley and Lord Shaftesbury, who in 1663 took possession of the land between Virginia and Florida—Carolina.[126] All of these founded feudal undertakings based on slave labour, and the semi-feudal character of the capitalist plantations in the " Negro " States right down to the Civil War bore testimony to the fact. Only after the war did the commercial spirit carry the day over " the Southern gentlemen " ; only then was ended the attempt to found, " in an environment of farmers and traders, industrialists and free wage-earners, a plantation system of *grands seigneurs* and their petty imitators, based on force and customary dues." [126ᴬ]

3. THE CIVIL SERVANT.

It is possible to conceive the modern state as a huge capitalist undertaking, seeing that its aim is more and more to get gold and money. Such indeed has been the case ever since the discoveries and conquests of the Spaniards cultivated in ruling princes the taste for a share of the booty, and when India also came within their horizon, that taste became even more marked.

But even when conquering expeditions in the Dorado were not uppermost in their minds, statesmen were constantly occupied with the problem of amassing gold. How to get money?—that was the alpha and omega of their thoughts. Sometimes it was for the expenses of the state ; sometimes for economic progress. But the problem was the same. Recall Colbert's reason for the policy of Mercantilism. " I believe," he said,[127] " that most people would be agreed that the quantity of gold in a state alone determines the degree of its greatness and power." Put " profits " instead of " gold " in this dictum, and you have the first principle of every capitalist undertaking.

But in calling the civil servant an early type of the capitalist undertaker, I am thinking neither of the goal which mercantilism set itself nor of the policy which modern states pursued to reach it. We shall have occasion to refer to both, when we deal with the sources of the capitalist spirit; and we shall then observe that many a regulation of the Mercantile system nurtured the seeds of the capitalist spirit in the average citizen.

My object here is to call attention to the fact that ruling princes and their servants, the state officials, were among those who kept alive the spirit of capitalist undertaking; and that both played a rôle of no small significance among the earliest representatives of the modern economic outlook.

What a reliable authority says of Gustavus Vasa holds good for all the important princes of the *ancien régime.* " He was the chief undertaker of his nation. Not only did he know how to discover and utilize for the crown the mineral wealth of Sweden, but by commercial treaties and protective duties, and last but not least, by engaging himself in foreign trade on a large scale, he acted as an example to his merchants. Everything was due to his initiative." [128]

It would require a whole treatise were we to attempt to chronicle all those activities of monarchs in modern times that stamped them as founders of capitalist industries. There is the less need to do so, seeing that the facts are pretty generally known. The mere reference to them must therefore suffice. But what I will do is to consider the peculiar importance of these state enterprises, and demonstrate the special qualities of civil servants which mark them as capitalist undertakers.

First and foremost, state enterprises appeared as activities on a large scale where before there had been no activities whatsoever. Often enough it was the initiative of the monarch himself that was responsible for the undertakings. Consequently, in many cases it may be said that the monarch was the fount wherein the first beginnings of the undertaking spirit lay hidden. A German mercantilist writer points out what is appropriate for private initiative and what for public ; and the opinion may be regarded as classical. To improve manufactures, says this worthy, you need cleverness, thought, and money ; and he concludes, " These things are for the state ; the merchant continues in his work just as he learned it and is accustomed to it. The general advantage of his native land is no concern of his." [129] These simple words speak volumes. True, they were written down in a Germany which was as yet in a backward condition. They hold good nevertheless (possibly in a weaker form) for all cases of early capitalist economic activities. How, for instance, would mining have fared, in more places than one, if the ruling prince had not stepped in at the right moment and dragged the disused carts out of the mire? You need only refer to the history of the mining industry in what is to-day the Ruhr district. " With a system of mining that was without plan (and such it had been for centuries, until about the middle of the 18th), it was hardly possible to expect a far-sighted policy. In the mining regulations issued in the Mark of Cleves in 1766, the state took over the technical and commercial management of the concern. The guardians brought up the neglected child." [130] It was the same in a thousand other cases.

Now while the undertakings of the state were of great importance for the development of capitalism, their quality was of no less significance. State enterprises were always on a large scale ; there was something big about them.   In an age when the accumulation of capital was not extensive, the state was able to devote considerable sums of money to its undertakings, and often enough the state was the only agency with sufficient means to commence an undertaking.   As illustrations we need only recall the transport enterprises both by land and sea, which even into the 19th century were made possible because the state was behind them.

Similarly, the state had at its disposal the necessary organization for these undertakings.   To appreciate the full value of the civil service let us call to mind that earlier ages lacked trained intelligence for administrative work of all sorts.   The advantage in this respect which the state possessed over the private undertaker goes without saying.   The state had the administrative machine ready ; the private undertaker had first to provide it.

Nor is this all.   State undertakings had a large prospectiveness about them.   Who so well as a reigning monarch could make plans for the future ?   And so, the characteristic marks of all capitalist undertaking, that your schemes should be far-sighted and your energy continuously active, both sprang from the very nature of state enterprise.   In the same way, for creative ideas, extensive knowledge, and scientific training, who so well situated as the ruler of the state ?   Where else could you find so much capacity as in the council chamber ?   In those days, gifted citizens placed their capabilities at the disposal of the state.   Of course, a good many princes were nonentities.   But I am thinking rather of the competent ones, and of them and of their equally competent ministers, history has a fairly long list. Was any one more capable as a capitalist undertaker, in the France of those days, than Colbert? [131] And in the Prussia of Frederick the Great, who was more distinguished in the same way than Freiherr von Heinitz, the founder of the state's mining works in Upper Silesia?

In the process of time, state undertakings began to manifest certain weaknesses—slow and cautious movement, red-tape, and so on. But these things were not yet in the earliest stages of capitalist development. On the contrary, in those days the civil servant represented a most important type of subsidiary capitalist undertaker, who by his special gifts made a lasting impression on the history of capitalism.

4. THE SPECULATOR.

How does the speculator come in as a type of capitalist undertaker? The answer is simple—as soon as he appears as the organizer of a speculative undertaking. A case in point is when a " projector " obtains the necessary means for putting his idea into execution ; when, as I have already said, projecting unites with undertaking. This must have been the case towards the end of the 17th century. We are told that the projectors at that time were beginning to find favourable consideration at the hands of the financiers, and that in consequence " flotations " of all kinds made their appearance. Speculative undertakings these are best called ; and Defoe informs us about them in his own inimitable fashion [*On Projecting* (1697), pp. 12–14] :—

There are, and that too many, fair pretences of fine discoveries, new inventions, engines and I know not what, which being advanced in notion, and talked up to great things to be performed when such and such sums shall be advanced, and such and such engines are made, have raised the fancies of credulous people to such a height, that merely on the shadow of expectation they have formed companies, chose committees, appointed officers, shares, and books, raised great stocks, and cried up an empty notion to that degree, that people have been betrayed to part with their money for shares in a New-nothing ; and when the inventors have carried on the jest till they have sold all their own interest, they leave the cloud to vanish of itself, and the poor purchasers to quarrel with one another and go to law about settlements, transferrings, and some bone or other thrown among 'em by the subtlety of the author, to lay the blame of the miscarriage upon themselves.   Thus the shares at first begin to fall by degrees, and happy is he that sells in time, till like brass money it will go at last for nothing at all.   So have I seen shares in joint-stocks, patents, engines, and undertakings blown up by the air of great words, and the name of some man of credit concerned, to £100 for a 500th part, or share, some more, and at last dwindle away till it has been stock-jobbed down to £12, £10, £9 or £8 a share, and at last no buyer ; that is, in short, the fine new word for Nothing-worth, and many families ruined by the purchase.   If I should name linen manufactures, saltpetre works, copper-mines, diving engines, dipping, and the like for instances of this, I should, I believe, do no wrong to truth, or to some persons too visibly guilty.

There is in reality no need to appeal to the evidence of so excellent an authority as Defoe in order to characterize that age, and more especially the first decade in the 18th century, as a period of company promotion on a large scale.   So far as I am aware, it was the first of its kind in which the desire to establish capitalist undertakings became a veritable epidemic, particularly in England and France.   It was the time of the South Sea Bubble and of Law's Financial Scheme, both of which so dominated the period that we are apt to forget that around each of these giant enterprises hundreds of lesser ones were clustered. Together they present the true picture of the age.

A new world burst upon the horizon of mankind in those days.   Some idea of it may be conveyed by a bird's-eye view of the extent and ramifications of the company promotions of the period—not only the first in history, but models for the future.   The contemporary official inquiries furnish a mine of information in their reports, to say nothing of Anderson's treatise.[132]   In this, speaking of the year 1720, he says it was " a year remarkable beyond any other which can be pitched upon by historians for extraordinary and romantic projects, proposals, and undertakings, both private and national ; . . . and which therefore ought to be held in perpetual remembrance, not only as being what never had its parallel, nor, it is to be hoped, ever will hereafter ; but, likewise, as it may serve for a perpetual memento to the legislators and ministers of our own nation, never to leave it in the power of any hereafter to hoodwink mankind into so shameful and baneful an imposition on the credulity of the people."

A few illustrations from Anderson may therefore not be out of place.

The centre of greatest attraction in England was, of course, the South Sea Company.   In its origin it was no more than one of the numerous colonial companies established long before.   Its charter provided for a monopoly of trade on the eastern coast of America from the river " Aronoca " to the southernmost part of Tierra del Fuego, and on the west coast from Cape Horn northwards.   Like its prototypes, the South Sea Company was granted sovereign rights over the regions wherein its activities were to lie.

But the significance of the South Sea Company lay not in its own speculative undertaking, but rather in its serving as a concern which lent itself to speculative activities.   It achieved this by being mixed up with the national finances.   According to the custom of the time, the company took over a considerable portion of the National Debt, gradually having over 31 millions incorporated in its stock.   Which means, and this is the important point, that a large part of the national capital,

hitherto invested in gilt-edged securities the interest on
which was fixed, was now an investment subject to variations in dividend.   In 1720 the directors were allowed to
carry out their scheme of absorbing the National Debt by
purchase or subscription.   So frenzied was the speculative
fever among the wealthy classes that the stock rose to
£1,000 for every £100 subscribed.   Once the gambling
rage had become acute, crafty projectors utilized it to
float innumerable new undertakings.   It would be tiresome
to give a complete list of these bubbles, but some among
them may be of interest.   [The details are from
Anderson.]

	Original Money paid in or due.			Highest Prices sold for in 1720.
	£	s.	d.	£
Million Bank	100	0	0	440
York Buildings Company	18	0	0	305
Lustring Company	5	2	6	120
English Copper Company	5	0	0	105
Welsh Copper Company	4	2	6	95
Royal Fishery Company	10	0	0	25
Company for making the River Douglas navigable	5	0	0	70
Company for fresh water to be brought to Liverpool	10	0	0	20
Temple Mills Brass Works	10	0	0	250
Hamburg Company	15	0	0	120
The Orkney Fishery Company ...	25	0	0	250
Fire Insurance Company	0	2	6	8

There were besides 12 companies for fishing, 4 for
salt-mining, 8 for insurance, 2 for remittances of money,
4 water companies, 2 sugar companies, 11 for trade or
settlements in different parts of America, 2 building
companies, 13 for agriculture, 6 oil bubbles, 4 for
improving harbours and rivers, 4 for supplies for London,
6 for manufacture of hemp and flax, 5 for cotton, 15 for
metals, mines, and minerals, to say nothing of others of a

miscellaneous character, including one for cleaning and paving London streets (with a capital of two millions sterling), for trading in human hair, for employing the poor, for a grand dispensary (three millions), for the discovery of perpetual motion, for paper manufacture, and many more.

Altogether 200 companies (bubbles) were promoted in that one year, 1720. The figure is for a year of average business in our own time, neither particularly good nor particularly bad. But for the England of those days it was tremendous. Moreover, the list we have enumerated bears testimony to flourishing imaginations in the promoters themselves.

What was the " spirit " of these enterprises, the spirit that gave them birth ? In other words, what are we to understand by speculation (not generally, but in so far as it affected capitalist undertakings) ? We shall find a reply in the analysis of the speculator's soul.

Speculative capitalist undertakings differ from the three already mentioned in that both for their conception and execution they call for far different qualities. In the three previous instances, we saw a common basis of outward force or pressure. The directors of these undertakings are able to carry out their schemes by the aid of their might. In the case of the freebooter, might comes to the fore very much ; in the case of the landlord and the civil servant it takes a secondary place. But the speculator depends on a new power, which is within himself—the power of suggestion ; and this alone enables him to realize his schemes. Instead of outward force he looks to an inner force ; in place of fear he sets hope.

And this is how he accomplishes his task. He himself, with all the passionate intensity he is capable of, dreams the dream of the successful issue of his under-

taking.   He sees himself already rich and influential, the
idol of his neighbours, the hero of famous deeds which
his fancy so magnifies that they become like elongated
shadows on a wall.   Let him but have completed the
work in hand and others will be added unto it, until the
two hemispheres resound with the praise of his enterprises.   He sees visions of giant undertakings ; his pulse
beats quickly like a person's in a fever.   The exaggeration of his own ideas grows by reason of its own momentum.   His soul may be said to be in a condition of
lyrical enthusiasm.   And the result of all this ?   He
carries others along with him, who help him to realize
his plan.   If he is a specially able type of speculating
undertaker, he may possibly possess the poet's gift of
calling up to the minds of his audience ravishing pictures
of realms of gold, in order to show the marvels he is
capable of producing and the blessings his enterprise will
shower on the world, as well as on those who co-operate
with him.   He promises the treasures of Midas, and
knows how to make his words sound plausible.   He
stirs up the imagination ; he arouses faith.[133]   He thus
awakes mighty instincts, and contrives to make them
subservient to his ends.   Above all, he tickles the
gaming propensities, utilizing them to his advantage.
In short, there is no speculative undertaking on any large
scale without stock-exchange gambling.   The gamble is
the soul of the business, or the flame that glows right
through it.   " Eh bien ! " cries Saccard, " no speculation,
no business.   Why on earth do you expect me to fork
out my money, to risk my future, when you make no
promise of an extraordinarily tempting return, of some
unlooked-for happiness, or that the heavens will open to
my gaze ?   Legitimate and moderate payment for work
done, rational equilibrium of everyday activities—bah !
Life with these only is an extensive waste of deadly dull-

ness ; a morass in which man's powers and capacities go
to sleep, and then waste away. But let a dream picture
of a sudden appear on the horizon, proclaim that with a
single *sou* you can get a hundred, hold out to the sleepy
souls the probability of chasing the impossible, show
them the millions to be earned in a short hour . . . and
the race commences at break-neck speed, energies are
whipped to boiling-point, and the crowd is so dense that
though everybody is working for his own selfish ends,
they produce living things magnificent in their beauty."

In a word, you must stir up desire. Never mind what
means you adopt, if only the end is achieved. Attract
people's attention, appeal to their curiosity, make them
want to buy. For all this, the louder you shout the
better. The speculator's work is done, he has reached
his desired haven, when large numbers of people are
thrown into a state of feverish restlessness, ready to
provide the wherewithal for the completion of the speculator's undertaking. And the less simple the plan of any
undertaking is, the more difficult for the mind to grasp
it in its entirety, the better fitted it becomes for the
speculator's purpose, and the more marvellous the results
he can promise. Accordingly, immense undertakings,
whether they be in banking or oversea commerce or
transport (the Suez and Panama Canals at once spring to
the mind), lend themselves best of all for the exercise of
the speculative spirit. Such has been the case from the
very first, and it has continued so to this day.

5. The Trader.

Whenever a trader, from plain money-dealing or the
selling of wares, developed a true capitalist undertaking,
he also may be regarded as a type of undertaker. The
earliest businesses had something of the handicraft about

them ; bit by bit they were extended, until ultimately and imperceptibly there was a transition from one economic order to another.   Whereas before quality had been the main determinant factor, now quantity has taken its place.   This must have been quite a common process. The early *negotiatores* developed into capitalist under-takers, whether we turn to the Florentine wool merchants, the English tradesmen, or the French *marchands*. Obviously, a series of auspicious circumstances must have contributed to enable this metamorphosis to take place. The nature of these circumstances does not for the moment concern us ; it is sufficient to observe that the metamorphosis was a frequently occurring phenomenon. How frequent it is impossible to say ; but certainly frequent enough.

Traders turned capitalist undertakers in yet another way : they became manufacturers.   A very important process, this, whereby craftsmen, and sometimes even agricultural labourers, were financed by the wealthy, until they sank down to the position of wage-earners in a capitalist undertaking.   The " clothiers " in England in the 18th century are a case in point.   We have already seen that the middlemen who supplied the necessary cash hailed from all manner of social groups.   Of course, these became capitalist undertakers only when they themselves engaged in commerce.   Often, too, the richer craftsmen employed their less favoured brethren in this fashion.

Let us glance at a few of the early instances.   The *Arte della Lana di Pisa,* in the 14th century, forbade its members to entrust to any of their workmen more than 25 pounds of wool, if they lived in a town, or 50 pounds if they lived in the country.   No *Lanaiulo* of the city of Pisa might erect more than one weaving shed in which work was done for wages (*ad pregio*).

In England, in 1537, we are told that in the gild of

sheep-shearers the richer masters had lent their poorer colleagues two sums of £100 and £50 respectively. There was some disagreement about these debts, and it would seem that the borrowers had been obliged to work them off. "Davy Ellys had commandment to work with Humphrey Hitchcock or with Thomas Saunders until such time as they be both satisfied of their debts which is due to them by the said Ellys." [134] Again, a law of 1548 forbade the rich leather-sellers to provide their poorer brethren with leather ; next year the law was repealed, because "most of the artificers are poor men and unable to provide such store of material as would serve their turn." [135] About the same time a similar tale came from France. [136]

Despite these instances, however, the ranks of the middlemen or "clothiers" were recruited for the most part from among traders ; so much so that this tendency may be regarded as having been the general rule. The process has not escaped the observation of historians, Marx among them, who, reducing it to a simple formula, speak of a gradual application of commercial capital to the work of production. It was not quite so simple as all that, as we have already seen. Nevertheless, cases of plain traders who became directors of manufacturing enterprises occurred in great abundance, and in some industries more than in others. Here are a few illustrations.

The textile trade stands first. From the 14th century onward, and possibly even earlier, clothsellers (and often, too, silk-mercers) in almost every land gave out work to craftsmen in their homes. The "clothiers" in England, *marchands drapiers* in France, the members of the "Calimala" gild—all were middlemen of this kind. Mining must be assigned the second place. The third is occupied by *articles de luxe*, while the fourth must

be accorded to tailoring, in which, certainly in the
17th century, the sellers of clothes (mostly Jews)
blossomed out into tailors on a large scale.[137]

Now, what manner of men were these newcomers,
creeping in silently to conquer the world? We shall be
in a position to answer this question if we direct our
attention to the then prevailing method of trade and
traffic, as well as to undertakings generally, among the
three peoples in whom the commercial spirit manifested
itself, not only earlier than elsewhere, but also in a more
perfect form. I refer to the Florentines, the Scotch, and
the Jews. Let us glance at each in turn.

It is a striking fact that the method of the Florentines[137A]
in the Levant, certainly from the 13th century, differed
considerably from that of the Venetians, Pisans, or
Genoese. These fought; Florence traded. The former
looked to their mighty armies and their fleets; the
Florentines, even in the most flourishing period of their
commerce, had no navy, and not even any mercantile
marine to speak of. Their goods were carried by foreign
vessels chartered for the purpose, and if these required
protection the Florentines engaged the Provençal or
Genoese galleys. But they avoided dangerous routes if
they could, selecting land routes wherever possible, or
making long detours, in order to escape the pirates that
infested the Archipelago or the ships of neighbouring
states. Their success in foreign countries was due to
three things—money, treaties, and special knowledge, both
commercial and general. From the first the Florentines
were more financiers than ordinary traders, money-dealers
rather than dealers in commodities. As for their treaties,
whole lists are extant of advantageous agreements. But
their knowledge was, perhaps, of most importance.
For this the books of Balducci (Pegolotti) and Uzzano
are eloquent witnesses; the merchants of Florence

obtained their knowledge of commerce, of geography, and other useful subjects from these sources. Pagnini adduced these writers as a proof of the experience of the Florentine merchants (*prova della perizia de' nostri mercanti*). They were the camp-followers of the warlike nations ; when these were exhausted they took their place; when these by their rude conduct lost the favour of sultans and rulers, the Florentines knew how to ingratiate themselves into their confidence by gifts and fair promises. "That Venice should bleed to death by fighting the Turks single-handed was the silent hope of the Florentines. Accordingly they manœuvred so that the war should not be made the common cause of the West (1463). And when Pope Pius II invited the Florentines to participate in it, they excused themselves by saying that their merchants and ships could not be recalled from Turkey in time." All the while they were angling for the Sultan's favour, "they sat in his council, celebrated his victories, and knew so well how to derive the greatest possible advantage for themselves as traders, that the Genoese in Pera and all other Italians in the Levant were bursting with jealousy and anger." No wonder, then, that when the Venetians made a request to the Florentines to join them against the Turks, the Signoria replied that " the invitation had come just too late, seeing that a great deal of cloth had already been made, and other commodities purchased for export to Turkey." A policy such as this often brought with it the sacrifice of personal dignity, but there was no need to shrink from that if commercial advantage ensued. Thus, in the island of Cyprus, the Florentines were not among the privileged nations. In order to enjoy the discount of 2 per cent. on customs dues which the Pisans had obtained, the Florentines pretended they were Pisans, even though the latter made them pay dearly for the ruse by the contempt with which they treated them. But what is contempt when profit is assured? Similarly, the Florentines thought nothing of purchasing two harbours from the Doge of Genoa, who required ready cash in order to keep his enemies at a distance. The Florentines provided the 100,000 florins, and took over the harbours on June 24, 1421. But the transaction apparently brought them little joy, for in 1500 their goods were once more carried in foreign bottoms. Drapers and bankers, it would seem, are spoiled for shipping. For in all shipping enterprises, then even more than now, there is a goodly dash of the freebooter. Freebooters, however, the Florentines were not. That is just wherein their trade differed from that of their neighbours.

And as with trade, so with industry. Florentine cloth-making, perhaps the first capitalistically organized industry in the world, was an offspring of the trade in wool. Once again, therefore, we meet with the commercial spirit. Indeed, this spirit was reflected in the public life of the city. Recall how it allowed its great men to suffer, and behaved in a niggardly way to its artists. What else could you expect, seeing that ever since the 14th century the city had been governed by bankers and drapers! It was only the finishing touch, when, appropriately enough, a family of money-dealers became the princes of the state.

So much for the Florentines. We turn now to the Scotch, who may be called the Florentines of the North, despite the many characteristics that differentiated the two types. As the rise of the Medicis was probably the only case in history of a family of bankers becoming ruling princes, so, too, it must have been a unique historical fact for one people to sell their king to another for a lump sum, as did the Scotch with Charles. I ought to add that in speaking of the Scotch I mean the Lowlanders ; the Highlanders are an essentially different type of folk. Indeed, the two are as opposed as the poles.

Like the Florentines, the Scotch Lowlanders had little love for a seafaring life, though the ocean washed their coasts on both sides. The Scotch were never what might be termed a maritime people on a large scale. About the middle of the 17th century, the English East India Company owned some 15,000 tons of shipping ; as early as 1628 there sailed on the Thames estuary 7 Indiamen of 4,200 tons, and 34 other craft with a tonnage of 7,850. How did the largest Scottish harbour, Leith, compare with this ? It had 12 ships, of a total tonnage of 1,000 ; while Glasgow had 12 ships likewise, totalling together 830 tons ; Dundee had 10 ships of 498 tons.[138] Until well into the 18th century the Scotch possessed no fleet to speak of ; before that their goods were carried in English bottoms. *132877*

Their principal commerce was inland. They were the middlemen between the Highlands and London. In so far as they adventured abroad, they took fish, coal, or plaiding to Ireland, Holland, Norway, and France, bringing back hops, corn, flour, and butter. But throughout their trafficking a mighty desire for gain burned within them. During the 16th and 17th centuries it was covered by an unparalleled bigotry ; towards the end of the 17th century it burst out into flame, so that the Scotch at home and abroad became successful undertakers. The spirit of their enterprises is illustrated by a proverb of theirs, which Karl Marx quotes somewhere, " If you have made a little profit it cannot be difficult to make a lot. The difficulty lies in making a little." [" Many a mickle makes a muckle."]

In a word, the commercial spirit dominated Scotch trading activities. A clever observer wrote as follows

about the Florentine-Scotch commercial attitude at the
beginning of the 19th century, contrasting it with that of
the Irish.¹³⁸ᴬ " Were it possible for the Irish by a
sudden *coup de main* to attain to the enjoyment of wealth,
they would seize upon it with alacrity. But ask them
to get rich slowly by cultivating double-entry, sitting over
miserable accounts until they are round-shouldered, and
they cannot do it. But the Scotchman can. His desire
to climb to the top of the tree is keen enough in all
conscience, but he can wait. He may not have the
momentary outburst of passion, but he does possess the
staying power that succeeds in the end." The Irishman
jumps about like a squirrel ; the Scotchman is content to
climb from branch to branch. " This admirable trait in
the Scotchman, his extraordinary capacity of submission
to his superiors, and the speed with which he unfurls his
sail to every favourable breeze, have resulted not only
in filling London commercial houses with Scotch clerks,
but also in providing many an undertaking with a Scotch
partner."

Put Florentine in place of Scotchman, and does not
the statement continue to hold good ? It will hold good
also if in place of Scotchman you put Jew. I would refer
to my book on the Jews * for an elaborate study of the
Jewish commercial spirit. Besides, I should only be
repeating myself, were I to go into it here, seeing
that Florentine, Scotchman, and Jew are interchangeable
terms. Marti, in his commentary on Ezekiel, asserts of
the Jews in the Roman Empire that " right down to this
very day the Syrians (Jews) still possess such a strongly
marked talent for commerce, that they traverse the two
hemispheres in search of gain. So great is their desire to
be constantly trafficking, that everywhere in the Roman
Empire they are on the look-out to draw their. profits

* [*The Jews and Modern Capitalism.* T. Fisher Unwin.]

from war, murder, or assassination." How apposite for
the position of the Jews in the world ! They derive their
profits *from* war, murder, or assassination ; while other
peoples seek to derive it *by means of* war, murder,
or assassination. Without a navy, without an army, the
Jews work their way up to the position of being
the mighty ones of the earth, using as their weapons
those of the Florentines—money, treaties (i.e. contracts),
and knowledge. All undertakings that they establish are
born of the commercial spirit ; all Jews who become
capitalist undertakers are types of the trader. Hence our
mention of them here.

6. The Craftsman.

One last type of undertaker remains. At first sight,
it may seem contradictory to class the craftsman as an
undertaker. What I mean by craftsman, however, is
what is termed in English " manufacturer," and in
French *fabricant* (in contradistinction to the *entrepreneur*,
who is a child of commerce).[139] I have in my mind the
" manu-facturer," the man who works with his hands,
striving hard to extend his concern, until ultimately it
becomes a capitalist undertaking. You know the type :
his hands are toil-scarred ; his head is almost four-
square ; his manners are a bit rough ; until his silver
wedding-day he lives in the old house amid the old
furniture, and then, at the wish of his only daughter,
whom he worships, and who has had the education which
he so painfully lacks, he engages an architect to put up
a mansion for him. It is our old friend, the self-made
man. His commercial aptitudes are limited ; but he is
the father of the big capitalist undertakers.

In some important industries, such as machine-building,
this type was the rule in all the earliest capitalist under-

takings. But he is to be found scattered over all the industries. In the development of the woollen manufacture his part was no small one.[139A] All countries are acquainted with him, and it was in the large towns that he was most frequently met.[140] To estimate his influence by reference to statistics is of course quite impossible ; just as it is in the case of the other types.

The craftsman as an undertaker bears the mark of the trader ; both have much in common. And though a whole world separates them from the speculative undertaker, they do share with him their abhorrence of appeals to force, or reliance on anything approaching seigniorial rights—which is the characteristic of the three first types of undertakers on our list. It is clear that the craftsman who has won for himself the position of a capitalist undertaker must be a negotiator or dealer, carving out his way by peaceful efforts, by silver-tongued oratory, by skilful contracts with those who supply his raw materials, with his employees and with his customers. But he must be more than this. He must possess certain moral qualities to a greater degree than is required by the other types of undertakers. Put into two words, he must be able to calculate and to save. Thus a new spirit must dominate him—him first, and the other types of capitalist undertakers later ; until it becomes a component part of the spirit of capitalism. What is the nature of this new spirit ? The following chapters will give the answer.

SECTION II

THE MIDDLE-CLASS OUTLOOK

CHAPTER VII

MIDDLE-CLASS VIRTUES

WHAT to-day is called the capitalist spirit comprises
within itself, besides the spirit of enterprise and the desire
for gain, a complexity of certain qualities, to which I
shall apply the term "middle-class virtues." These
include all the views and convictions (and, of course, the
actions and conduct based upon them) of a respectable
citizen and head of a family, no less than of an honest
tradesman. Expressed a little differently, it merely
means that in every perfect capitalist undertaker you will
a respectable citizen. And this respectable citizen—
vhat manner of man is he? Where did he first appear?

To the best of my knowledge we make the acquaintance
of the citizen—the "Compleat citizen"—for the first
time in Florence, at the close of the 14th century;
undoubtedly he is the child of the Trecento. And by
this statement it at once becomes apparent that by citizen
I do not mean every town-dweller, nor yet every trader
or craftsman. I apply the term to a peculiar complex
which developed from all these groups of pseudo-citizens,
to a being with a psychology all his own. And to
describe him I can find no better word than that which,

when in inverted commas, we take to represent a type and not a social class, i.e. the " bourgeois."

Now, why do I suggest Florence as the cradle of this type? Only because the evidence for his existence there already in the 15th century is remarkably abundant.[141] A whole list of tradesmen and others intimately acquainted with trade (and who was not in the New York of the Quattrocento ?) have bequeathed to us their views, set down in valuable memoirs or books of edification, from the pages of which there steps a perfect picture of Benjamin Franklin, the incarnation of the spirit of respectable citizenship. The maxims that should govern life, the rules that make for respectability (which we usually first associate with the 17th and 18th centuries), meet us here in the pages of the Florentine money-changers and cloth merchants, in whose lives they became a dominating influence already as early as the year 1450.

L. B. Alberti was the most perfect type of the " bourgeois " of those days, and his works provide a mine of information for obtaining an insight into the outlook of that generation of middle-class folk. *Del governo della famiglia* ("On the government of a family ") is from his pen, and you may find in it the same opinions which in a later age were expressed by Daniel Defoe and Benjamin Franklin. Alberti's book is of still greater value because, as we know, it was already a classic in its own time. It was much admired and widely read ; and other wise fathers of families quoted it either in full or in a shortened version.

We are justified, therefore, in assuming that Alberti's views were generally shared by a large number of people ; and that they express the outlook on life then current in tradesmen's circles. What those views were I shall record in outline, supplementing them by those of some of the contemporaries of Alberti. Of course, we shall deal only with such of his opinions and maxims as have any bearing, direct or indirect, on economic activities.

The views fall naturally into two groups, one dealing with the internal organization of business, and the other with the relationship between shopkeepers and customers and shopkeepers and the greater world beyond. I have labelled the first group " Holy Economy," and the second " Business Morality."

1. HOLY ECONOMY.

Alberti speaks of thrift as being " holy "—*sancta cosa la masserizia*. What exactly he means by *masserizia* he does not say in any one place. But scattered up and down his book are references to it. If we sum them all up we shall find a more or less complete conception.

A wise economy, according to Alberti, calls for certain fundamental things.

1. It calls first for thought. A good manager always carefully thinks out what it is he has to do. He concerns himself with ways and means ; devotes himself entirely to the task before him ; is not ashamed to speak of it, in no wise deeming it low or menial ; indeed, he is rather proud of it. What was new about all this was that it received general recognition, even by the rich and the great. The chapman had always to be careful of the pennies, and the small shopkeeper's life was taken up with making both ends meet. That was only to be expected. But the wealthy man and the man of influence, the man who had as much as a feudal lord of old—that he, too, should give a thought to balancing income and expenditure, that was the novelty !

The mere statement of this already implies that a new standpoint had been reached. The maxims of the old seigniorial way of life were now utterly rejected. Expenditure had dominated the feudal economy, as we have already observed. The feudal lord needed so much to live on or to spend ; consequently, that amount had to be forth-coming. But now income was the governing factor in all economic activities. " Be mindful, O my sons, never to let your expenditure exceed your income. "[142] That is the last word of wisdom in the third volume of Alberti's work, as, indeed, it is the conclusion of Pandolfini's treatise ; it is the alpha and omega of all successful domestic economy, the *credo* of every good " bourgeois," the motto of the new age, the quintessence of the worldly philosophy of all worthy folk.

2. All middle-class capitalist economic activities rested on this foundation, so that the thought that was called for as the first fundamental need was given an objective—thrift, which became the second.

Not enforced thrift, mind you, but thrift exercised willingly. Poor folk knew the first kind of thrift from bitter experience. But now rich men became thrifty, and this was the unheard-of thing. Before long, the original doctrine of not spending more than you were earning gave rise to its corollary of actually spending less than you were earning. The idea of saving thus came into the world ; of saving not as a necessity but as a virtue. To manage economically now became the ideal even of the rich, in so far as they belonged to the middle class. A man like Giovanni Ruccellai, who owned thousands, adopted the maxims of a country yokel, that "to save one penny is more honourable than to spend a hundred."[143] Seigniorial conduct was no longer regarded as the ideal to aim at ; a well-ordered economy was what mattered most.[144] Thrift was loved ; thrift was elevated to the position of being the one virtue of economic activities. A passage or two from Alberti's writings will illustrate how much it was held in reverence.

In a thousand variations you will find the doctrine expressed that the way to riches is not merely to earn much but also to spend little ; the way to poverty to be wasteful and extravagant.[145] " Beware of unnecessary expenditure as of a deadly foe " ; " it is madness to spend one penny more than is absolutely essential " ; " just as being a spendthrift is bad, so to be economical is good, useful and praiseworthy " ; " thrift hurts no one, while it is useful to the family " ; " thrift is holy." " Do you know in whom my soul finds most pleasure ? In those who spend their money on just what they need and no more, laying by the surplus ; these I call thrifty, successful managers." [146]   Or once more : " Who is a good manager ?   One who can hold the balance evenly between Too-much and Too-little.   But what is Too-much, and what Too-little ? It is not difficult to say. No expenditure should surpass what is absolutely needful, nor should it fall below what is required for decent living." [147]

Alberti actually has a table of different kinds of expenditure.   Those for food and clothing he regards as necessary ; any others he divided into three categories. First, those that are desirable, because without them your credit, or the good name of your family, might be endangered.   Of this sort is expenditure on your house, or your country residence, or your warehouse.   Then comes that expenditure which is not really essential, but at the same time not blameworthy.   If you incur it, you derive pleasure ; if you don't, there is no harm done. Expenditure of this sort is that for livery stables, or books, or mural paintings.   Finally, the third class of expenditure is to be condemned, for it is madness.   Such is the upkeep of retainers, who are worse than wild beasts.[148] (Note the hatred of anything smacking of feudalism.)

Moreover, necessary expenditure should be incurred

at once; unnecessary should be put off as long as possible. " Why ? " ask the disciples of their master. " We should like to hear your reasons, for we know you do nothing without careful consideration." " I will tell you," replies Gianozzo. " If I postpone spending, the desire may possibly vanish, and I shall thus save what I had intended spending. If, however, the desire remains, at any rate I have sufficient time to look around for the cheapest way of getting what I want." 149

For a perfect economy in business (and in life) you require not only thrift (which may be termed economy of matter) but also the proper co-ordinating of actions, and the profitable employment of time (what may be termed the economy of mind). This the master preaches insistently and incessantly. We are to be scrupulously careful in the management of three things—our soul, our body, and, most of all, our time. How ? By being usefully and properly occupied. " Throughout the whole of my life I have striven to do useful and honourable things." 149ᴬ But occupation in itself suffices. " I use my body, my soul, and my time in as reasonable a way as may be. I try to save as much as I can of each, and to lose as little as possible." 150 Therefore, avoid idleness. Idleness and extravagance are the two deadly sins. Idleness corrupts the body no less than the mind ; 151 it breeds dishonour and shame. Ever since the world began the heart of the idler has been the fount of all evil. There is nothing so hurtful and noxious to public and private life as idle citizens. Idleness leads to luxuriousness, and luxuriousness to breaking the law. 152

Once the disciples protested that they could not possibly remember and obey all the wise teachings of the master. Whereupon he replied, the remedy lay close at hand : let them but economize their time. " Whoso loses no time can accomplish almost everything ; and he who has the gift of employing his time wisely will very soon be master of every circumstance." 153 Gianozzo then proceeds to give directions as to how time may be most usefully employed. " To lose not even one iota of that most precious good, Time, I follow this rule. I am never idle ; sleep I flee from, and I lay me down only when weariness overcomes me. . . . How I flee from sleep and idleness ? I make it my business always to have some occupation. And to achieve my aim successfully, I provide myself every morning with a time-table for the day. I enumerate my duties, assigning to each a definite time. This shall be done in the morning, that in the afternoon, the other in the evening. In this wise I accomplish my tasks with perfect smoothness, almost without any effort. . . . In the evening before I retire to rest I recall everything I have done. . . . I had much liefer lose sleep than time." 154

Sermonizing in this strain continues with endless repetition (which, by the way, does not say much for his economy of words).

But the main thing for the business man to remember is this : Diligence and application are the sources of wealth. " Profit increases with the extension of business, because the extension of business increases our diligence and work." 155

If there are any details still wanting in this sketch of the spirit that filled the soul of the respectable, middle-class Florentine citizen of the 15th century, they will be completed by reference to the description, from the pen of a gifted writer,156 of the relations of Leonardo da Vinci.

Leonardo's brother Lorenzo was much distressed at the rumours current as to Leonardo's lack of religion. This Lorenzo, scarcely out of his teens, was a diligent disciple of Savonarola, had a business of his own, and belonged to the wool-combers' craft in Florence. Many a time and oft in the presence of his father he would turn the conversation with Leonardo to the Christian religion, and the necessity for penitence and humility, warning him against the heterodox opinions of certain of the newer philosophers, and once he presented him with a book on the soul's salvation, of which he himself was the author.

Leonardo, seated at the fire in the family sitting-room, drew out the carefully written volume. *Tavola de confessionario descripto per me, Lorenzo di Ser Pierro da Vinci, Fiorentino, mandata alla Nanna, mia cognata*—such was its title. (A book of confessions, written by me, Lorenzo di Ser Pierro da Vinci, a Florentine, and dedicated to my sister-in-law Nanna.) Then followed the legend written in smaller script : " An exceedingly useful handbook for all those who desire to confess their sins. Take up the book and read therein. And when you come across your sins in the table of contents, be sure and mark the passage. But about those sins of which you feel yourself guiltless, you need not read. Such passages as these, however, will no doubt be of service to others. For, rest assured, a thousand tongues would be unable to complete the entire list."

Then came an inventory of sins most scrupulously compiled by this wool-comber, with all the precision of a linendraper.

Leonardo directed his attention to the allegorical description of the four cardinal Christian virtues—Wisdom, with its three countenances in token of its insight into the Present, the Past, and the Future ; Justice, with sword and scales ; Strength, resting on a pillar ; and Moderation, a circle in one hand and in the other a pair of scissors, " with which to cut off every superfluity." Leonardo seemed to recognize the spirit that breathed in the leaves of the volume. It was the old fear of God he knew so well in the days of his childhood, the fear of God which had been passed on from one generation of his family to another.

Already a hundred years before he was born, his ancestors had been just such honourable, thrifty, God-fearing officials of the Florentine municipality as was his own father, Ser Pierro. As early as 1339, there was mentioned for the first time in the city records the artist's great-grandfather, a certain Ser Guido di Ser Michele da Vinci, who appears to have been *Notajo* to the government. Quite easily the artist recalled the picture of his grandfather, Antonio, with his wise saws, that were but the duplicates of those of his own brother, Lorenzo. The old man taught his children never to aim too high, neither at glory, nor honours, positions in the state or in the army, nor yet at great riches or great learning. " The surest way of life," he used to assert, " is to keep to the proper mean."

Leonardo could almost persuade himself that he heard the gentle, insistent voice of the old man laying down the life-maxim of the golden mean. " My children," he would say, " take as your model the ants, who to-day already have a care for the needs of the morrow. Be thrifty and moderate. To whom shall I compare a prosperous householder, or a good paterfamilias? I will liken him to a spider, sitting in the centre of her wide-spread web, yet ever on the alert to strengthen and repair if any one thread tremble never so lightly." He expected of his family that all its members should assemble every evening at the sound of the Ave-Maria bell. He himself went the round of the house, shut the gates, took the keys to his bed-chamber, and placed them under his pillow. Not the smallest detail of the household escaped his attention. He knew whether the cattle had had too

little hay or not, whether the maid turned up the lamp
wick too high, and so used too much oil. His eye was
everywhere, but withal he was not miserly. The best cloth
money could buy was furnished for his attire, and he
counselled his children to do likewise. The high prices
did not frighten him, for, as he remarked, you did not
have to replace clothing of excellent material so frequently.
And was not this cheapest in the end?

According to the old man's conception, the family was
to live united under one roof, "for," so he reasoned,
" when all eat at one table, one tablecloth and one light
suffice. But if there are two groups, they require two
tablecloths and two lights. Moreover, one fire can warm
the whole company. For two, however, you need two
fires. And so in all things."

Towards women he was somewhat supercilious.
" Their sphere was cooking and children ; they should
never interfere in their husbands' concerns. Whoso
relies on a woman's wisdom is a fool."

Now and again the old sage became subtle. " Children
dear," he exclaimed, " be charitable as our Holy Church
ordains. Nevertheless, cultivate rather your fortunate
than your unfortunate friends, and the rich rather than
the poor. The highest art in life is to appear charitable,
and to use craft to overcome the crafty."

It would seem that he was rather inclined to craftiness.
He directed his children to plant their fruit trees on the
extreme boundary of their field, so that the shade might
fall on the neighbouring domain. He taught them to
refuse an appeal for a loan with polite excuses, adding,
" You have then a twofold superiority—you retain your
money, and you can mock at the man who schemed to
cheat you. But if he who asked the favour was an
educated man, he will understand you, and will only
appreciate you the more for the courtesy with which you

said him nay. A knave takes; but he who gives is a fool. But if it be a question of helping relatives or members of the household, your policy is clear. Put at their disposal not only your money but your very life, your work, your honour. For the family a man should sacrifice his all. It is more honourable and profitable to help your kith and kin rather than strangers."

And now, as after an absence of thirty years Leonardo sat once more under his grandfather's roof, while the wind moaned without, and the fire burned brightly on the hearth, he realized to the full how his whole life had been one long contradiction of the wisdom of his ancestor. It had overflowed with abundance and super-fluity, that superfluity which, according to his brother Lorenzo, should be clipped off by the iron shears of the Goddess of Moderation.

If we trace the development of the middle-class virtues through the centuries, we shall have to take stock of their intensive and extensive growth alike; that is to say, of the enlargement of the sum-total of the virtues them-selves, and of their acceptance by the great body of the people. The first is not difficult, seeing that we are well informed as to the details by a number of treatises still extant; but as for the latter, we shall be able only to make deductions from certain given circumstances.

An intensive growth of the middle-class virtues from the stage in which the Italian writers of the 14th century left them never, as a matter of fact, really took place. Later generations of tradesmen were taught nothing different from that which Alberti asked his disciples to lay to heart. Between the mode of life of Leonardo's grandfather and that of Benjamin Franklin there is not the least divergence. The fundamental doctrines are the same, reappearing in later centuries almost in the identical wording ; and the standard authorities on the subject in the 16th, 17th, and 18th centuries sound almost as though they were translations of Alberti and no more.   A reference to one or two representative treatises will prove this right up to the hilt.

Thus we find that in the 16th century the characteristic books were those on husbandry, and they abounded in every country.

The Spaniard Herrera had little sympathy tor trade. But the virtues he counsels the husbandman to acquire are none other than those which Alberti laid down for the prosperous draper.   The farmer should carefully plan out his course of action ; he should avoid idleness like the very Devil ; he is to be thoroughly acquainted with all branches of his business.[157]

And what says Etienne, the Frenchman ?   The good husbandman should spend his spare time in thinking over his concerns, not neglecting them for the chase, or conviviality, or the entertainment of friends.   Above all, he is to map out every minute of his time ; and as for his expenditure, it should never exceed his incomings. Industry will enable the patient farmer to win produce from even the least fertile soil.   Moreover, as the old proverb hath it, the skilful husbandman is more concerned with profits and making things go as far as possible, than with the satisfaction of momentary wants and immediate use.[158]

Our Italian instance is Tanara,[159] whose principal watchword is Utility.   He advised the farmer never to plant in his garden those flowers that yielded no return. The farmer should occupy himself with marketable produce alone.   Was it not the goodly appearance of Eden that brought Adam to sin, and with him, all of us likewise ?   Riches cannot be obtained by service at court, or in the army, or even by alchemy.   There is only one sovereign method : to be thrifty.

The 17th century produced numerous "Books for Merchants" and "Commercial Dictionaries," wherein business-men, young and old, were admonished to order their lives and their affairs in accordance with reason and virtue. The same doctrines again ! Think over everything ; arrange everything carefully, be sober, industrious, and thrifty, and the good things of the earth shall be yours. You will become an honoured citizen and a wealthy man.

One of the best known of these text-books is Savary's *Le parfait négociant*, dedicated to Colbert. It is mainly concerned with the art of commerce, but commercial morality is not omitted either. The tradesman's success, according to Savary, depends on five things—perfect knowledge, orderly arrangement, industry, and economy (*de l'épargne et de l'æconomie de leur maison*), and commercial morality.[160]

Commercial morality occupies an even more important place in Daniel Defoe's *Complete English Tradesman*.[161] " Diligence and application in business " is the title of his fifth epistle, and the author lays an immense amount of stress on both. " Let the man have the most perfect knowledge of his trade, and the best situation for his shop, yet without application nothing will go on." The tradesman should also avoid all pleasures and diversions, even of the most harmless kind ; they are a cause of disaster. " Of innocent diversions, as they are called, how fatal to the tradesman, especially to the younger sort," is the heading of the ninth chapter, in the fourth edition of the book. But sporting and seigniorial amusements he denounces most of all. " When I see a young shop-keeper keep horses, ride a-hunting, learn dog language and keep the sportman's brogue upon their tongues, I will not say I read their destiny, for I am no fortune-teller, but I do say I am always afraid of them." As for expensive living, " it is a kind of slow fever . . . a secret enemy that feeds upon the vitals . . . it feeds upon the life and blood of the tradesman "—and more in the same strain. The wise tradesman avoids " (1) expensive house-keeping or family extravagance, (2) expensive dressing or the extravagance of fine clothes, (3) expensive company or keeping company above himself, and (4) expensive equipages, making a show and ostentation in the world." The merchant should remember that " trade is not a ball where people appear in masque and act a part to make sport . . . but 'tis a plain, visible scene of honest life . . . supported by prudence and frugality." And the end of the matter ? That " prudent management and frugal living will increase any fortune to any degree," and that " if the expense is kept under the revenue, the man will always grow ; if not, I need not say what will follow."

The numerous editions of the writings of Savary and Defoe lead us on well into the 18th century. The thread they had spun was taken up and continued by men like Benjamin Franklin. Indeed, Defoe was one of Franklin's favourite authors.

In Benjamin Franklin, the man who (according to Balzac) was the inventor of the lightning rod, the hoax, and the Republic, the middle-class view of life reached its zenith. The sobriety and exactness of this American almost take one's breath away. Everything with him became a rule, and was measured by the proper standard, and his every action was governed by economy. Indeed, he worshipped economy. He relates how on one occasion he was present at a social gathering where a new lamp was being admired. The guests inquired whether the new lamp cost more than the one it had replaced, for it was eminently desirable to make the illuminating of rooms as cheap as possible. " I was delighted," says Franklin, " to note this general tendency to economy, which I specially love." [162] That was the high-water mark of his philosophy and his life.

His insistence on the value of time is universally

known; as is also the oft-quoted dictum that "Time is money," which is from his pen.[163] "But dost thou love life, then do not squander time, for that's the stuff life is made of. . . . How much more than is necessary do we spend in sleep, forgetting that the sleeping fox catches no poultry, and that there will be sleeping enough in the grave. . . . If time be of all things the most precious, wasting time must be . . . the greatest prodigality."[164]

Economy of time is only paralleled by economy of money. "If you would be wealthy . . . think of saving as well as of getting. The Indies have not made Spain rich because her outgoes are greater than her incomes. Away then with your expensive follies.

> Get what you can, and what you get, hold ;
> 'Tis the stone that will turn all your lead into Gold![165]

In short, the way to wealth, if you desire it, is as plain as the way to market. It depends chiefly on two words, industry and frugality ; that is, waste neither time nor money, but make the best use of both. Without industry and frugality nothing will do, and with them everything. He that gets all he can honestly, and saves all he gets (necessary expenses excepted, cf. Alberti), will certainly become rich, if that Being who governs the world, to whom all should look for a blessing on their honest endeavours, doth not, in His wise providence, otherwise determine.[166]

Franklin's whole life was one long worship of "holy economy." In his memoirs he set forth what virtues were the best, and how he educated himself to be a "virtuous" man in the light of these virtues. In his scheme the "bourgeois" view of life received its final and highest expression. The following passage from his *Autobiography*[167] is more than usually instructive.

It was about this time I conceived the bold and arduous project of arriving at moral perfection. I wished to live without committing any fault at any time ; I would conquer all that either natural inclination, custom, or company might lead me into. . . . I concluded at length that the mere speculative conviction that it was our interest to be completely virtuous, was not sufficient to prevent our slipping ;

and that the contrary habits must be broken, and good ones acquired and established, before we can have any dependence on a steady, uniform rectitude of conduct.   For this purpose I therefore contrived the following method.

In the various enumeration of the moral virtues I had met with in my reading, I found the catalogue more or less numerous, as different writers included more or fewer ideas under the same name. . . . I proposed to myself, for the sake of clearness, to use rather more names, with fewer ideas annexed to each, than a few names with more ideas ; and I included under thirteen names of virtues all that at that time occurred to me as necessary or desirable, and annexed to each a short precept, which fully expressed the extent I gave to its meaning.

The names of the virtues, with their precepts, were :

1. *Temperance.*—Eat not to dullness, drink not to elevation.
2. *Silence.*—Speak not but what may benefit others or yourself ; avoid trifling conversation.
3. *Order.*—Let all your things have their places ; let each part of your business have its time.
4. *Resolution.*—Resolve to perform what you ought ; perform without fail what you resolve.
5. *Frugality.*—Make no expense but to do good to others or yourself, i.e. waste nothing.
6. *Industry.*—Lose no time ; be always employed in something useful ; cut off all unnecessary actions.
7. *Sincerity.*—Use no hurtful deceit ; think innocently and justly, and if you speak, speak accordingly.
8. *Justice.*—Wrong none by doing injuries, or omitting the benefits that are your duty.
9. *Moderation.*—Avoid extremes ; forbear resenting injuries so much as you think they deserve.
10. *Cleanliness.*—Tolerate no uncleanness in body, clothes, or habitation.
11. *Tranquillity.*—Be not disturbed at trifles, or at accidents common or unavoidable.
12. *Chastity.*—Rarely use venery but for health or offspring, never to dullness, or the injury of your own or another's peace or reputation.
13. *Humility.*—Imitate Jesus and Socrates.

These virtues Franklin, as he tells us, attempted to acquire one by one.   Then—

Conceiving that, agreeably to the advice of Pythagoras in his

Golden Verses, daily examination would be necessary, I contrived the following method for conducting that examination.

I made a little book, in which I allotted a page for each of the virtues [this "little book" is dated July 1, 1733]. I ruled each page with red ink, so as to have seven columns, one for each day of the week, marking each column with a letter for the day. I crossed these columns with thirteen red lines, marking the beginning of each line with the first letter of one of the virtues, on which line, and in its proper column, I might mark, by a little black spot, every fault I found upon examination to have been committed respecting that virtue upon that day.

Form of the page.

TEMPERANCE						
Eat not to dullness. Drink not to elevation.						

	S.	M.	T.	W.	T.	F.	S.
T.							
S.	•	•		●		•	
O.	• •	●	•		•	•	
R.		•	•			•	•
F.					•		
I.			•				
S.							
J.							
M.							
C.							
T.							
C.							
H.							

He determined to give a week's attention to each of the virtues in succession, so that after thirteen weeks' daily examination he hoped that the clean pages would set forth the story of his final achievement.

Observe the verisimilitude in the outlook of Leonardo's grandfather and the father of the American Republic. There is an interval of four hundred years between them, but how little has changed. They are " bourgeois " both.

But the important question at this stage is, Did the multitude live up to the high standard of the wise preceptors? Did every tradesman model his life in accordance with Benjamin Franklin's scheme of virtue?

From the complaints of the wise preceptors themselves, it rather looks as though they were prophets crying in the wilderness. Savary and Defoe, for example, lash the wickedness of their generation, more especially its luxury and good living. Nevertheless, things were not quite so black as might at first sight appear. I am inclined to believe that the spirit of industry, thrift, and moderation, in a word, the spirit of those virtues that made the good " bourgeois," slowly settled upon the capitalist undertakers of modern times, anyhow upon those who sprang from the trading and craftsman class (types 4, 5 and 6 in the last chapter). There may have been variations in different lands in the degree of the intensity of this spirit. Perhaps the French of the 17th and 18th centuries were less under its influence than the Dutch or the Americans. Certainly, there is evidence to that effect.[168] But on the whole it was spreading, and the " bourgeois " spirit came to be a component part of the capitalist spirit. Were this not so, how comes it that the earliest representatives of Capitalism spoke with the voice of the " bourgeois "? Does it not follow that it was only in the nature of things that they should have done so? The books which set forth the middle-class virtues were amongst the most popular of the day. Consequently, a very large number of people must have been acquainted with the " bourgeois " spirit. " Frugality, Industry, Moderation " was the motto that might have been observed hung up in letters of gold in many a warehouse and shop. This is not surprising, if we remember that Alberti became a classic, Defoe was read in two continents, and as for Benjamin Franklin's teaching, was there ever a literary man whose works were so scattered over the globe ? The quintessence of Franklin's teaching is to be found in *Poor Richard's Almanac*, which he published annually for quite a number of years. " Father Abraham's Speech to the American People at an Auction," which appeared in the *Almanac* for 1758, is the best sermon ever preached upon industry and frugality. Reprinted as *The Way to Wealth*, it became at once familiar to the world. It was copied into all the newspapers of the Continent and scattered broadcast over the face of the earth. " Seventy editions of it have been printed in English, fifty-six in French, eleven in German, and nine in Italian. It has been translated into Spanish, Danish, Swedish, Welsh, Polish, Gaelic, Russian, Bohemian, Dutch, Catalan, Chinese, modern Greek, and phonetic writing. It has been printed at least four hundred times, and is to-day as popular as ever." [169]

Does not this tend to prove that the author's influence was widely extended ?

2. BUSINESS MORALITY.

To be a successful tradesman it is essential not only to arrange one's business most economically internally, but also to have a proper relationship to the world beyond. The rules and regulations that govern the nature of this relationship, I term business morality ; and I use the second word in a double sense—morality in carrying on business, and personal morality as a business man. We may say morality *in* business, and morality *for* business.

In the first sense of the word, I am thinking of such things as making contracts, or one's relation to one's customers. Commercial honesty it has sometimes been called ; meaning thereby trustworthiness, making your word your bond, serving customers with consideration, punctuality in payments, and so on. Only as capitalist undertakings have grown up has this form of morality become more and more necessary. It is thus included in the entity middle-class virtues. For, can you imagine " honesty " (using the word in the sense here indicated) as applied to a peasant farmer or a craftsman? Hardly. You could only use the word when status had given place to contract, when economic relationships had lost the personal touch that was theirs in the earliest times. Call it " contract morality " and the meaning is apparent.

In its earliest form this, too, was a personal virtue. Those same Florentine drapers who, as we have already noted, were the fathers of middle-class virtues, cultivated this one likewise. " There was never (!) any one in our family who at any time broke his word," says Alberti. " We kept our promises simply and truthfully, and so we became known in Italy and in foreign parts as great merchants." 170

The principle was preached by all the subsequent mentors of tradesmen ; the wording is almost identical in each case.

But the degree of " commercial honesty " was not the same among all nations at all times. As a general rule, it may be observed that it increased in strength with the development of capitalism. It is interesting to note in this connection how Englishmen, who in later centuries were looked upon as the model of commercial honesty, had a poor reputation in this respect in the 17th century. A mass of evidence would go to show that the Dutch were regarded as superior to the English, so far as this point was concerned.[171]

As for the second sense in the usage of the term "business morality," I have in mind the personal morality of the business man. This likewise became an integral part of the middle-class virtues with the rise of capitalism. From that time onwards it appeared advantageous, from a business point of view, to cultivate certain virtues; at any rate, to appear to possess them. Their sum total comprises middle-class respectability. You must live in accordance with the moral code of your class—that became the first commandment of the successful business man. In essence this meant—eschew all irregularities; appear in respectable society; avoid drinking, gambling, and women; go to church regularly; in a word, always wear the aspect of true respectability, and all for the sake of your business. Such a moral rule of life will assure your credit.

Alberti calls this middle-class respectability *onestà*, and it is the backbone of his moral code. All other virtues branch off from this; they derive their significance from it. *Onestà*, in Alberti's view, should always accompany us as a public, righteous, practical and wise middleman, weighing, measuring, valuing our every act, our every thought, our every wish. *Onestà* gives the final polish to all our conduct. From of old she has been and remains the best teacher of virtue, a true companion of morality, the admirable mother of a peaceful and happy existence. Besides, and this is the main point, *onestà* is of exceeding great use to us. Hence, if we cultivate her, we shall attain to riches, fame, popularity, and honour.[172]

It is the same story through the ages. Italian *onestà*

becomes French *honnêteté* and English *honesty*. In all three instances the meaning is clear—the totality of all that is respectable. Often enough an air of sanctimoniousness accompanies it, seeing that for business purposes the mere appearance of respectability is sufficient. As a matter of fact, it does not by any means suffice actually to *be* respectable. You must be regarded as such. Hence Benjamin Franklin resolved that " in order to secure my credit and character as a tradesman, I took care not only to be in reality industrious and frugal, but to avoid the appearance to the contrary. I dressed plain, and was seen at no places of idle diversion ; I never went out a-fishing or shooting." [173]

CHAPTER VIII

THE ART OF CALCULATION

A GREAT part of capitalist economy is taken up with the making of contracts and agreements concerning commodities and services that have a money value (as, the purchase of the means of production, the sale of the finished products, the engaging of labour, and so forth). Moreover, the beginning and the end of capitalist economic activities is a sum of money. Consequently, calculation forms an important element in the capitalist spirit, and this was recognized quite early in the history of capitalism.[174] By calculation I mean the tendency, the habit, perhaps more—the capacity, to think of the universe in terms of figures, and to transform these figures into a well-knit system of income and expenditure. The figures, I need hardly add, always express a value, and the whole system is intended to demonstrate whether a plus or a minus is the resultant, thus showing whether the undertaking is likely to bring profit or loss.

The mechanism of calculation rests on two branches of study, commercial arithmetic and book-keeping.

Three ways are open to us for the study of the rise and growth of the calculating habit. We may trace its history by directing our attention to stages in the development of technical apparatus ; or we may see from extant ledgers, day-books and kindred memoranda how people in any period calculated ; or, finally, we may judge of the progress of the calculating habit from the opinions on it expressed by the men who lived in successive epochs.

The history of the calculating habit since the Middle Ages has already been sketched in my *Modern Capitalism*. I shall therefore merely summarize it here, adding one or two conclusions that have since been established.[175]

The cradle of commercial arithmetic was in Italy ; or, to be more precise, in Florence. The appearance of Leonardo Pisano's *Liber Abbaci*, in 1202, laid the foundations of correct calculation. But the foundations only, for the true art of calculating was learned but slowly. It was not until the 13th century that the Arabic numerals became acclimatized in Italy, and every one can see how without them quick and exact calculation would be well-nigh impossible. Yet as late as 1299 the use of Arabic numerals was forbidden the brethren of the Calimala gild. That the process of their adoption, even in Italy, was a slow one is plain from the manuscript of the *Introductorius liber qui et pulveris dicitur in mathematicam disciplinam*, which dates from the second half of the 14th century. Its author used Arabic and Roman numerals promiscuously.

But from the 14th century in Italy, and from the 15th and 16th in northern lands, the art of reckoning made swift progress. Calculations with figures supplanted the unwieldy method of calculating by tallies. Obviously this was an advance, and in the words of Simon Jacob, teacher of arithmetic in Coburg, "just as a pedestrian walking without any burden is at an advantage, compared with one who is bent under a load, so a calculator operating with numerals is so much better off than one who uses tallies."

Long before Tartaglia, the mathematical genius of the

16th century, who perfected the art of commercial arithmetic, a new kind of "total" calculation in respect of goods had become popular among Italian tradesmen. It was spoken of as the "welsh" [foreign] practice, and, indeed, its origin was in France and Germany, whence it had been brought to Italy at the beginning of the 16th century. Its first German exponent was Heinrich Grammateus, who set it forth in his *Arithmetic* (1518). In the 15th century the decimal fractions were "discovered," and from 1585 they became more and more generally used through the influence of Simon Stevin. Furthermore, 1615 is the birth-year of the reckoning machine.

As books on arithmetic came to be increasingly printed, commercial arithmetic was gradually simplified. Then the arithmetic schools, which had been growing up since the 14th century, more especially in trading cities, helped to spread the knowledge far and wide. In the 14th century Florence (Florence again!) had six such schools, which, as Villani informs us, were regularly attended by 1,200 boys, who were taught "the abacus and the elements of commercial arithmetic." Luebeck was the first town in Germany to have schools of this kind ; in Hamburg the need for them arose about the year 1400.

The beginnings of well-ordered book-keeping stretch back into the 13th century. The accounts of Pope Nicholas III, of the year 1279–80, and the expenditure book of the city of Florence of the year 1303, alike bear witness to the fact that simple book-keeping was practically perfected at that time. Nor was double entry of a much later date. It is doubtful whether it was being applied in the 13th century, but the researches of Cornelio Desimonis have proved that, anyhow in the year 1340, the government of the city of Genoa kept its books on a system of *partita doppia*, the perfection of which was so complete as to lead to the conclusion that it must have been pretty well established for a long time. Evidence of its use in the 15th century, both for private and public accounts, we possess in plenty. The completest and most instructive instance is the extant ledgers of Soranzo Brothers, of Venice (1406). The first theoretic treatise on double entry was that of Fra Luca Paciuoli, in the ninth section of the first part of his *Summa arithmetica*.

And so we see that in those centuries of budding capitalism people in Italy calculated more or less exactly. Commercial arithmetic and book-keeping were both well known among middle-class undertakers, who in those days of beginnings must have themselves done much of what is now assigned to paid book-keepers.

Messer Benedotto Alberti used to say that it was becoming in the keen tradesman constantly to have ink-stained hands. Indeed, he held it to be nothing less than the duty of every merchant and tradesman who came into contact with many people always to jot down everything— every contract, every item of income and expenditure ; and revise everything so frequently, that his pen will be but seldom out of his hand.[176]

Certainly, Italy was first in the field as the land where commercial arithmetic was in vogue. Its place was taken by Holland in the succeeding centuries. Not only was Holland the model for all middle-class virtues, but for exact calculations also. Even as late as the 18th century the contrast in this respect between Holland and America was noted. Benjamin Franklin relates [177] how a partner of his, an American, living at a distance, would send him no accounts of their business ; it was only after his decease that his widow, who was a Dutchwoman, provided him with a clear statement of all transactions.

" The knowledge of accounts, as I have been informed, makes a part of female education in Holland," Franklin adds. Certainly that held good for the 1730's.

England caught up the Netherlands in so far as this matter was concerned, and at the beginning of the 19th century German tradesmen pointed to England and Holland as the lands which had an advanced commercial education. In Germany itself Hamburg was pre-eminent in this respect.[178]

It goes without saying that even in the less developed countries calculation was a strengthening element in the capitalist spirit.

The last few points in the story of the middle-class virtues have already touched upon national differences as they come to light in the gradual growth of capitalism. In the next section we shall give these more attention.

SECTION III

THE NATIONAL EXPRESSIONS OF THE CAPITALIST SPIRIT

CHAPTER IX

THE DIFFERENT POSSIBILITIES OF EXPRESSION

THE rise and growth of the capitalist spirit are pheno-mena common to all the European and American peoples of modern times. Evidence for this has already been adduced in abundance in the preceding pages, where our illustrations have been drawn from the history of all countries.

But not all lands show the same tendencies in the growth and development. Naturally, there were varia-tions, first in different localities, and then also in different periods. Our business here will be with the first category of variations, and to begin with we shall examine the different possibilities of development.

1. Not all nations were caught in the stream of capi-talist growth at the same time. Consequently, the date of the genesis of the " bourgeois " will vary. (I use the word " nation " broadly to represent any group. In the following chapter I shall consider the great national entities of history.)

2. The duration of the influence of the capitalist spirit in a nation may vary in length. Consequently,

there would be differences in the time capitalism took to develop.

3. The intensiveness of the capitalist spirit may be different in different lands. Consequently, the expansion of the spirit of enterprise, the desire for gain, the degree of middle-class respectability, would all vary.

4. The extensiveness may also be different. I mean that there may be differences in the degree in which the various social groups were influenced by the capitalist spirit.

5. The relationship of the component parts of that spirit may vary in different lands. Some may have the spirit of enterprise in a more marked degree than others ; others again may possess larger portions of the " bourgeois " spirit. And so forth.

6. The component parts of the capitalist spirit may have different capacities for development in different lands, and may need varying lengths of time in which to come to full bloom. Some of the parts may develop at the same pace, others separately.

In view of all these possibilities it is apparent how complex in different countries may be the development of the " bourgeois " outlook as a whole. The most important differences in national development depended, however, on the following conditions :—whether a country was strong or weak capitalistically ; whether all or only some (in that case, which) of the component parts of capitalism reached maturity ; whether the development commenced early or late in history ; and whether it was temporary, intermittent, or permanent.

The manner in which these possibilities actually occurred in different countries and the specific characteristics which the capitalist spirit took on in each in consequence, will form the subject matter briefly (and no doubt imperfectly) sketched in the next chapter.

CHAPTER X

DEVELOPMENTS IN DIFFERENT COUNTRIES

1. ITALY.

THE capitalist spirit first manifested itself in Italy. From the 13th century onward it extended over all the trading republics of Lombardy ; by the 14th century it was fully developed there ; and throughout the Middle Ages its intensive growth in Italy was unparalleled in Europe. As we have already observed, the evidence that is available for Italy for this period is abundant enough. It was just that state of mind which I have termed the " bourgeois spirit " that was found in the Italian cities earlier than elsewhere, and it reached its highest development in the Tuscan Republics.

We have already taken note of the differences which distinguished the undertaking spirit of the Tuscan from that of the other towns, especially the two great seaports of Venice and Genoa. But here I would once more like to emphasize the fact that it was from Florence that the strongest impulse for the development of the " bourgeois " outlook came. As early as the 14th century the Florentines were filled with a feverish (I had almost said an American) desire for gain, and a devotion to business that almost amounted to a passionate love. Florence was that state " which was requested by dying fathers in their last wills and testaments to fine their sons one thousand florins if they had no regular occupation " ; [179] it was here that affairs were first conducted on a thoroughly business-like basis ; here that men like Alberti first taught and cultivated the middle-class virtues ; here that the art of calculation received its final form in the treatises of Fibonaccio and Paciouli ; and here statistical surveys were first in vogue and greatly extended. Burckhardt somewhere reviews a statistical table compiled by a Florentine and one by a Venetian, both dating from about the same year, 1442. The latter undoubtedly referred to a much greater fortune, greater profits, and a larger scene of activities, but, says Burckhardt, " who will not admit the superior intelligence displayed in the work of the Florentine ? " And it is in this connection that he speaks of " the inborn talent of the Florentine in adapting calculations to all the varied needs of existence."

But all this capitalist splendour came to a speedy end. True, the calculating gift and the practice of thrift remained unchanged ; indeed, as we may gather from 15th and 16th century writers, they became more strongly marked than ever. But the spirit of enterprise decayed. It is possible to trace its decline in Southern Italy from the end of the 15th century, elsewhere in the country from about the 16th. The joy of acquisitiveness and the devotion to business made way for a comfortable mode of life, partly that of the aristocrat, partly that of the man of independent means.

Of one South Italian town—La Cava—we hear the general complaint even before 1500, that the place had been proverbially rich so long as it was inhabited by builders and weavers. But now that the demand for building materials and cloth had been replaced by that for spurs and gilded belts, seeing that every citizen aspired to be either a doctor, a lawyer, an officer or a knight, the direst poverty was experienced there.[180]

The same inclination towards a feudal state of society

became conspicuous in Florence. It was spoken of as the "Spanish way of life"; its chief characteristic was to despise work and to seek after titles of nobility. The change set in under the first Duke Cosimo; and he it was who made all those young men who despised trade and industry members of the Order of Stephen. But the Florentine wealthy classes generally strove to obtain patents of knighthood, which were coveted so much because they alone enabled the holders to participate in tournaments. And just then tournaments were revived in good earnest in Florence. With real middle-class frailty, the Florentines invented a less dangerous kind of tournament, to which everybody was passionately devoted without being in the least conscious of the caricature presented by the medley of middle-class and aristocratic elements. The first of the Medici patronized this craze with a zeal that can only be explained by their desire to prove to the world that they, though commoners, had a court life not one whit inferior to that of princes of the most ancient lineage.[181]

It was the same in other Lombard towns; the period of the change was the beginning of the 16th century. Just as the most cherished ideal of the middle classes who had become opulent was to be dubbed knights, so for those beneath them in the social scale the goal most diligently sought for was to live on their incomes, to live a life free from work, if possible in a country house of their own. The *vita temperata*, the *stato pacifico*, were pointed to as Nirvana, principally in the numerous books on husbandry with which extracts have already made us familiar.[182]

2. THE IBERIAN PENINSULA.

It would seem that capitalism blossomed early in several towns in the Iberian Peninsula. We do not know much about Barcelona in the Middle Ages, nor of its commercial and maritime law. But what little has come down to us tends to strengthen the conviction that there was a broad streak of the capitalist spirit in the commerce of Barcelona, certainly in the 14th century. Besides, look at the many voyages of discovery that started from Spain and Portugal in the 15th century, culminating at the century's end in the two well-known splendid geographical finds. Is it not certain that an unquenchable thirst for gold, together with a bold spirit eager for adventure, were to be found among the people in the coast towns? It was the combination of the two that brought about, in the 16th century, conquests in America and colony plantations. Nor did the capitalist spirit of the Spanish and Portuguese exhaust itself in these enterprises. Lisbon merchants began to trade with the new lands in the West and in the East, and the volume of this commerce far surpassed that of the Italians; while the traders of Seville loaded the silver-ships with wares for their return journey to America. Industry, too, appears to have flourished; its aspect leads to the belief that it was permeated with the spirit of capitalism. Seville boasted 16,000 looms, which gave employment to 130,000 people.[183] In Toledo no less than 430,000 pounds of silk were spun by 38,484 workers. Segovia likewise had important silk and woollen industries.[184]

Then came total paralysis in the 17th century, of which every schoolboy has heard. The spirit of enterprise faded away, and all interest in business vanished. Instead, the nation turned from economic activities to religion, court life, or knightly exercises. Business had now the same low taint that appertained to agriculture; a man of noble birth was contemptuous of both. This is just what foreign observers—Italians, Dutchmen, French, or English—could not understand; they spoke of it as

Spanish indolence. "Everybody," so Guicciardini relates, "everybody imagines he is a nobleman. In 1523 the Cortes petitioned the King to allow every Spaniard to wear a sword; two years later the same body laid it down that the Hidalgos were far superior to the tax-payers."[185] "The Hidalgos," as Ranke[186] informs his readers, "were regarded as the core of the nation; they were appointed to the offices of state . . . and enjoyed universal popularity. Every one aspired to a life like theirs—with much honour and no work. Many were the claimants of real or imaginary rights of the Hidalgia, and so numerous did these pretensions become that the law courts sat specially on Saturdays to decide them. It was only natural that gradually a distinct disinclination for work and business, and a contempt for industry and frugality, should be the result." "Material interests are much like other human affairs," continues the same writer. "What is not deeply rooted in a nation's life cannot thrive in its midst. The Spaniards' whole outlook was coloured by the religious practices of Catholicism and by the conception of a hierarchy; their mission in life, they seem to have thought, was to get as much as they could from both; it was their pride to hold fast to the attitude which enabled them to do this; and apart from that they sought to live a life of ease in a constant round of sunny days."[187]

Their way of life, then, was totally opposed to the capitalist spirit. And wherever Spaniards and Portuguese established themselves in colonies the ideals of the mother country accompanied them.[188]

3. France.

France has at all times been blessed with great and gifted undertakers, especially endowed for speculation:

men who formed their plans with lightning speed
and made them comprehensive ; men of quick action and
vivid imagination ; boastful sometimes, but energetic and
high-spirited ; running grave risks of failure or possibly
also of ending their days behind prison walls, unless
mental or physical decline intervened. Such a type was
Jacques Cœur in the 15th century, who by his natural
gifts brought French commerce to a high pitch of
perfection for a brief space of years. He owned seven
galleys, employed 300 factors, and was in communication
with all the great seaports of the world. " He was
Charles VII's Treasurer, and the royal favour he enjoyed
was of considerable assistance to him in his commercial
enterprises ; so much so, that no other French trader was
able to compete with him. His counting-house was the
centre of a mighty commerce, rivalling that of the
Venetians, the Genoese, and the Catalonians." The money
he acquired in trade, and also, it must be added, in
financial manipulations not altogether of an unquestion-
able kind, he lent to needy courtiers, making them his
debtors, and subsequently his enemies. His end is well-
known ; accused of high-treason, coining, and much else,
he was arrested, deprived of all his property, and banished.

The career of Fouquet in the age of Louis XIV, which
is famous enough, is almost parallel. Nor were these
alone. A whole series of them continued right down
almost to this very day ; some of them were adventurers
who speculated in a large way, others were merely small
fry. Think of Lesseps and Boncourt and Rochefort and
the Humberts and the Deperdussins and the Saccards !
Quite a French speciality.

Montaigne may have been a little hard on his countrymen in his characterization of this somewhat "gassy"
sort of undertaking, but he certainly hit the mark. These
are his words : " I am afraid that our eyes are bigger

than our stomachs ; and (in conquering a new land) we
possess more curiosity than perseverance ; we embrace
everything, but we retain nothing but wind." [189]

At the same time complaints have been loud in France,
from Colbert's days to these, that the French tradesman
is deficient in the spirit of enterprise.   There is no contradiction here.   The plaints clearly refer to the great body
of middle-class business men and to sound undertakings.
" Our merchants," wailed Colbert, " have not the capacity to
take up any matter with which they are unacquainted." [190]
He spoke from bitter experience.   It is generally known
that the enterprising statesman had the greatest difficulty
in combating the indolence of his compatriots, when it
was a question (say) of founding an oversea trading
company, such as the East India Company.   There were
meetings and conferences (no less than three took place
between the 21st and the 26th of May, 1664) at which
wealthy merchants and manufacturers had to be persuaded
to take up shares. [191]   (It reminds one almost of what
happens to-day when moneyed men have to be wheedled
into providing the necessary financial assistance for
establishing learned academies, Oriental societies or
similar institutions.)

Nor was Colbert the only one who diagnosed this
weakness.   Turn to the pages of Sayous, Blondel, or any
other authority who was acquainted with French economic
life, and the same jeremiad will meet you everywhere.
The French tradesman of an earlier age was accounted
indolent, if not altogether lazy.   *The Patriotic
Merchant* (about the middle of the 18th century)
complained that in French businesses there was so little
work done.   The writer wished his son to work " night
and day, and not the paltry two hours that had become
the custom in France." [192]   This very book is testimony
enough that Franklin's spirit was not universal among the

French tradesmen of that period. Despite its manifest longings for American conditions it is yet full of romance, flights of imagination, and chivalrous notions.

This under-development of capitalist tendencies in the French people was only in accord with its positive ideals (and one may add, is so still, for, during the last hundred years or so, the national spirit in this respect has, remarkable to relate, remained fairly constant). What were these ideals ? To begin with, there was a strongly marked inclination towards the aristocratic way of life. Does not the author of *The Patriotic Merchant* vent his spleen on his countrymen for their extravagance ? He blames them for wasting their substance on unnecessary expenditure on luxuries instead of investing it in capitalist undertakings. As a result, you could not obtain money in France for trade and industry under between 5 and 6 per cent., whereas in England and Holland the rate varied between $2\frac{1}{2}$ and 3. Whereupon he moralized thus : business investments at 3 per cent. are much more profitable and sane than the purchase of beautiful country estates that bring in nothing.[193]

Secondly, the French have a strong preference for the assured (and respected) position of the official. This may be observed throughout the whole economic history of the country, like a red thread in the fabric ; it was a tremendous obstacle in the path of capitalism. " This plague of bureaucracy," as one critic [194] termed it ; " this French civil-service mania " to use the words of another,[195] began in the 16th century and has not yet disappeared. It was accompanied by a disdainful attitude towards commerce and industry, and so bore witness to the constant weakness of the capitalist spirit in France. Whoever was able to do so retired from business or avoided entering it, using what fortune he had to procure an office for himself, and this was quite usual until well on into the 18th century. The history of France shows that this ideal was common to all sections of the population.

This disdainful attitude towards commerce and industry has just been enlarged upon. Regarded as cause or effect, it prevailed until the July Revolution. I am not thinking so much of the desire of the rich to be ennobled, or of the accepted practice of considering the nobility as the most privileged class. These things were to be found in England too, and it is doubtful whether even there they have wholly disappeared. No. What I have in mind is the supercilious, almost insulting, attitude towards commercial and industrial avocations, and the contemptuous utterances concerning their social value, which even as late as the 18th century were found broadcast nowhere else (if we except Spain) so much as in France.

" If there is contempt in the world, it is reserved for the tradesman." Thus a reliable witness [196] to the prevailing opinion of the upper classes in France in the 16th century remarked. The hard saying might have held good for the Germany of the time ; but it could not possibly apply to England. Montesquieu's dictum, however, dating from the middle of the 18th century (and it was by no means unique), would have been inconceivable even in the Germany of those days. What was it ? " All is lost when the profitable calling of the financier begins to be an honourable one. All other professions are disgusted, Honour loses its value, the slow and natural ways of winning distinction have no further attraction, and the government is attacked at its very foundations." [197]

4. GERMANY.

There can be no doubt that the capitalist spirit began to develop and extend in Germany in the " age of the Fuggers " ; here and there even earlier. Bold undertakings may be observed in that period, side by side with careful trading.

Nevertheless, it is well to sound a note of warning. Let no one imagine that the capitalist spirit in Germany, even in the 16th century, could compare for influence and intensity with what prevailed (say) in the Italian city states in the 14th. To form a true estimate of its extent in Germany in the 16th century when, as is generally acknowledged, it reached its zenith, it is necessary to observe certain facts.

1. Those undertakings in which the capitalist spirit was expressed were special cases, and limited in number. Public opinion, the judgment of the learned, and the views of the nation's leaders were all alike and unmistakably opposed to the new spirit. Luther's strong language on " Fuggering " is a good instance, and coincides with that of Ulrich von Hutten and Erasmus of Rotterdam.[198] Do not imagine, however, that only the learned shared these views. They had the masses with them. Sebastian Franck translated Erasmus into the vernacular [199] and his work enjoyed great popularity. "The stinking merchant class "—so Franck spoke of them. Even more in vogue was Cicero's tractate on Duty, which was available in many translations, and became a sort of household guide to conduct. This contained Cicero's well-known description of trade as a low kind of occupation (though he was probably thinking of higgling).[200] In view of all this, it is just to conclude that if there was anything of the capitalist spirit in the Germany of those days it had not penetrated very deeply.

2. Now it may be urged that the strong criticism of capitalism by contemporary thinkers can be taken as evidence that capitalism was maturing rapidly. The objection is not altogether invalid. There certainly were large undertakings at that time ; to cut prices was a common practice ; and monopolies were being sought for in all directions. Capitalism thus seemed to have reached a fairly high degree of development. But recall the other component parts of the capitalist spirit. These were as yet in their infancy in Germany. Take the art of calculation. It was only just beginning to be known in Germany in the 16th century, as I have already indicated. Ledgers such as those of Ott Ruland (15th century), trade reports such as those of Lucas Rem (16th century), can hardly bear comparison with similar Italian documents of the 14th and 15th centuries. And even in the 18th century, Germany was far behind England and Holland in this respect.

3. It is clear, therefore, that what development of the capitalist spirit there was lasted for only a brief space. A feudalizing process soon made itself felt in Germany even before the end of the 16th century ; it was much like what had happened in Italy, and before long it caught up in its onrush all the famous families of undertakers. Successors they had none, or very few ; the " bourgeois " stream was a thin one. It was not until the 18th century that a pulsating industrial and commercial life made itself noticeable, and, even so, it seems to have spent itself by the beginning of the following century. It is no exaggeration to assert that the capitalist spirit awoke in Germany once more only after 1850. To-day it has grown so mighty that, as no one can deny, Germany is catching up the United States of America as the land wherein that spirit has reached its utmost development. The characteristics of modern capitalist undertakings in

Germany are thus those that mark the modern type of undertaker generally, and these you will find set forth in the twelfth chapter of this book. The German undertaker (together with the American, whom he is approaching very closely) represents to-day the most perfect type of this species of the human race. He is distinguished from other modern types possibly in the following ways [201] :—

(*a*) *His adaptability.* German dominance in the world-markets owes much to the German's capacity of adapting himself to the wishes and peculiarities of his customers. Numerous observers have noted this fact many a time and oft. The quality is also exercised in his quick understanding of any set of conditions and in accommodating himself to them.

(*b*) *His great organizing talent.* See what this has done for German shipping, banking, and electrical works. No other nation has it in so great a measure, not even the Americans.

(*c*) *His attitude to science.* This too is universally admitted—that Germany's great industries, especially the electrical and chemical industries, have become so mighty because of their careful attention to the results of natural science, and the utilization of those results in their methods of production.

The attitude of the German undertaker to economic science is on the point of being determined. For the moment it seems that it is going to be another characteristic of the German undertaker that he will recognize as a condition for success the need to organize his business in accordance with the results of economic teaching. This much can even be asserted now : method in business enterprise, or, in other words, commercial calculations, have reached their most complete form in the German schools for capitalist undertakers.

5. HOLLAND.

In all probability the United Provinces were the land in which the capitalist spirit for the first time attained its fullest maturity ; where this maturity related to all its aspects, which were equally developed ; and where this development had never been so comprehensive before. Moreover, in the Netherlands an entire people became imbued with the capitalist spirit ; so much so, that in the 17th century Holland was universally regarded as the land of capitalism *par excellence* ; it was envied by all other nations, who put forth their keenest endeavours in their desire to emulate it ; it was the high school of every art of the tradesman, and the well-watered garden wherein the middle-class virtues throve. The Dutch were a maritime and bellicose people, yet at the same time unmatched in their knowledge of the trader's entire bag of tricks ; now and again (as we have already had occasion to observe) they were completely carried away by some speculating madness ; later on they became the centre of international stock-exchange activities. All these facts are well known ; they need only be recalled.

It will be giving my readers a treat to quote at this juncture the fairly brief and comprehensive description from Ranke's pen of the commercial prosperity enjoyed by Holland in the 17th century.

" Henceforth Holland levied tribute on the products of the universe. It was first the middleman between the eastern and western coasts of the neighbouring seas. The timber and the corn of the former it exchanged for the salt and the wine of the latter. It sent out its ships into the northern waters to catch herrings, and distributed the harvest of the deep in the estuaries of all the rivers, from the Vistula to the Seine, that flowed through southern lands. Down the Rhine, the Maas, and the

Scheldt it carried the fish itself. It shipped it to Cyprus and brought back wool, to Naples and brought back silk, and thus the coastlands of the ancient Phœnicians paid tribute to a distant Germanic people whose home their own early navigators had never been able to reach. Marketable wares of all sorts accumulated in Holland. In 1610 Contarini found in its granaries 100,000 sacks of good wheat and a similar quantity of corn ; while Raleigh is positive that the Dutch were never without a minimum supply of 700,000 quarters of corn, so that if their neighbours were in need they could hasten to relieve them. Naturally, not without drawing some advantage to themselves. Indeed, one year of scarcity brought them as much profit as seven of plenty. Nor were they content to distribute commodities in their raw state ; they usually added their own labour. Thus they imported annually from England 80,000 pieces of cloth, but these were undyed. The Dutch saw to this themselves, and thereby increased their gains.

"Great as was their participation in European commerce, their greatest trading achievements, which yielded them profit no less than fame, were those connected with their ventures in East Indian waters. Of all their attacks on Spain, their expeditions to India were what king and people alike most dreaded ; their effects were twofold : they hit the Spaniards very hard and widely extended Dutch activity. Contarini marvelled at the perfect arrangements for sending annually to India some 10 or 14 ships. This was about 1610. He estimated the capital of the Dutch East India Company at about 6,600,000 florins. This magnificent and all-embracing business led them further afield to unknown lands.

" And in Holland itself every harbour and creek, every inlet of the sea, was filled with ships, and every canal with barges. There was significance in the popular saying that in Holland as many people lived on the water as on the land. It was estimated that the country possessed no less than 200 large ships and 3,000 of moderate size, and Amsterdam was their main port. Their masts looked almost like a forest in the city's vicinity. Was it surprising, then, that Amsterdam expanded? Within the short space of thirty years its boundaries were considerably enlarged on two occasions. In 1601, 600 new houses were erected. Contarini reported that a foot of land cost as much as a scudo. For the year 1610, according to the same authority, there were 50,000 inhabitants in the Dutch capital.

"Industry throve, and the quality of the work done was splendid. The rich continued to be moderate in their habits and thrifty; and many a one who sold fine cloth to others was content himself with a rougher material. The poor had their needs provided for, and idleness was a deadly sin which merited and received condign punishment. To export to India was a common affair, and every wind that blew was made subservient to shipping. Indeed, there was no house but was a maritime training school, no habitation but had its map of the ocean. Need they fear an enemy when they had conquered the sea? Dutch sailors were famed for their policy of burning their ships with their own hands rather than surrender to the foe."

To this picturesque narrative I would only add that Holland became classical likewise for its cultivation of the middle-class virtues, and the extension and elaboration of the art of calculation. Evidence for this we have already noted above.

Now what became of this highly developed capitalist spirit? Parts of it, especially those last mentioned, have continued to exist; others either fell into decay or totally disappeared. Even before the 17th century had drawn to a close, we may observe a diminution of that military ardour which from the earliest times had given a special colouring to all oversea undertakings. In the 18th century the spirit of enterprise itself dwindled away ; and the "bourgeois" did not, as in some other countries, become feudalized. Here he waxed fat. He lived on his income, which, like a stream flowing gently and regularly, was derived either from the colonies or from invested capital. Is it not generally known that in the 18th century Holland became the money-lender of all Europe? Even the smallest interest in capitalist undertakings was no longer to be met with. "The Dutch have ceased to be merchants ; they have become commission agents ; and then from being commission agents they have finally taken on the rôle of financiers" (Luzac). Whether the credit was that of the state or only of bill-accepting is of little moment. The point is that whenever bill-discounting becomes the principal occupation of the "bourgeois," the spirit of undertaking is broken.

6. Great Britain.

The fate of the capitalist spirit has been very different in each of the three component parts of the United Kingdom.

Ireland as a country with a capitalist civilization may be almost entirely neglected. Down to this very day there is scarcely another land which has been so little affected by the capitalist spirit. Ireland, therefore, does not come within the purview of our considerations.

Of England we have already said a good deal in these pages. We noted that the heroic age of capitalism began in the 16th century, when the land was filled with a mighty spirit of undertaking, born of the love of adventure and the impulse for conquest. We saw how the landowning class transformed themselves into capitalist undertakers. We observed the stormy period, towards the end of the 17th century and the beginning of the 18th, when all manner of speculative enterprises were floated. We perceived how until the end of the 18th century middle-class virtues and the art of calculation both attained a very high degree of perfection, so much so that England became the model for less developed countries, like Germany and France. Finally, we are aware that England was the birthplace of modern industrialism.

From the end of the 17th century onwards, but more especially since the union with Scotland, the course of capitalist development in England was greatly influenced by the fortunes of the capitalist spirit in the Northern kingdom.

Nowhere else in the world did the birth of capitalism come about in so curious a fashion as in Scotland. Nothing is more surprising than the suddenness of its appearance. It is as though a pistol-shot had given the signal for the capitalist spirit, fully grown, to come into the land and dominate it. You cannot help thinking of the Victoria Regia, which blooms overnight.

Until the 17th century the Scotch, as we have already seen, carried on trade of a sort with neighbouring countries, not even having any ships of their own to speak of. As for the capitalist spirit, they were completely untouched by it. The 17th century brought few changes into this state of things. The only marked changes were in religion, and here a vast spiritual wave swept over the land, in the wake of the Reformation. It was towards the end of the 17th century that the sudden emergence of capitalism to which we have alluded came about. Everywhere you might have observed an unbridled desire for gain and undertakings innumerable. There is abundant evidence in proof of this, and we shall here review one or two expressions of opinion.[202]

" Soon after the establishment of the Revolution settlement, the ardent feelings of the Scottish people were turned out of their old channels of religious controversy and war in the direction of commercial enterprise," writes Burton in his *Criminal Trials in Scotland*. And under the year 1695 Burnet's *History of his own Time* records that " the lords and commons of Scotland were then desirous of getting into trade." In 1698, Fletcher of Saltoun writes : " By no contrivance of any man, but by an unforeseen and unexpected change of the genius of this nation, all their thoughts and inclinations, as if united and directed by a higher power, seemed to be turned upon trade, and to conspire together for its advancement." At this the Puritan clergy became uneasy. They stood like a duck on the river brink that sees its little ones swimming off. In 1709 the Rev. Robert Woodrow expressed an opinion in one of his letters that " the sin of our too great fondness for trade, to the neglecting of our more valuable interests, I humbly think will be written upon our judgment." In the same year some ships were taken by the French and part of the loss fell upon Glasgow. Thereupon Woodrow wrote expressing the view that this was Heaven's punishment. " I am sure the Lord is remarkably frouning upon our trade . . . since it was put in the room of religion."

The inwardness of the new spirit we have already discussed. There can be no doubt that it contributed in large measure to the high state of capitalist development which has been manifest in England and Scotland since the middle of the 18th century. What has been the course of that development ? What is the position to-day, comparing England with other lands, say with Germany ?

All reliable and authoritative observers appear to agree that to-day a condition of " capitalist decline " [203] has made its appearance in England. You may observe it in several ways.

1. Clear thinking has ceased to be an active and compelling influence in economic activities. The English undertaker, unlike the German, has not kept pace with progress ; he has not taken technical science into his service. Indeed, in the field of technology he is miles behind. The Englishman declares the adoption of the newest methods to be impossible. When raw material is delivered to him he would never dream of testing its quality in his laboratory ; the name of the supplying firm suffices him. As for his machines, they are ancient models of which he is proud ; whereas in reality they are only fit to be thrown on the scrap-heap.

You will find a similar instance of traditionalism in commerce reported in a Blue Book of 1897. " The Germans take their goods to the customers ; the English tradesman waits for the customers to come to him." British agents and commercial travellers live in too grand a style. Then, English packing cases are too heavy ; the foreigner packs his wares lightly and according to requirement. The Englishman neglects the finish of his commodities, which is quite independent of the quality, and he does this principally with the cheaper goods. He demands cash payments and gives little attention to the genuine credit needs of his customers. He does not cultivate advertisement. English goods are frequently of too high a quality, and therefore too expensive. The Englishman forces his tastes upon the market ; he will deliver goods in the way he thinks best or not at all.

A certain rigidity in the English banking system has also been observed.

2. The spirit of enterprise, interest in business, and

love of industry are all declining. The old business ideal is disappearing and a new outlook on life is taking its place. The Englishman finds pleasure in luxury, in an aristocratic manner of living, and above all in sport. All these are spreading, and as they spread they weaken the energies needed for economic activities. " Among members of the Idle Rich class the German bookworm is looked upon with the same pitiful contempt as the American Dollar-king, who at least may be useful as a father-in-law. Though differing from each other widely, they yet are both of the kingdom of fools, for they work. This opinion, hitherto the speciality of the aristocracy, is now also beginning to be shared by the upper middle classes in England. . . . It is significant that the most popular forms of the national sports have a strong pluto-cratic taint. They presuppose an aristocratic race that lives upon Negro, Chinese, and Hindoo labour, and draws dividends and economic rent from every country under the sun ; while the soil of their own land they regard (and value) solely as an article of luxury." [204]

7. THE UNITED STATES OF AMERICA.

In this book I shall say little about the United States of America, although they are of the utmost importance for the development of the capitalist spirit. That little may be placed under three headings.

1. The elements of the capitalist spirit have had a niche in the American national character ever since the foundation of the colonies, and even before that spirit took form and substance, i.e. before ever there was an economic order inspired by it.

2. The early stages of the capitalist spirit changed into the later and fully perfect stages sooner and more completely in America than anywhere else. There is

conclusive evidence [205] showing that the ideas of modern Americanism had already taken root at the beginning of the 19th century, and had even as far back as that day commenced to shape life according to their own liking. The peculiarities of this perfected capitalist spirit I shall deal with in Chapter XII.

3. Whatever the results of the capitalist spirit may be, you will find them developed to their utmost in the United States to-day. There the strength of that spirit is as yet unbroken ; there the whirlwind still rages.

SECTION IV

THE BOURGEOIS—PAST AND PRESENT

CHAPTER XI

THE BOURGEOIS—OLD STYLE

By now we have come to know the component parts
of the undertaker's soul as it aspires to perfection.
Acquisitiveness and enterprise, middle-class respectability
and calculation all go to compose the complex entity,
though various combinations are possible owing to the
variety of shade in each element, or owing to the
way the elements are combined. That is why we have
reviewed the different resultant types of capitalist undertaker. Moreover, we have also observed that in different
countries the development of the capitalist spirit varied
considerably. There remains one further question. Is
the capitalist spirit constant ? Does the bourgeois remain
immutably the same ? In other words, is there anything
common to all the types that have come under our notice,
and to all the national expressions of capitalism, so that
it may be possible to sketch the picture of the bourgeois
from them ?

With one qualification the answer is in the affirmative.
And the qualification is that we should be allowed to
divide one age of capitalist growth from another according
to its characteristic spirit, for it was this that marked off

one type of bourgeois or undertaker from another. This
means that there was not one persistent type of undertaker at all times, but different sorts at different times.

Now, so far as I can judge, capitalist undertakers from
the first dawn of capitalism to about the middle of the
18th century—the period which I have christened that of
early capitalism—had, with all their variation in details,
a good many characteristics in common. These were so
definite that they form a clear dividing line between the
undertaker of the early capitalist period and his prototype
in modern times. What manner of man, then, was he,
this bourgeois of old ?

To begin with, he also was a capitalist undertaker.
Profit was his end, undertakings his means ; he speculated
and calculated ; and ultimately he cultivated the middle-
class virtues, though not all in the same degree. What,
then, was his distinguishing mark, you ask ? How did he
differ from his modern brother ? You may sum it up in
a sentence : in all his thoughts and actions, in all that
he did or left undone, he was actuated by the weal or
woe of the living, breathing human being. The central
doctrine of the pre-capitalist period had not lost its
efficacy. *Omnium rerum mensura homo ;* man still continued to be the measure of all things. Life was still
natural. Even the bourgeois as yet walked bolt-upright
on his two feet ; he did not yet run about on all fours.

Of course, only fragments remained of the pre-capitalist
man who was still met with in the first faint beginnings
of capitalism, when the Genoese noble merchants built
them towers, or when Sir Walter Raleigh sallied forth in
search of El Dorado. These fragments you may come
across in Defoe or Benjamin Franklin. But the remainder
of that early natural man with his healthy appetites has
disappeared ; he has been forced to accustom himself to
the strait-waistcoat of middle-class respectability and

the tyranny of the calculating habit. His claws have been trimmed, his carnivorous teeth blunted, and his horns encased in leather.

But all those who bowed the knee to capitalism—the rich landowner and the great oversea trader, the banker and the speculator, the manufacturer and the draper—all these never ceased to accommodate their economic activities to the healthy demands of life ; for all of them business was but a means of livelihood. Their own interests and those of their fellow-men, for whom and with whom they laboured, determined the extent and direction of what they did. In support of this, you need only examine the views of these old-fashioned bourgeois.

1. First and foremost, consider their conception of riches and their attitude towards profit. Wealth was undoubtedly prized, and to obtain it was the passionate desire of every heart. But wealth was not an end in itself. Its only virtue lay in the creation or preservation of life-values. This is the tune on which all our informants harp, from Alberti to Defoe and Franklin.

The true value of money, says Alberti, can be appreciated only by him who has at any time been obliged to say to another " that bitter word, which all free spirits hate—' I pray thee.' " [206] Riches should bring you independence and liberty, should get you friends, should make you honoured and renowned.[207] On the other hand, " What you cannot make use of is but a heavy burden." [208]

It will suffice to add to these expressions of opinion, dating from the childhood of capitalism, others that were current in the latest period of this early capitalist era. The similarity in sentiment will be apparent.

Our first witness shall be Benjamin Franklin. A man, he says, who has been granted wealth and a soul to use it aright has received a special and splendid gift of grace.

Once in possession of riches it is a paramount duty to use them well. " A wise man will desire no more than what he may get justly, use soberly, distribute cheerfully, and live upon contentedly." [209] Riches must be constantly increasing through industry and skilful application. They should never be allowed to lie fallow, but always be adding to their owner's wealth and spreading happiness all around. It is sensible to accumulate goods and money ; but to use them well is wise. It is not riches that give happiness, but rather their proper utilization.[210] Riches bring fame, guarantee security, and provide means for many an honourable and useful undertaking. Moreover, wealth must be acquired in just and right ways,[211] for only those riches bring joy that are gotten honestly, or *onestamente*, as Alberti says.[212] If you are selling anything for profit, hearken to the still, small voice of conscience, and be content with fair gain ; and take no advantage of the buyer's ignorance.[213]

Now, it may quite rightly be objected that this wise counsel is easily given. In all probability it is the leisure-thought of the writers ; possibly the voice of conscience heard in the quiet of the study but neglected in the stress and heat of the day. Consequently, it is evidence that must be ruled out of court.

2. To see that such an objection would be invalid, observe (and this is the second point) the attitude of all our authorities to business itself, their conduct as business men, the way they carried on their affairs ; in a word, their " style " (as it may be called), and you shall find the same spirit in it as that in their attitude towards wealth.

Their business pace was as yet slow ; their whole activity was calm and unruffled. There was no stormy whirlwind in their work. Recall Franklin's decision to spend his time as profitably as possible and his view that industry was the prime virtue. His working-day was mapped out thus : six full hours were devoted to his business ; seven to sleep ; the rest he gave up to prayer, reading, and social diversions. And this was the type of the diligent undertaker, though Franklin was then only in a small way of business. His own words are worth recording.[213A]

The precept of order requiring that every part of my business should have its allotted time, one page in my little book [cf. p. 119 above] contained the following scheme of employment for the twenty-four hours of a natural day.

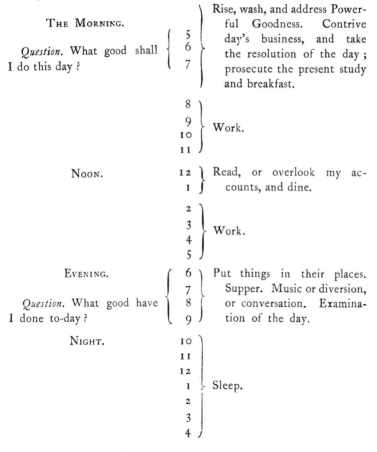

THE MORNING.

Question. What good shall I do this day ?

5
6
7

Rise, wash, and address Powerful Goodness. Contrive day's business, and take the resolution of the day ; prosecute the present study and breakfast.

8
9
10
11

Work.

NOON.

12
1

Read, or overlook my accounts, and dine.

2
3
4
5

Work.

EVENING.

Question. What good have I done to-day ?

6
7
8
9

Put things in their places. Supper. Music or diversion, or conversation. Examination of the day.

NIGHT.

10
11
12
1
2
3
4

Sleep.

Or take the case of the wholesale traders of Bozen. They closed their businesses for the whole summer and spent the time in the health resort of the highlands near.

Leisure was thus appreciated. And just the same as you left yourself an abundance of it during the day and during the year, so, too, you sought to obtain the maximum amount of leisure for life as a whole. It was a common practice for people who had amassed a fortune in business or in industry (even though it were not of great proportions) to retire in middle age, and if possible purchase a country seat where they might end their days in contemplative ease. Jacob Fugger with his " Let me earn so long as I am able "—a dictum typically characteristic for a full-blown capitalist economic out-look—was undoubtedly far in advance of his age. It was for holding such a view that Anthony Fugger described him as a queer fish. He was regarded as abnormal. And so he was, judged from the standpoint of those who in their demands on life placed the ideal of the retired private gentleman first and foremost.

This yearning for a peaceful existence in a country house may be found in all the Italian books on trade ; in the German Renaissance there was the same tendency to feudalize the traders ; and in the 18th century the English commercial world still continued to look longingly at this end-all of business. The ideal of the retired private gentleman may thus be regarded as an article of faith in the early capitalist economic creed everywhere. That it had yet another significance we shall see presently.

The domination of this ideal in England in the first half of the 18th century is attested by Defoe's remarks [213B] on the common English practice to retire from business comparatively early. When a man has

amassed £20,000, "why should he trade any farther?
and what need he desire any more, that has such a bank?
'Tis time to leave off and have done; 'tis time to leave
labouring for the world, when he has the world, as they
call it, on a string." Such a one "changes his situation
in the world, that is to say, he lays down the tradesman
and takes up the gentleman with a £1,000 a year estate."
Defoe gives him two "seasonable hints." Let him live
within the compass of his income. Of his £1,000 a year
he should spend half and lay up the remainder, thus
ensuring "a rising family under him." Secondly, he
should keep far from speculation, for has he not retired
from business to enjoy what he has got? Why then
adventure it? All he has to do is to be "quiet when he
is arrived at this station of life." After all, "if a tradesman is leaving off, it is with the usual saying of the rich
men that withdraw from the world—That he may enjoy
himself; that he may live in quiet and peace at the latter
end of his days, without noise and without hurry."

That was all very well when they had made their
fortune. But while making it, what of their work?
Let it be said at once that it was slow. Business
methods were such that in any given time you accom-
plished the least possible transactions. The extensive
development of commerce was small; its intensive
development was only in accord with it. The spirit
in which business was carried on appears to me to be
exemplified in the ancient saw to demand as high prices as
possible so as to obtain a great rate of profit on a small
capital. Small turnover, large profits, seems to have been
the ruling principle of the undertakers of those days.
And not merely of the lesser men, some of whom had
not yet thrown off entirely the shackles of the gild
system; the very big trading companies had it too.
Thus it was the policy of the Dutch East India Company

to carry on "small transactions that brought in a great deal." That was why it always destroyed spice plants, burned rich harvests and the like ; though another motive was to deprive the poor of the opportunity of enjoying colonial products.

Quite generally it was the aim of all business to satisfy the demands of the wealthy, which is always easier than to deal with demand on a large scale.[214] This was quite justifiable according to the economic theory of the 17th and 18th centuries, which made out a good case for high prices.[215]

The dignified aspect of the old-fashioned bourgeois, his stiff and pedantic bearing, were only the outward garb of his inward calm. Can you imagine a man in the long fur cloak of the Renaissance, or in the knee-breeches and powdered wig of the subsequent centuries, as ever being in a hurry ? Reliable authorities, indeed, describe the old-fashioned tradesman as one who walks with careful step and slow, who is never in haste just because he is occupied. Messer Alberti, himself a very busy man, tells us that he had never observed a busy person walking otherwise than at a slow pace,[216] and this applied to 15th-century Florence. Of 18th-century Lyons a contemporary tells the same tale. "Here," he says, "our walk is slow because every one is busy ; in Paris people are in one continuous haste—because there is nothing to do there."[217] So in Glasgow about the same time. We read of its merchants "how in scarlet coats, cocked hats, and powdered wigs, they strutted up and down the Planistanes, the only bit of pavement then in Glasgow, covering three or four hundred yards of road in front of the Town Hall and the adjoining offices, talking grandly to one another and nodding haughtily to the humbler folk who came to do them homage." [218]

3. The attitude of the old-fashioned traders towards

competition and to their customers sprang naturally from their business style. Above all else they wanted quiet. This "static principle," which had dominated the whole of pre-capitalist economic activities, had not yet lost all its influence in the early capitalist period. And the circle of your customers was like a fenced-off preserve ; it was wholly yours—to be compared to the territory assigned to the trading company in lands beyond the sea for its exclusive exploitation.

With this point I have dealt fully in another book ; [219] it must here suffice, therefore, to indicate its importance briefly. Let me refer to one or two business principles, all of them naturally resulting from a static economic order, all of them included in the economic outlook of the old-fashioned bourgeois.

All "custom hunting" was looked at askance; to take away your neighbour's customers was contemptible, unchristian, and immoral. A rule for "Merchants who traded in commodities" was : "Turn no man's customers away from him, either by word of mouth or by letter, and do not to another what you would not have another do to you." It was, however, more than a rule ; it became an ordinance, and is met with over and over again. In Mayence its wording was as follows : "No one shall prevent another from buying, or by offering a higher price make a commodity dearer, on pain of losing his purchase ; no one shall interfere in another's business undertaking or carry on his own on so large a scale as to ruin other traders." In Saxony it was much the same. In the Ordinances of 1672, 1682, and 1692, paragraph 18 reads : "No shopkeeper shall call away the customers from another's shop, nor shall he by signs or motions keep them from buying." [220]

It followed from this that all tricks to increase your custom, of whatever sort they were, were rather despised.

Right into the 19th century there was still a certain prejudice in many a high-class firm against even the simplest form of advertisement. Some houses in New York had not got rid of the prejudice by the middle of the century. "No respectable house would overdo the thing. There was a sort of self-respect about the articles advertised." 221

But even in an advertising age it was for long considered nefarious to praise your goods or to point out wherein your business was superior to others. The last word in commercial impropriety was to announce that your prices were lower than those of the man opposite. "To under-sell" was most ungentlemanly: "No blessing will come from harming your neighbour by underselling and cutting prices."

Bad as underselling itself was, it was beneath contempt to advertise it. "Since the days of our author," remark the editors of the fifth edition (1745) of Defoe's *Complete English Tradesman* (Defoe died in 1731), "this underselling practice is grown to such a shameful height that particular persons publicly advertise that they under-sell the rest of the trade."

For France there is extant a particularly valuable document, dating from the second half of the 18th century, which proves even more strikingly how heinous this offence was thought to be, even in Paris. It is an ordinance of the year 1761, and it proclaims to all and sundry in the French capital that to advertise that you are selling your goods at a price below the customary one must be regarded as the last resource of a merchant in difficulties, and that such action deserved severe con-demnation. The ordinance proceeded to forbid the wholesale and retail traders of Paris and its suburbs "to run after one another" trying to find customers, and above all to distribute handbills calling attention to their wares.

Other methods of drawing advantages for yourself at the expense of your neighbours or of poaching on others' preserves were equally disreputable. The author of the *Complete English Tradesman* has some reflections on this manner of competition which help us exceedingly in gaining a true estimate of the business ethics of those days. They prove that economic activities were still in a static state and that tradition and custom ruled them. Remember that Defoe was not unskilled as a trader, and that generally he is filled with the capitalist spirit.

This is his story.[222] Before Wiltshire broadcloth reaches Northampton, where it is retailed, four people find employment. "The clothier, when it is finished, sends it up by the carrier to London to Mr. A, the Blackwell Hall factor, to be sold. Mr. A, the factor, sells it to Mr. B, the woollen-draper; Mr. B, the woollen-draper, sells it to Mr. C, the shopkeeper at Northampton, and he cuts it out in his shop and sells it to the country gentlemen about him . . . also 'tis sent down by the carrier from London to Northampton."

Now in Northampton is another shopkeeper, " perhaps an Alderman, a rich overgrown Tradesman," who has more money than his neighbours and therefore wants no credit. " Prying about into all the secrets of the trade," he discovers where the cloth comes from, communicates with the clothier in Wiltshire, and buys his goods direct, then has them brought by horse-packs to Northampton. Possibly by tempting the clothier with ready money he obtains the cloth a penny per yard cheaper than the factor in London sold it to the woollen-draper. What is the result? The overgrown tradesman will save in cost of transport, so much so that his cloth will cost him half-a-crown per yard less than his neighbour. Hence he will be able to undersell, and thus obtain his neighbour's custom. Not only that, but

he will have taken away the occupation of several people :
the carrier who brought the goods to London from
Wiltshire, the carrier who took them from London to
Northampton, and finally Mr. A, the Blackwell Hall
factor, who " also loses his employment and may sit and
blow his fingers for want of trade." Mr. B likewise is
ruined by the loss of his wholesale trade. " And what
is all the benefit which is made by this spoil upon trade ?
Only this, that Squire D. E. of Northamptonshire buys
his suits half-a-crown a yard cheaper," and a covetous
man has been made richer. And the moral ? " This is
cutting off the circulation of trade ; this is managing
trade with a few hands ; and if this practice, which is
indeed evidently begun, was to come to be universal,
a million of people in England that now live handsomely
by trade would be destitute of employment and their
families in time might want bread."

This passage speaks volumes. How utterly inconceivable must the line of thought appear to a modern
business man !

Like the producers, the consumers also received
attention. In a certain sense the consumer received even
more, for the conception that all production was in the
interests of consumption had not yet disappeared. It
was the old " natural " view ; production for use was still
the rule of all economic activities. Hence the stress
laid throughout the whole of the early capitalist period
on *good* wares, and on the principle that commodities
should really be what they pretended. Innumerable
were the ordinances that were everywhere promulgated
to this intent, more especially in the 17th and 18th
centuries ; and the state deemed it part of its work itself
to regulate the quality of wares. It is idle to assert that
this very state control is evidence of the decline of the
" natural " view ; in other words, that the custom

of producing for use was on the decline. Such was not the case. The interference of the state was intended to check the conduct of some few unscrupulous manufacturers. For the rest, the old tradition prevailed that you should make good and genuine commodities ; it was the tradition of the gild system, and industry in the early capitalist period continued to be tinged with it.

It was long before the purely capitalist notion gained acceptance that the exchange value of any commodity was what influenced the undertaker most. We may observe how slow its progress was from the conflicting opinions on the subject in the 18th century. Sir Josiah Child appears to have been in the minority on this, as on most other questions, when he formulated the demand that every manufacturer should be allowed to judge for himself as to the kind of commodity, and the quality, that he brought into the market. It is curious enough now-a-days to read Child's plea for the right of the manufacturer to make shoddy goods. " If we intend to have the trade of the world," he cries,[223] " we must imitate the Dutch, who make the worst as well as the best of all manufactures, that we may be in a capacity of serving all markets and all humours."

4. Finally, the attitude of the old-fashioned bourgeois to technical inventions is significant for the spirit within him. The old view of life appears once more : technical improvements are to be welcomed if only they do not overthrow man's happiness. True, they may cheapen commodities ; but the odd pence thus gained are too high a price for the tears and the sufferings of the families of the workmen who are thrown out of employment. Once more, then, human welfare is the pivot of the whole economic organism, even though this time it be but the welfare of the wage-earning class. The interests of this class were by no means absent from men's thoughts

in those days, although the reason for this may have been a selfish one.

There is abundant testimony to the dislike of labour-saving machinery in the early capitalist period. Let us glance at one or two instances.

In the second year of Elizabeth's reign a Venetian inventor (a type whose acquaintance we have already made) offered a labour-saving machine to the Court of the London Clothworkers' Company (whose industry by that time was already capitalistic in its organization). The Court carefully considered the offer and decided to refuse it, for the new invention would probably have deprived many a workman of his living. " It wolde be a grete decay unto the companye, whereupon the Master and Wardens gave the said stranger grete thanks and also xx*s.* in money towards his charge, and so parted." [224]

In 1684 the knitting-frame for stockings was forbidden to be used (again in a capitalistically organized industry), and once more the reason was that it might reduce the wages of the craftsmen.[225] Even a professional " projector " and inventor like John Joachim Becher shared this view. " I should certainly advise no one to invent instruments that might do away with human labour or reduce wages ; but there can be no objection to such as are of advantage and utility, especially in those places where there is more work than workers can accomplish." [226] Colbert's language is stronger still ; the inventor of time-saving devices is a " foe of work." And these are the sentiments of Frederick the Great : " It is not by any means my intention that the spinning machine should be generally used. . . . If it were, a large number of people who depended for their livelihood on spinning would be thrown out of employment into starvation—which cannot possibly be tolerated." [226a] After all this we shall not be surprised to find that a man of such noble sentiments and good taste as Montesquieu should be conservative in this respect. He believed that machines, even including water-mills, were not an unmixed blessing.[227] Finally, so thorough a business man as Postlethwayt is very reserved in his judgment on new inventions. A people without commerce may safely refuse to admit machines, but commercial states should only allow them after careful scrutiny and should anyhow exclude such as manufacture goods for home consumption. " What we gain in expedition, we lose in strength." [228]

What comes to the fore throughout ? The old conception of producing in order to satisfy wants, no more and no less, the traditional way of life, or moral scruples. But be the reason what it may, it is always a stumbling-block to the unfettered development of acquisitiveness, of the undertaking spirit, and of economic rationalism.

With the dawn of the 19th century all this changed, at first slowly, then with a rush. The results of the change will form the subject of the succeeding chapter.

CHAPTER XII

THE MODERN BUSINESS MAN

How has the economic outlook changed in the last century? What characterizes the capitalist spirit of our own day—the zenith of capitalism; and how does that spirit differ from the one which filled the old-fashioned bourgeois?

Before attempting to answer these questions, let us realize that there is no one single type of undertaker to-day, any more than in earlier epochs; that, as in the early capitalist period, a different spirit moves different capitalist undertakers. Let us, then, place the various types in groups. Surprising as it may seem, they are the types we already know as having existed in the past. To-day, too, we find the freebooter, the ground landlord, the bureaucrat, the speculator, the trader and the manufacturer.

Recall the career of a Cecil Rhodes. Does it not remind you of the Genoese merchants on their towers, or possibly even more of Sir Walter Raleigh and Sir Francis Drake? Cecil Rhodes was of the stuff that robber-knights were made of. He was a discoverer and a conqueror whom no stumbling-blocks could retard; beside the sword and the rifle he wielded another mighty weapon —modern stock-exchange gambling. He was partly politician, partly capitalist undertaker; rather more of a diplomat than a trader; he recognized no other power than

brute force. It is strange to find in him even one iota of
the Puritan spirit. And if we are to compare him with
earlier generations, he must be placed alongside the men
of the Renaissance.

How different from Cecil Rhodes's world is that of
(say) Stumm, or some Silesian mine-owner! Here we
are in the atmosphere of the old feudal landed nobility;
the ancient relationship between master and man is still
met with; the staff of the establishments are arranged
in a kind of hierarchy, and business is deliberate and
cumbersome. Such are a few of the characteristics
of these concerns, the directors of which have much
in common with the capitalist landed proprietor of days
gone by.

Then there is a third kind of undertaker nowadays
who reminds us of the bureaucrat of old—exact in his
work, methodical to a degree, nicely balanced in his judgments, highly gifted as an organizer, very careful before
committing himself, an excellent executive official, who
to-day may be town clerk of a large town and to-morrow
manager of a bank, who frequently enough gives up the
control of a Government department for that of a trust.*
You will find him at the head of state and municipal
enterprises.

Different from all these is the speculator of our time,
who appears to be twin-brother to the 18th-century
projector. Recently the daily papers reported the exploits
of a French speculator, and the story is worth recalling.
Rochette was the man's name; his age scarcely thirty.
Yet he had allowed millions to slip between his fingers.

---

* [This is a type common in Germany. Perhaps Bernard Dernburg
is the best known. He was Director of the Darmstädter Bank from
1901 to 1906, and German Minister for the Colonies from 1907 to
1910. On his resigning his portfolio he again became a banking
magnate.]

He started life as an under-waiter in a railway station restaurant; before long he was a full-fledged waiter in a café in Melun. Coming to Paris, he made himself acquainted with book-keeping, and entered the service of Berger, the financial swindler. On his master's bankruptcy Rochette took over the business with the 5,000 francs dowry brought him by a typist whom he married. He then began to float companies, and in the space of four years no less than 13 came into existence. There was the Crédit Minier, with a capital of 500,000 francs; the Laviana Coal Mines, with 2 millions; the Liat Coal Mines, with the same amount; the Banque Franco-Espagnole, with 20 millions; the Minier Trust, with 10 millions; the Union Franco-Belge, with $2\frac{1}{2}$ millions; the financial paper *Le Financier*, with 2 millions; a number of copper and tin companies; a Moroccan Fishery Company; an incandescent lamp company, with $4\frac{1}{2}$ millions; and many more. He issued altogether some 60 million francs' worth of shares, which by skilful manipulation rose to 200 millions, though a tenth of that figure was more nearly their true value. He had opened no less than 57 branch establishments in France; and the total number of people who participated in his scheme was close upon 40,000. Most of them were ruined, their total losses amounting to more than 150 millions. Why, it may be asked, was Rochette able to take in so many people? The explanation will be found in his marvellous power of surrounding himself with "solid," respectable folk. Just to show how cunning he was in blinding his victims, it may be mentioned that he founded a large factory for utilizing a filament lamp patent. Everybody rushed to get shares in the company; the huge factory was the talk of the town; its tall chimneys belched forth smoke day and night, to the great satisfaction of the shareholders. In reality, however, there was only one solitary individual working in the building, and he was the stoker!

Does not this story read like a report of doings in England in the 1720's?

How different is the persevering tradesman who makes a fortune because of his sure eye for the right conjuncture, or by clever calculations and advantageous agreements with his wholesale house, his customers, and his employees. What has such a man, say a Berlin draper, in common with Cecil Rhodes? What the director of a multiple shop with a gold-mine speculator? And what all these with the manufacturer who runs his factory as was done 100 or 200 years ago, in Bradford or Sedan?

These old friends are still among us, and seemingly their form is unchanged. Nor are they the only types of the modern undertaker. Others have joined the group, which thus becomes quite picturesque. A very common one, usually found in America, may be termed the master-undertaker (since super-undertaker is an ugly word). His great characteristic is that he unites within himself several independent types. He may be freebooter, unscrupulous calculator, landlord, and speculator all in one. Any trust-magnate will serve as an illustration.

Finally, a phenomenon of our age is the collective undertaker, who is not an individual at all, but a group of capitalist undertakers at the head of a giant enterprise. They form a kind of syndicated undertaker, each of them exercising special functions, and in their corporate capacity they represent undertaking in all its comprehensiveness. We need only think of such industrial organizations as our electrical concerns, our iron foundries, our cannon factories.

In short, modern undertaking in all its types presents a variegated picture. But in our own days, as in those of long ago, all the types have certain features in common, all are filled with the same spirit. It is only a difference of degree that distinguishes the one from the other. In olden times, as we saw, the undertakers were children of the early capitalist spirit; in modern times, they are the children of the perfected capitalist spirit.

What manner of thing is this perfected capitalist spirit? And what have all the types of the modern capitalist undertaker in common ?

1. The ideal of both must be our first consideration. What is it ? What are the life-values that govern the latter-day business man ? What strikes us here is that there has been a peculiar change of perspective in the evaluation of man, a change of perspective which seems to have affected the whole of the rest of life. Man, the flesh-and-blood man, with his joys and sorrows, with his needs and demands, has been forced from his place as the centre round which all economic activities rotate ; his throne is now occupied by a few abstractions, such as Acquisitiveness and Business. Man has ceased to be what he was until the end of the early capitalist period—the measure of all things. The economic subjective agent now aims at as high a profit as he can, and strives to make his business flourish exceedingly. The two aims are closely intertwined, as we shall presently observe. Their relationship may be expressed thus : The undertakers wish to see business thriving ; as for acquisitiveness, it is forced upon them, even though they may never have set out with that as their goal.

The real interest of undertaking does not always lie in mere gain, certainly not for the dominating personalities who determine the type. Walter Rathenau was, as I think, perfectly right when he once said : "I have never yet met with a business man whose chief aim was to acquire wealth. I will even go so far as to assert that he who is out to make money cannot possibly be a great business man." [229] Something very different occupies the thoughts of the undertaker. His heart is set on seeing his business thrive. Once more Walter Rathenau has expressed it well. " The object of the business man's work, of his worries, his pride and his aspirations is just his undertaking, be it a commercial company, factory, bank, shipping concern, theatre or railway. The undertaking seems to take on form and substance, and to be ever with him, having, as it were, by virtue of his bookkeeping, his organization, and his branches, an independent economic existence. The business man is wholly devoted to making his business a flourishing, healthy, living organism." [230] This view is shared by all the capitalist undertakers of the day in so far as they have expressed themselves on the inner meaning of their activity.

Now, what is really meant by making a business, that is, a capitalist undertaking, flourish? Observe that a business begins with a sum of money and ends with the same, and that therefore its existence is bound up with the realization of a surplus. Success in business can only mean success in realizing this surplus. No profits, no business success. A factory may make very dear or very cheap goods, and their quality may establish their maker's name as a household word throughout the globe, but if the business continues to show a deficit from year to year, it is a failure from the capitalist point of view. To flourish, a concern must be profitable ; to prosper, it must pay. [231]

You see now what I meant when I made the statement that the undertakers wish to see business thriving, and as for acquisitiveness, it is forced upon them.

Such being the goal of the capitalist undertaker, the end of his activities is necessarily projected into infinity. In earlier times, when the needs of the community determined economic activities, these had natural boundaries

or limits. There can be no such limits when economic
activities are determined by acquisitiveness and by flourishing businesses. There is never a point in the future when
the total profits are sufficiently great for the undertaker
to say : It is enough. Should the development of a
business be such that its prosperity ceases to increase, the
many-sidedness of modern enterprise will see to it that
before long a second, and possibly a third, business is
added to the original one. Thus it is that in modern
days two equally strong tendencies show themselves—
expansion of one and the same business, and the branching
out into subsidiary or additional businesses. This very
often leads to a kind of inner pressure in the mind of the
undertaker. It frequently happens that he really does not
want to expand further, but he must. Many a captain of
industry has confessed as much. We were always hoping,
says Andrew Carnegie in his *Autobiography*, that there
would come a time when extension of business would no
longer be necessary ; but we invariably found that to put off
expanding would mean retrogression.[232] Rockefeller tells
the same tale. The first reason for starting his trusts was
the desire to unite his capital and his capacities " to carry
on a business of some magnitude and importance in place
of the small business that each separately had heretofore
carried on. After some time, when the possibilities of the
new conditions became apparent, we found that more
capital was necessary. This we provided, as also the
people, and founded the Standard Oil Company with a
capital of a million dollars. Later we discovered that
even more money could be profitably invested, and we
raised our capital to $3\frac{1}{2}$ millions. The more the business
grew the more capital we put into it, the object being
always the same : to extend our business by furnishing
the best and cheapest products."[233] A kind of mono-
mania this ; capital is piled on capital *because* the business

grows. Extension of business is the end; furnishing cheap and good products the means. A famous German undertaker—Strousberg—says exactly the same thing. " The first wedge calls as a rule for a second, and so the great railway I was building made further demands upon me. To satisfy these I extended my activities, departed more and more from my original intention, and, finding so much promise in the new prospect, I devoted myself wholly to my business." [234]

Most capitalist undertakers think of nothing else but this constant desire for extension and expansion, which to the outside observer appears so meaningless. If you ask them what purpose the expansion is intended to serve, they will regard you with a kind of mild surprise and reply a little testily that the purpose is self-evident ; it is to make economic life more vigorous, and, moreover, is demanded by economic progress.

But what is meant by " economic progress " in this quite general and fairly stereotyped answer? What is the association of ideas in the minds of the people who give it ? Examine carefully and you shall find that it means an expansion in what may be called the "economic apparatus"—the production of largely increased quantities at the cheapest possible price ; enormous output ; enormous extent of communications ; the quickest transportation of goods, people, and news.

But the answer, like the phenomena that prompted the question, sounds meaningless too. It is therefore unsatisfactory. There must be method in all this madness ; it must surely be explicable. The people concerned in the activities do not seem to be alive to any life-values at their base. But life-values in them there must be, or you would not find whole generations of men intellectually sound and strong engaged in the activities mentioned. An analysis of the soul of the modern capitalist undertaker therefore repays the trouble, and at the very outset you stumble across—the child. In very truth, the psychology of the modern undertaker appears to me to resemble greatly that of the child. Understand the one and you will understand the other. For all the processes in the mind of the undertaker (and indeed of modern man generally), if reduced to their simplest elements, show a kind of relapse into the days of childhood.

Let us consider the matter more in detail.

The child possesses four elementary " values " ; four ideals dominate its existence. They are—

(*a*) Physical bigness, as seen in grown-ups and imagined in giants ;

(*b*) Quick movement—in running, bowling a hoop, riding on a roundabout.

(*c*) Novelty—it changes its toys very quickly ; it begins something and never completes it because another occupation attracts it ; and

(*d*) Sense of power—that is why it pulls out the legs of a fly, makes Towzer stand on his hind legs and beg nicely, and flies its kite as high as it can.

Curious as it may sound, these ideals, and these only, will be found in all modern " values." Let us take them in turn.

(*a*) We attach importance to quantities, to mere size. It is what interests us, what we admire most. That, I fancy, will be generally admitted. There is a universal tendency (to use the words of Lord Bryce) " to mistake bigness for greatness." It matters not wherein the bigness consists : it may be the population of a town or a country, the height of a monument, the breadth of a river, the frequency of suicide, the passengers carried by a railway, the size of a ship, the number of players in an orchestra, or what not. Of course our greatest admiration is reserved for a huge sum of money. Besides, money makes it possible to measure the size of otherwise unmeasurable things and to compare them. It is a natural and easy step from this to the belief that that is valuable which costs much. We say this picture or this jewellery is twice as valuable as that. In America, where this modern tendency may be studied better than anywhere else because there it has reached its greatest perfection, people come to the point at once, and prefix to every commodity its monetary value. " Have you seen the 50,000-dollar Rembrandt at Mr. A's house ? " is a not unusual question. " To-day Mr. Carnegie's 500,000-dollar yacht entered the harbour of " (say) Boston—so you may read in the daily paper.

Get into the habit of looking at the mere quantity of things and you will naturally tend to compare any two phenomena that may come under your notice ; you will weigh the one against the other and pronounce the larger to be the more valuable. Again, if of two things the one becomes larger than the other in a given space of time, it is said to have been successful. So that the inclination towards what is measurably big brings with it necessarily another tendency—worship of success The modern business man is appraised only in accordance with his success. Now success means to overtake others ; to do more, to achieve more, to possess more than others ; in a word, to be great. The pursuit of success holds out the same unlimited possibilities as the chase of profits ; the one complements the other.

To illustrate the influence on the inner workings of the mind of this quantitative valuation of things, so characteristic of our day, let us refer to the attitude of people to sport. What is invariably the main question of interest ? Is it not, who will win ? Who will score most ? A match is but a quantitative balance between two results. Imagine such a standpoint in an ancient Greek wrestling school ! Imagine it at a Spanish bull-fight ! The thing is impossible. In both these cases qualitative values were looked for, e.g. the highest personal artistic skill.

(*b*) Speed is of almost the same consequence to the modern man as massivity. To rush on in a 100-h.p. motor-car is one of the supremest ideals of our age; and he who cannot speed madly along contents himself with reading of record-breaking velocity. Perhaps the express between Hamburg and Berlin was ten minutes in advance of its scheduled time; perhaps the latest ocean-liner reached New York three hours earlier than it was expected ; perhaps the postman now comes at 7.30 instead of at the customary 8 o'clock ; perhaps one news-paper published a declaration of war (probably a fictitious one) an hour before its competitor—all these things are of tremendous interest to the queerly constituted folk of our day ; they seem to be of vital importance to them.

Moreover, a curious concept has sprung into existence, that of "beating the record." In terms of record-breaking you impress on your memory the speediest achievements as the most valuable ones. In its fullest meaning the new concept refers to great size and great speed combined. All the megalomania, all the mad hurry of our time, is expressed in record-beating. I think it most likely that the future historian of our time will speak of it as "The Age of Record-breaking."

(*c*) Whatever is new nowadays attracts merely because it is a novelty. It attracts most when the assurance is possible, "There never has been anything like it." Sensational we call its effect on the mind. That the love of sensation is a marked feature of the age requires no expatiation. Modern journalism is perhaps the best proof.

But recall also how fashions in dances, no less than in
clothes, change from season to season.   Is it not because
nothing is so attractive as what is new ?

(d) The sense of power is the fourth characteristic of
the modern spirit ;   it is felt in the consciousness of
superiority over others.   But in reality it is only an
expression of weakness ;   hence its importance in the
child's world.   For, after all, any one gifted with true
greatness, which is usually inward, will be hardly likely
to estimate the outward semblance of power at all highly.
Power has no temptation for Siegfried ;   only a Mime
thirsts for it.   Bismarck in all probability did not bother
much about the power he exercised ;   but in Lassalle the
desire for power must have been tremendous.   A king
possesses power ;   it is therefore of small moment in his
sight.   But the financier of humble origin, who keeps a
kingly borrower waiting in his ante-chamber for some
little time, suns himself in this power because his soul has
none of it.   An undertaker who employs 10,000 men and
experiences a sense of power in consequence is like a little
boy who makes his doggie bring back the stick he keeps
on throwing from him.   Moreover, when neither by
money nor any other outward force power over mankind
is given us, we talk of the conquest of nature.   That is
why our age is so childishly delighted with epoch-making
discoveries—say, the mastery of the air, and such-like
achievements.   The truly great man, however, will be
comparatively unmoved at the sight of a biplane in the
air.   A truly great generation concerned with the deepest
problems of life will not be enraptured because it
made some discoveries in technical science.   Power of
this sort it will assuredly regard as " superficial."   Our
own age lacks true greatness ;   accordingly, like a child
it admires the power which new inventions bestow,
and it overrates those who possess it.   Hence the high

esteem in which the populace holds inventors and millionaires.

It is just possible that these visions float before the gaze of the undertaker more or less clearly. But certain it is that they take form and substance in his goal—the expansion and growth of his business. Acquisitiveness and interest in his enterprise thus direct his activities as a capitalist undertaker.

2. His ideal we have reviewed. It remains now to review these activities as influenced by the ideal. In essence the activities of the modern capitalist undertaker remain the same as before. He must conquer, organize, deal, speculate, and calculate. But the extent of each of these factors varies, and consequently the resultant whole is not quite like that of an earlier age.

In modern times the trading function has become of more and more significance. I use the word "trading" in the sense indicated earlier in the book of dealing or negotiating. It is on this that commercial success now increasingly depends; on the skill and strength of suggestion in making contracts of all kinds. In olden days knots were cut; to-day they must be unravelled.

Next in importance to dealing comes skilful speculation—by which I mean stock-exchange manipulations. Modern undertakings are drawn more and more into the vortex of stock-exchange activities. Trust development such as we find in the United States is in reality only the transformation of manufacturing and commercial enterprises into purely stock-exchange speculative concerns. Consequently the directors and managers of such businesses have new problems to solve, and this opens up new activities for them.

As for calculation, it becomes more and more delicate as well as increasingly difficult, both because of the need for absolute exactitude and also because it has become so extensive.

Finally, the activities of the capitalist undertaker have become much more many-sided ; that is to say, in so far as specialization has not set in. Economic activities have branched out in all directions ; what wonder then that those who direct them should be called upon to be many-sided ?

So much for the nature of the activity itself. What is new is its boundlessness. So long as the needs of the living human being governed economic activities, so long did these have a limit. But with the disappearance of the governing factor, the natural limit fell away. Accordingly the activities of the capitalist undertaker have no bounds. *Non sunt certi denique fines.* Which means that the expenditure of human energy in modern economic activities, extensively and intensively, is strained to the uttermost. Every minute of the day, of the year, nay, of life itself, is devoted to work ; and during this working period every power is occupied at highest pressure. Everybody is acquainted with the hard-worked man of to-day. Whether employer or employed, he is constantly on the verge of a breakdown owing to overwork. That he tends to be excited, that he is always on the move, is generally known too. Speed and yet more speed— such is the cry of the age. It rushes onward in one mad race.

The influence of such a life on body and soul is not difficult to gauge. It corrodes the former and dries up the latter. Everything is sacrificed to the Moloch of work ; all the higher instincts of heart and mind are crushed out by devotion to business. How much the inner life of modern man has been shattered is best seen if we cast a glance at the kernel of all natural life—the relationship to women. These men have no time for the enjoyment of delicate passions, nor even for gallant flirtations. They seem to be quite incapable of deep erotic emotions. Either they are wholly apathetic so far as love is concerned, or they are content with a brief sensual intoxication. They either do not bother about women at all, or they buy what they require in this respect.

3. Business principles likewise have undergone a change. That was only to be expected when the goal of enterprise has become different. To-day, it may be said, five main rules regulate economic activities.

(*a*) Absolute rationalism is the first. Economic activities are ruled by cold reason, by thought. As we have already seen, that has always been the case ; it showed itself in the making of plans, in considering whether any policy was likely to be successful or no, and in calculation generally. The modern capitalist spirit differs from its predecessors only in the degree in which this rule is obeyed. To-day the rule is strictly, one might almost say sternly, enforced. The last trace of traditionalism has vanished. The man of to-day (and the American undertaker may stand as the most perfect type) is filled with the will to apply cold reason to economic activities ; moreover, he possesses the determination to make the will effective. Accordingly, he is ever ready to adopt a newer method if it is more rational, whether in the sphere of organization, of production, or of calculation. This naturally implies that, no matter what the cost may be, he is able to leave the old methods the moment the newer ones are available.

(*b*) Production for exchange (as opposed to production for use) is the motto of economic activities. As much profit as possible is their ideal ; consequently what matters is not the goodness or the kind of commodities produced but their saleability. How they are sold is secondary, so long as they are sold. Consequently the

undertaker is wholly indifferent to the quality of his
wares ; he will make shoddy goods or cheap substitutes,
if only it pays. If cheap and nasty boots yield more
profit than good ones, it would be a deadly sin against
the holy spirit of capitalism to manufacture good ones.
It is no argument against the truth of this to point
to a movement in certain industries (the chemical industry
is one), the object of which is to improve quality. As
well say that the bonuses which the general store offers
to its employees on the sale of more expensive articles
proves the same thing. What both instances do prove
is that they are cases where there is more profit from
high-class goods than from inferior articles. The
greatest gain is the only criterion in these matters, and
an undertaker will make now cheap goods, now dearer,
according as the one or the other yields more profit.
From the capitalist's standpoint that is only natural.

What follows from this is plain. Since it is inherent
in acquisitiveness to enlarge incomings to the uttermost ;
and since, again, the greater the sale the larger the
profits, it is only to be expected that the undertaker
will try all he can to increase his sales. Apart from the
greater gain, more extended sales will give him certain
advantages over competitors. Hence it is by no means
remarkable that the desire for greater sales, for new
markets, for more customers, is one of the mightiest
motive powers in modern capitalism. It is directly
responsible for a number of business principles, all of
which have one end in view—to make the public buy.
The more important of these principles deserve to be
mentioned.

(*c*) The first (and the third in the general scheme)
may be enunciated as follows : Search out the customer
and attack him. That is to-day as self-evident a maxim
in all branches of business as it was strange and wrong

in the age of early capitalism. In practice it means that you set out to attract the customer's attention and to stir up within him the desire to purchase. You attract his attention by shouting in his ears, or catching his eye by loud, coloured indicators ; you strive to make him purchase by suggestion ; you seek to convince him that the articles for sale are extraordinarily good or valuable. Advertisement serves both ends—as every one knows ; and advertisements, as every one knows also, shatter all sense of propriety, of taste, of good manners, and of dignity. Is it not true to say that modern advertising in its extreme forms is both unæsthetic and immoral ?

(*d*) Secondly, sell as cheaply as you can ; reduce price to the lowest possible figure so as to attract the public. In the early capitalist age low prices were an abomination. The motto then was (as we have already noted) little business but great profits. To-day we are at the opposite extreme : as much business as possible but small profits. Small profits, quick returns—is not this nowadays the universal motto ?

(*e*) Elbow-room is demanded in order to arrive at the wished-for goal. Which means, first, that you require freedom of action, liberty to enter upon or to abstain from any course, as seems best to you. It means emancipation from the trammels of law or morality ; it means that you should be allowed to poach on your neighbour's preserves just as he may be allowed to poach on yours ; it means that you should be allowed to oust him if you can ; it means that you object to interference either from the state or from working men's organizations in making your contracts. You want none of the restraints of an earlier age. The free exercise of your powers shall alone determine economic success or failure.

And in the second place it means—what follows quite naturally—unrestricted competition. If acquisition is the first consideration, unrestricted competition is a matter of course. You need no longer be bound by considerations of any kind, whether moral, æsthetic or social. Unscrupulous is the adjective for your actions.

Look at the extensive American trusts and you will see what unrestricted competition means. The recent doings of the American Tobacco Company are a case in point; they outdistanced the accepted practices of Europe and illustrate to what lengths an unscrupulous undertaker will go. No considerations give him pause; he leaves no road untried that promises success. The trust threw its goods away at ridiculous prices in order to conquer new markets; middlemen received enormous commissions; well-known brands were imitated and poor quality wares were sold in wrappers that misled the public. If it became involved in litigation, the trust by its superior financial strength was able to draw out the cases until its opponents were utterly exhausted. Even retail trading received careful attention, for the trust opened shops at effective points, and by underselling forced the old-established tobacconists to close their doors. Finally, the trust monopolized the raw material, and so came into conflict with the tobacco-growers of Kentucky. In 1911 the trust was proceeded against under the Sherman Law, and the presiding judge in delivering sentence characterized the activities of the undertaking against their competitors as having been carried on with extraordinary cunning, precaution, and devilry. Every human creature that by energy or skill threatened to stand in the way of the trust was mercilessly crushed.

Perhaps the most perfect type of the unscrupulous, smart business man was Edward H. Harriman, who died a few years ago. An obituary notice [235] declared that the secret of his victorious career was his utter lack of moral scruples. Had he not cast these overboard he would have stumbled almost at the very first step he took. He began by breaking the man who had opened for him the gates of the railway paradise; following this up by his brutal campaign against Morgan, who, however, knew how to utilize for his own ends the capacities of his opponent. Harriman's fight with Hill was as unscrupulous as the policy that brought him into the Standard Oil Trust. But Harriman's delinquencies were not merely personal; they form part and parcel of American speculation.

Of the great victors on the racecourse of modern capitalism it may be asserted, what was recently said of Rockefeller, that they know how to glide over every moral restraint with almost childlike disregard. The mirror of this naïve view of life will be found in the memoirs of John Rockefeller, who once summed up the faith within him by saying that he was willing to pay a substitute a salary of a million dollars, if beside other positive qualities he had no scruples whatsoever, and was ready to kill off thousands of victims without a murmur.

Another undertaker, this time a German, who considered himself rather backward in this respect because he was " too good-natured and considerate "—I refer to Werner Siemens—urged his brother Charles to become a smart business man in these terms : " Always be determined and unscrupulous. That in so large a concern is called for. Once begin to be considerate of private interests and you will fall into a morass of demands and intrigues " (letter of March 31, 1856).

4. The middle-class virtues—industry, frugality, and honesty—are they of any consequence for the modern capitalist undertaker ? It is as difficult to reply to the question in the affirmative as in the negative. The place of these virtues in modern economic life is so very

different from what they occupied in the early capitalist system. As a matter of fact, they have ceased to be necessary to the undertaker. Nevertheless, they still play their part in undertaking. Before, these virtues were still in the sphere wherein personal will-power was exercised ; now they have become part of the mechanism of business. Before, they were characteristic of living beings; now, they have turned into objective principles of business methods.

This may sound difficult. I will explain my meaning by considering each of the virtues in turn.

In the olden days when industry was preached as a prime virtue in the tradesman, it was necessary to implant a solid foundation of duties in the inner consciousness of men. Everybody had to be urged to exercise his will-power in a certain direction, and when the habit was once formed the industrious tradesman went through his day's work in conscious self-mastery. To-day all this is changed. The business man works at high pressure because the stress of economic activities carries him along in spite of himself. He is no longer exercising a virtue ; necessity drives him to this particular course. The general business pace determines what his own business pace shall be. He can no more be idle than a man at a machine ; whereas a craftsman with his tools can be idle or industrious as he chooses.

The objectiveness of frugality is even more marked, for the private and the business "housekeeping" of the under-taker are now separate. In the latter frugality is needful more than ever. " Extravagance even in the smallest things should be avoided. It is not petty to have a care of this, for extravagance is a consuming disease difficult to localize. There are great undertakings whose existence depends on whether all the sand is removed from the carts or whether one shovelfull is left behind." [236] Recall the careful, almost miserly, economy of Rockefeller in his management of the

Standard Oil Company ; recall how not a drop of oil was wasted ; the wooden boxes in which tin was brought from Europe were sold to florists or were used as firewood.237 But in the private housekeeping of the undertaker you will find none of this fanatical thrift. Neither Rathenau's nor Rockefeller's castle is a centre of that frugality so much beloved of Benjamin Franklin ; and the festive boards of our rich undertakers know nothing of sufficiency and moderation. And if the head of the family is content to go on in the old-fashioned bourgeois style of his youth, his wife, his sons, and his daughters will all see to it that luxury and superfluity and pomp become part and parcel of the new bourgeois spirit. Bourgeois the style of life still is, even in the case of the wealthiest. The old doctrines of Alberti still hold sway. Never let your expenditure exceed your income, he urged his disciples. And calculate. To-day this advice is faithfully obeyed by the modern bourgeois. Herein his mode of living differs from the seigniorial. The seigneur scorns money.

Commercial honesty comes last. Can any one doubt that honesty is to-day—to-day perhaps more than ever— a factor in business life ? In business life only, however. For the conduct of the undertaker as a man may differ widely from his conduct as a tradesman. Commercial honesty is a complexity of principles that are intended to apply to business but not to the personal conduct of the business subject. An honest tradesman to-day may certainly be unmoral in his private life. When you say he is " good," you mean that he is reliable in his business ; that he will pay ; that his firm has a good name. You pass no judgment on his personal conduct, which is governed by other principles. Indeed, the firm may not have an individual head at all. It may be an impersonal limited company, the directors of which change from time to time. Their personal morality stands in no relationship to the business. The " name " of the business is all that matters. Thus, here, too, what before was a personal quality has now become a matter of business routine. You can see it best by considering modern credit. A bank in olden days was relied upon because it could point to an ancient and honoured name ; it was " good " for personal reasons. To-day a bank inspires confidence by the size of its invested capital and its reserves. To-day you assume that business is carried on honestly—anyhow until some swindle comes to light to prove the contrary. In this virtue then, as in the others, what before was organic has now become mechanical.

All this applies to the large undertakings. In the small and middle-sized enterprises, however, you may still find the principles prevalent in the early days of capitalism. The middle-class virtues are still cultivated, and the undertaker's personal characteristics determine his economic progress. It is in the large undertakings and their directors and managers that we find the spirit of capitalism fully developed in all its shining purity.

Now, why has the capitalist spirit developed in this fashion ? Why did it not take on another guise? What forces moulded it ? What nourished it during its growth ? These are questions that require consideration by themselves, and so the sources whence the capitalist spirit sprang will be reviewed in the following section of this book.

BOOK II

THE ORIGINS OF THE CAPITALIST SPIRIT

INTRODUCTION

CHAPTER XIII

THE PROBLEM

W H A T is the origin of the capitalist spirit ?   Whence did it spring ?   Two ways of answering these questions are possible.   The first is by a reference to external facts. You may point to the appearance of a capitalist under-taker in a land in which he had come to trade or where he had set up business.   Thus you may say the capitalist spirit in China owes its origin to the English ; or, the Jews introduced the capitalist spirit into Magdeburg.   In this sense the question is answered by the facts of the history of migration.   But we shall not deal with this aspect of the question here.   What we want to know in this book is, How did a capitalist economic outlook grow up in the minds of men ?   Why in any particular period did the capitalist spirit dominate economic activities, giving men a certain aim, calling forth in them certain capacities, making them obey certain principles ?   And what was responsible for the appearance from time to time, now in one generation, now in another, of certain people with strongly marked views and a particular out-look, with a certain will-power and a certain skill ?

I am bound to say that many people do not admit that there is any problem at all to be solved.   They take it as self-evident that the capitalist spirit was engendered by capitalism. They do not admit that the capitalist spirit has an independent existence. But this is by no means an axiom ; it certainly requires proof. It is possible, of course, that an economic outlook may be the result of economic conditions, but the exact relationship between the two has to be most carefully taken into account. We want to know how and why the one springs from the other.

There are other people who admit the problem, but deny that a scientific solution is possible. One of the younger scholars of the day expressed himself on the subject in some such terms as these. [238] The capitalist spirit and all that it conveys are merely very useful descriptive labels. We may talk of the development or the history of morals, but we cannot lay bare the stages in its growth by the aid of documentary evidence. So, in the same way, thrift, self-interest, and all the other qualities contained in the conception " capitalist spirit " have undoubtedly developed, but we cannot trace that development historically.

There is clearly a good deal of truth in this suggestion. No one can definitely show when certain outlooks or opinions first came into existence. It would obviously be an impossibility to demonstrate by reference to sources what the influence (say) of Puritanism was on the capitalist spirit. [239] But what can be done is to differentiate between natural capacities and tendencies and the influence upon such of environment in general or specific occurrences in particular. We can even lay down one or two rules to guide us in considering this contrast. These rules will exclude, for example, certain common denominators found among all peoples as sources of a given intellectual outlook ; they will make it impossible to account for certain aspects of the capitalist spirit by quoting authorities that come later in point of time

For instance, views of life in the 15th century cannot possibly be traced to religious doctrines which were first enunciated in the 17th ; or, the capitalist spirit of Germany in the 19th century cannot be regarded as the fruit of Puritan or Quaker religious teaching.

In order to arrive at a right view of the cause and effects, one or two facts must be borne in mind.

1. The component parts of the capitalist spirit vary so much that their origins will vary also. Some of the factors in that spirit may be what are termed "instinctive passions"—acquisitiveness, activity, the desire to plunder your neighbour. All successful undertakers have always had a goodly dose of these instincts. This is common knowledge, and there is ample proof in support of the statement.[240]

Take as an illustration what Gentz, in a letter to Adam Müller, says of the Rothschilds : "They are just ordinary, ignorant Jews with tolerably good manners, and in their business unspoiled children of nature, understanding the larger aspect of things but little. But they possess a marvellous instinct of always being able to decide upon what is right, and, of two good courses, to choose the better. Their enormous wealth is due entirely to this instinct, which the populace calls luck." Heine's description of James Rothschild is in almost identical terms : " He has the peculiar capacity of insight, or, if you will, the natural instinct of being able to take the measure of others in all spheres of action."

Again, the capitalist spirit may express itself in certain personal characteristics to which particular business principles or middle-class virtues may be sympathetic. Or we may see acquired skill—say, in rapid calculation or the arrangements of a business or something similar.

Accordingly, when we come to consider the variations in the root elements of the capitalist spirit the question

as to the origins of that spirit assumes a twofold importance. In the first place, the manner in which the
individual characteristics manifest themselves in one and
the same person is different according as the component
factors of the capitalist spirit are present in a larger or
lesser degree. Instinctive movement, instinctive capabilities, are always to be found—they are bred in the bone ;
they may be either repressed, neglected, or not made
use of, or they may be quickened, strengthened, and
broadened.

The nature of the two other factors is such that the
possibility of their acquirement is patent, and is as a rule
the result of tuition. The first factor—moulding the
character—is due to educative influences ; the second—
forming the mind—is due to instruction.

In the second place, the question of inheritance divides
the various factors into two sharply defined groups.
The first consists of those qualities which may be trans-
mitted from one person or from one age to another.
The second group is composed of all such characteristics
as are so intimately interwoven with the personality of the
individual that they can only affect others by the force of
example, and their existence ceases with that of their
possessor. Instincts and talents can never be accumulated
independently of the individual ; they are inherited, but
though they may have grown and developed, each human
has perforce to return to the old starting-point and to
pass through all transitory states. On the other hand,
virtues and capabilities, though the sum total of man's
single and united efforts, are quite distinct from personality, and the stages of their progress may be followed
and catalogued in codes and systems. Men die, but these
codes continue. In them later generations find the accumulated experience of their ancestors, and profit thereby.
It matters not that for a long time any particular precept

remains disregarded. So long as it is written down, some one or other may one day be inspired by it. Wise rules for conduct and for craftsmanship are transferable both as to time and space. The latter differ from the former only in that they are added to by each successive generation, seeing that experience is enlarged and technical inventions increased. But rules of conduct can hardly be said to gain by reason of any that were current before.

From all this it now becomes obvious that the process of growth of each of the elements of the capitalist spirit differed enormously among themselves.

2. Secondly, in tracing the origins of the capitalist spirit we must always bear in mind that the conditions vary fundamentally with each epoch of capitalist development. Above all, the era of early capitalism must be sharply distinguished from that of perfected capitalism. If you are to sum up the economic activities of each in a phrase, you might say that in the early capitalist age the undertaker produced capitalism, in the perfected capitalist age capitalism produces the undertaker. In the young days of capitalism, capitalist organization was by no means general ; it was mostly the creation of the non-capitalist genius. Its stock of knowledge and experience was not large ; both experience and knowledge had to be gained, garnered, and tested. It had little in the way of capitalist machinery, and that little had to be painfully acquired. And as for the primary foundations of all contracts and agreements, they had not yet been laid ; long and strenuous was the upward striving of credit and confidence and trust. Does it not stand to sense that under such circumstances the capitalist undertaker was bound to act on his own initiative, and possibly with a good deal of caprice ? To-day all this has been altered. Modern capitalist organization is, in the words of Max Weber, a huge cosmos into which the human unit is born, and

which represents for him as such an eternally unmodifiable structure in which he is compelled to live. And this cosmos imposes upon him, in so far as he comes into the market-place, economic laws of its own. The individual to-day stands face to face with a mountain of experience which threatens to crush him—book-keeping methods, calculating systems, wages customs, organization of management, business technics and what not. All these are so specialized that their application becomes a work of no small difficulty. So much so that specialists have to be called in to carry them through for the capitalist undertaker.

What conspicuous changes therefore in the "environment" in which the capitalist spirit grew up then and now ! All these distinctions must naturally be taken into account if we are to solve our problem with anything like exactitude.

The material at our command is enormous in extent ; it is indeed almost overwhelming. By two methods we may obtain the mastery over it. We may take each element of the capitalist spirit by itself, and try to discover the reasons for its genesis. For instance, what produced the greed of gold ; what gave an impetus to the spirit of undertaking ; why did the middle-class virtues arise ?—and so forth. Or we may trace back the manifold resultants of the capitalist spirit, and thus arrive at the complexity of causes that gave them birth. A good deal of repetition is necessarily involved in the first method, and so I prefer the second, which anyhow promises variety in outlook.

This is the course I propose to follow. One section shall be devoted to the biological foundations on which the history of the whole capitalist spirit is built up. Another section will consider the moral forces which have influenced mankind in determining how much, or how little, of the capitalist spirit it should imbibe. And in the third section the social conditions that have been effective find their place. In the last two sections our aim will thus be to make plain how outward circumstances helped to mould human beings with a capitalist turn of mind. These circumstances will be reviewed in all their details, from the earliest stages down to this very day ; and at the end we shall realize how manifold have been the influences at work on the capitalist spirit.

SECTION I

THE BIOLOGICAL FOUNDATIONS

CHAPTER XIV

THE BOURGEOIS TEMPERAMENT

Is one born a bourgeois? Are there people who are naturally " middle class," and thus different from others who are not? If this is so, shall we not have to describe the capitalist spirit as something temperamental? In any event, what is the true relationship between natural gifts and the capitalist spirit?

To answer these questions aright we must pay attention to the following general observations.

There is no doubt that all expressions of the capitalist spirit, as indeed soul expressions in general, may be traced to particular inherent personal characteristics ; that is to say, to original, inherited qualities of the organism, which account for the ability and tendency to exercise certain functions, or the inclination to acquire certain qualities.[241] We need not discuss for the moment whether the biological tendencies to capitalism are of a general nature, and so capable of development in various directions and not necessarily only into the bourgeois ideal ; or whether from the first they lead to this one goal, and to this only.

I repeat : there can be no doubt that all the expressions

of the capitalist spirit, that is to say, the mental constitution of the bourgeois, are rooted in inherited tendencies. This holds good equally of qualities that depend on the will, as of those that are instinctive ; of middle-class virtues therefore, as of inherent talents. All spring from certain qualities in the soul. It matters not whether or no these psychic qualities have physical parallels ; nor is it of consequence to discover how the tendencies themselves arose in any individual—whether he acquired them, and if so, when and how. It is sufficient for us that they are there at a time when we know capitalism to have been born. That is really the important point—to be alive to the fact that at that given moment man had already made these qualities so much his own that transmission was possible. In short, these qualities, the broader developments of primitive instincts, had become hereditary.

The question now faces us : are these tendencies toward the expression of the capitalist spirit general ; are they common in like degree to all mankind ? Alike, of course, they cannot be, since no two people possess the same psychological outfit. Even as regards such aptitudes as are almost universal—that of learning languages, for instance—there are differences in degree. Some people are able to acquire languages more easily and quickly than others. You can see it in children learning to speak their mother-tongue ; you can see it best of all in grown-ups learning foreign languages.

But I go further and believe that the qualities referred to are not common to humanity. They exist in this and not in that individual. Or, at least, some people possess them in such small doses that for all practical purposes the quantity is negligible ; whereas others are so imbued with them as to be at once distinguishable from their neighbours. Is it not obvious that many men have no great capacity or inclination to become freebooters, to organize and supervise the work of a thousand hands, to find a path through the mazes of stock-exchange business, to calculate with lightning rapidity, even to lay by for a rainy day, to economize their time or to lead a regular life ?   And should we not be agreed that not many people are gifted with a large number, less with all, of the qualities of mind that go to make up the capitalist spirit ?

Nevertheless, there are beings who impress you as born capitalist undertakers, who have the bourgeois temperament (even though they may never actually lead a middle-class existence).   We have in mind, of course, a more or less perfect bourgeois nature, and we ask, What is its specific mental constitution ?   How does the blood of such natures vary from that of other folk ?

Two souls dwell in the breast of every complete bourgeois : the soul of the undertaker and the soul of the respectable middle-class man.   The union of the two produces the capitalist spirit.   Hence in the bourgeois temperament we may distinguish two contributory factors —the undertaking nature and the nature of the respectable middle-class citizen.   We will take each of these in turn.

1. Undertaking Natures.

What mental or psychological qualities are essential to the capitalist undertaker if he is to be successful ?   I should say he must be intelligent, clever, and imaginative.

Intelligent means quick in comprehension, true in judgment, clear in thought, with a sure eye for the needful, enabling him to recognize the psychological moment (the Greeks called it Καιρος).   He must be endowed with quick-wittedness in a large measure, with that nimbleness of spirit which may be compared to the light cavalry of an army ; the quality which the French ascribe to all great undertakers—*vivacité d'esprit et de corps* ; he must be able to find his way through the complicated conditions of the market, much as the advance posts of an army are expected to render intelligence service. Above all, he must have a good memory—a gift all capitalist undertakers know how to value. Carnegie was glad to possess it ; Werner Siemens deplored the lack of it.[242]

Clever means the capacity for forming judgments about the world and men ; it postulates shrewdness in weighing up things, and instinctive tact in handling men aright ; it denotes ability in arriving at a correct valuation of situations of all kinds, and a knowledge of the weaknesses and disadvantages of one's surroundings. · The last especially is a predominant feature which is continually praised in great captains of industry. Pliancy on the one hand and suggestive influence on the other are indispensable to the negotiator.

Imaginative means fertile in ideas, resourceful, gifted with what has been termed the " faculty of combination," as opposed to the " intuitive faculty " of the artist.

All these great gifts of intellect must be accompanied by an abundance of the will to live, by " life energy," by that something (call it what you will) requisite for all undertaking, which produces satisfaction, nay, joy. This joy of work gives the undertaker the necessary resolution for the consummation of his enterprise. It makes him want to achieve, so that enforced idleness worries him. Then he must also be robust, with plenty of nerve, unshrinking. You know the type. He has determination, he persists in pegging away, he can hold on indefinitely, he is never at rest, he knows what he wants, he can risk much, and his boldness makes your hair stand on end. In a word, he lives greatly ; his vitality is above the average.

It is rather disadvantageous to be blessed with a strong sensitiveness. A capitalist undertaker should have no feelings. His intellect alone should rule his conduct if he is to scale great heights.

Contrast the undertaking nature with others, and you will discern its outlines clearly enough. Take the artistic temperament. The undertaker, especially where he has carried through some marvellous organizing work, has been compared to the artist. The comparison, to my mind, is a wrong one. The two are opposites, not parallels. All they have in common is a vivid imagination which helps them to create. But the imagination in each case is of a different quality. Apart from this superficial likeness, the two types differ from each other. Their respective souls draw their strength from very different sources. The undertaker works towards a goal ; to the artist an end in view is an abomination. The former is dominated by his intellect, the latter by his emotions. The former is hard where the latter is delicate and tender. The undertaker is practical and businesslike, the artist is the most unpractical and unbusinesslike fellow in the world. The undertaker's eyes look without to the macrocosm beyond, the artist's gaze is fixed on the microcosm within. That is why the undertaker is acquainted with men, while the artist knows only man.

Similarly, undertaking natures have little in common with those of craftsmen, private gentlemen living on their means, æsthetic folk, scholars, sybarites, strict moralists, and others of that ilk. On the other hand, they have a good many of the qualities of the general and the statesman, both of whom (more particularly the latter) are in the long run conquerors, organizers, and dealers. Single traits of the capitalist undertaker may be found also in the chess-player and the clever doctor. Skill in diagnosis enables you not only to heal the sick but also to do well on the stock exchange.

2. "Middle-class" Natures.

Either you are born a bourgeois or you are not. It must be in the blood ; it is a natural inclination. We all feel that. Everybody knows the middle-class nature ; it has a sort of aroma of its own. And yet it is difficult, we may even say impossible, to analyse its psychological qualities. We shall have to content ourselves with· a detailed sketch of the middle-class nature, and a comparison between that and other natures.

It would appear that the contrast between the natures we have described as middle-class and those not so represents a fundamental deviation between the two human types in modern society, anyhow so far as Europe is concerned. People are either· of the giving or of the taking sort ; either extravagant or economical. Deep down in our natures, as they recognized in classical antiquity and as the mediæval schoolmen philosophized, we are all of us inclined either to *luxuria* or to *avaritia*. Some are naturally spendthrifts, careless alike of material and spiritual riches ; others tend them carefully, store them, make the most of them, watch closely over the acquisition and expenditure of mental and bodily strength, of goods and chattels and money. Bergson has also called attention to this contrast ; he speaks of *l'homme ouvert* and *l'homme clos*.

These two types—those who spend and those who hoard, the aristocratic and the middle-class natures— stand facing each other in all human life. They appraise the world, they appraise even life itself, from opposite vantage-grounds. The ideals of the one are subjective and personal ; those of the other objective and material. The former are born for pleasure, the latter for duty ; the former are individualists, loving solitude ; the latter are gregarious ; for the one æsthetics is the supreme thing in life, for the other ethics. The former are like beautiful flowers wasting their perfume on the desert air ; the latter are like healing herbs and edible roots. It is only to be expected that they should hold conflicting views as to any man's occupation in particular, and the sweat of the world in general. The first class regard only those activities as worthy and noble which permit a man to become noble and worthy, which cultivate his personality ; the second values all activities alike, provided they contribute to the general good, provided, that is, they are useful. Is it not manifest that it makes an exceeding great difference in the prevailing outlook on life according as the one view or the other is in the ascendant ? The ancients had personal values ; we middle-class folk have material ones. Recall Cicero's polished statement : " Not what one has achieved is of consequence, but what one is." [243]

The two types are in everlasting contrast throughout life. In his threescore years and ten the one lives, sees, thinks ; the other organizes, trains, educates. The one dreams dreams and sees visions ; the other calculates. Even as a boy Rockefeller had a reputation for calculations. He made regular bargains with his father, a physician in Cleveland. " From my earliest childhood," so he himself relates in his *Memoirs*, " I had a little book in which I entered what I got and what I spent. I called it my account-book, and have preserved it to this day." You notice it was in his blood. No power on earth could have made Byron jot down his income and expenditure in a book, and not only that, but preserve the book !

The first type goes carolling through life ; the second is dumb. The first are many-coloured in all they say and do, the second are drab. The first are artists (not necessarily by profession) ; the second are

officials. The first are silk, the second wool. Wilhelm
Meister and his friend Werner — there you have the
types. The one talks as though he had kingdoms to
dispose of, the other like a person who carefully picks
up a pin.

It is in the erotic life of each that you find the
greatest contrast. After all, the love passion is the
mightiest force in human affairs, and the erotic temperament is as far remote from the middle-class nature as
pole is from pole. But what is the erotic temperament?
It cannot be defined; it can only be felt. Perhaps
Goethe pictured it in his " Pater ecstaticus " :—

> Endless ecstatic fire,
> Glow of the pure desire,
> Pain of the pining breast,
> Rapture of God possessed !
> Arrows, transpierce ye me ;
> Lances, coerce ye me ;
> Bludgeons, so batter me,
> Lightnings, so shatter me,
> That all of mortality's
> Vain unrealities
> Die, and the star above
> Beam but Eternal Love.*

" I suffered and loved ; my heart knew nought else."
Everything in the world is nothing worth, save only
love. There is only one abiding value : love. Is not
this the feeling of the erotic temperament? Sexual
love, all-comprehensive, all-embracing love—love of God
and love of man : anything beyond is vanity. Nor
should love ever be but means to an end. It should
not be for pleasure ; it should not be for the propagation

---

* [The passage will be found towards the end of the Second Part of
Faust. The version here given is by Bayard Taylor.]

of the species. "Be fruitful and multiply" expresses the most grievous sin against love.

Love is not lasciviousness. The lascivious and the cold natures are both equally far removed from the erotic temperament. On the other hand, they are closely bound up with middle-class natures. Indeed, sensuality and love are mutually exclusive terms, whereas cold and lascivious natures can easily accommodate themselves to the love of order inherent in the "middle-class temperament." Strong sexual passion, if restrained and controlled, may even be of great service to capitalism.

It need hardly be pointed out that erotic temperaments vary in strength and intensity, ranging from St. Augustine and St. Francis to the ordinary man of to-day, who spends his life in amorous adventures. But no matter what their degree, they have little in common with the middle-class nature. For there is only one of two alternatives. Either economic activities are the central interest in life or love is. You live for love or for business. Economic activity implies thrift ; while love is usually accompanied by extravagance. It is an old contrast, and the ancient economists did not overlook it. Listen to Xenophon.244 " I also notice that you seem to think you are rich, that you care nothing for business, that your mind is full of love. I am sorry for you on that account. I am afraid that before long you will be in difficulties." Or again : " Who is the best housekeeper ? She who is most capable of exercising moderation in food, drink, sleep, and love." In another passage he says that " those who are in love are useless in business." You will find the same opinion in Columella, the well-known Roman writer on agriculture. " Keep far from amorous adventures," he advises, " for whoso enters on them can think of nothing else. Such a one values one prize only—the fulfilment of his desire ; he fears only one punishment—to be crossed in love." [245]　A good housewife should give no single thought to men ; she must be *a viris remotissima.*

These indications must suffice. A more thorough investigation into the relationship between love and capitalism would lead us too far afield. Enough that we have realized that those mental gifts necessary for capitalism lie rooted in the sexual constitution.

We have thus observed how the capitalist spirit thrives in bourgeois natures (these being a hybrid between undertaking and middle-class natures). In other words, we have realized that there are people in the world who are so constituted mentally that they are able to develop the capitalist spirit more rapidly than others ; who incline in a more marked degree than those others themselves to become capitalist undertakers ; who cultivate the middle-class virtues much more easily ; who possess the qualities needful for success in economic life in a larger measure.

The consideration of the problem, however, is not thus exhausted. When all is said, it is of small moment whether one individual or another tends to capitalism. Overshadowing this question is a second of far greater magnitude. What is the aspect of these bourgeois natures in the mass ? To what extent are they represented among the different nations ? Is one nation more prone than another to develop such natures ? And can we say therefore that one nation is more gifted for capitalism than another ? Do racial or national characteristics in this respect remain constant, or vary from age to age ? If so, why ? The answer to these questions will show definitely what the biological foundation of capitalism is ; and the following chapter will be devoted to their consideration.

CHAPTER XV

NATIONAL TRAITS

WE saw in the last chapter that all expressions of the capitalist spirit are due to personal qualities inherent in the individual. And in our survey of the progress of capitalism in Europe we noted that the capitalist spirit manifested itself among all nations, though not in the same degree. In some it was more intense than in others ; or again its component parts were commingled in varying proportions in different nations.

Two conclusions follow :—

(1) All European peoples have the qualities necessary for capitalism ; and

(2) Each nation has these qualities in a varying degree.

When we speak of a nation having certain qualities, the explanation is that the national group in question possesses a large proportion of individuals with those qualities. Hence the conclusions noted above may be thus further amplified.

(1) All peoples have the qualities necessary for capitalism. That is to say that in the course of the history of the European nations there grew up in them a large number of capitalist variants (by which we mean variants specially gifted for the development of the capitalist spirit), and these made it possible for capitalism to thrive and extend.

(2) Each nation has the qualities in a varying degree.

That is to say, in the first place, the requisite gifts vary quantitatively in the individuals in each national group; and in the second place, they vary qualitatively.

From a biological point of view, how do these variations spring up? [246]

In all probability the nations must from their earliest origins have had a kind of germ-capacity for capitalism, and either all had it in the same degree or the degree varied in each nation. Suppose we take the first assumption. Then the variations that appeared later will have to be accounted for by saying that this germ-capacity was exercised unevenly, and so some nations ended with a strong tendency to capitalism, others with one less strong. As for the second assumption, it suffices itself as an explanation of variations. In theory both views are possible. But history rather shows that the second assumption was probably the correct one, at any rate for all but the prehistoric ages. Certainly the second assumption clears up many a difficulty, and as I see no reason against its adoption, it is on that basis that I shall proceed.

The tribes or races from which the modern European nations have sprung were partly over-inclined to capitalism and partly under-inclined. That the latter must have possessed some individuals with capitalist possibilities goes without saying; it would be absurd to imagine that there is any race wholly without capitalist tendencies of some sort. But these individuals must have been so few in number, and what capitalist tendencies they had so weak, that the capitalist spirit among the under-inclined peoples did not develop beyond its primary stage. The over-inclined peoples on the other hand had many richly-gifted individuals who were capitalistically inclined; in them, therefore, the capitalist spirit developed more rapidly and completely.

We see at once that the assumption of a varied degree of germ-capitalism cannot well be avoided. How else should we account for such differing results in the process of development? After all, was there much variation in the growth of Spain and Italy, of France and Germany, of Scotland and Ireland? Yet capitalism, as we have seen, fared differently in each. Varying original national traits seem to be the only explanation for this, as for most other phenomena in the life of a nation. Surely every people has the political system, the religion, even the wars which are in accord with its national qualities.

What peoples may be described as under-inclined to capitalism? I should say the Celts and a few of the Germanic tribes, the Goths in particular.* Wherever the Celtic element predominated capitalism made little headway. The nobility continued to live seigniorially with never a thought for thrift or the virtues of middle-class respectability ; and the middle grades of the community went on in the old ruts of tradition-alism, preferring a safe billet rather than adventurous careers in the field of commerce and industry. The Highlanders in Scotland are Celts,[247] more especially the nobility—a knightly race, a little quixotic, a little quarrelsome, holding fast to their ancient class traditions, untouched by capitalism down to this very day. The Scottish chieftain looks upon himself as an old feudal lord, and when the money-lenders begin to remove his possessions one by one, his family heirlooms he guards most jealously.

---

* [There is no need to regard all the Germanic peoples as having common traits. No doubt they had many qualities in common which made them different from other races (say, from Jews). But so far as their qualities that bear on economic life are concerned, they differed radically among themselves. Compare in this respect the Goths, the Lombards, and the Frisians.]

The Irish are Celts too. Do we not all know the plaint of the capitalist observers that the Irish are no good for business? Even in America, where the economic whirlwind storms, the Irish have managed to maintain their peaceful attitude, preferring above all else the secure harbour of an office in the service of the State.

There is a goodly admixture of Celts among the French. It is the Celtic blood that explains the strongly marked tendency to live on investments and the "plague of office-hunting" (a characteristic of the French people we have already noted). It is the Celtic blood also that probably accounts for that vivacity found more among French undertakers than others. John Law first met with a sympathetic understanding of his ideas in France. Perhaps that was because of his partially Celtic origin. On his father's side Law traced his descent from Lowlanders, on his mother's his family belonged to the Highland nobility.[248]

Lastly, the Spaniards are to some extent Celts. When the Visigoths came to the Pyrenean Peninsula the people there were a mongrel race of Celts, Iberians (a most un-capitalistic folk, for whom gold, desired of almost all peoples, had no attraction), and the descendants of early Roman colonists.[249] The Celts and the Goths were responsible for the slow development of capitalism in the Peninsula after its best strength had been spent in heroic and adventurous expeditions. What capitalism did thrive in Spain and Portugal was due to Jewish and Moorish influences.

But it is the over-inclined peoples that interest us most. Who were they?

Two groups meet our gaze. The one was more talented for forcible, all-conquering undertakings on a large scale, smacking somewhat of freebooting; the other for successful peaceful trading, with a tendency to middle-class respectability. The first we will call Heroic peoples, the second, Trading peoples.

The first introduced a touch of the heroic even in their economic activities. The warlike or semi-warlike undertakers with whom we have already made ourselves acquainted sprang from them. First in order we must mention the Romans, who formed an ethnical element in Italy, in parts of Spain, in Gaul, and in Western Germany. Their method of trading rested on force, and was governed by the idea that economic success can be won by the aid of the sword.[250] It was in accord with this idea that the different sorts of undertakings were variously appraised in classical antiquity. The attitude then was the same as that in England and France at a later period. There the shipping-merchant, with more in him of the soldier than the trader, was socially superior to the mere tradesman. Cicero's excellent contrast between the two is well known. "Oversea commerce to distant lands, bringing commodities from all quarters, taking no mean advantage over customers or talking their heads off, is by no means to be despised."[251] Put this into the terminology used in our pages, and what does it amount to ? A conqueror-undertaker—that is something, certainly ; a tradesman-undertaker—no one with any self-respect can sink so low.

Side by side with the Romans must be placed several of the Germanic races. The Normans, the Lombards, the Saxons, and the Franks all appear to have had the same all-conquering spirit within them, and their influence will account, together with the Romans, for undertakings, whether of the freebooting or the feudal sort, that were found among the Venetians and the Genoese, the English and the Germans.

You may see the true nature of these peoples by

comparing them with others equally gifted for the development of capitalism, but in another way. I mean the essentially trading peoples, who have the capacity strongly marked of doing successful business by peaceful contract-making, by diplomacy and by clever calculation. We have already noted what peoples helped to develop this aspect of the capitalist spirit in Europe : the Florentines, the Scotch, and the Jews. It remains only to adduce some testimony to prove that in all probability—and the evidence at our disposal suffices for a probability only—these peoples became what they were because of certain primary qualities which were theirs from the earliest times.

The Florentines became traders, became the foremost and greatest trading community in the Middle Ages, because of their Etruscan and Greek (i.e. Oriental) blood.

It is somewhat difficult to estimate exactly the influence of the Etruscans on the inhabitants of Tuscany throughout the ancient period of their history. But authorities seem to agree that the city on the Arno was more Etruscan in character than its neighbours.[252] Certainly Etruscan blood flowed in the veins of very many Florentines. Now the Etruscans,[253] possibly even more than the Phœnicians and Carthaginians, were the trading people of antiquity, and their commercial policy, so far as can be judged, was much like that of the Florentines in a later day. From the earliest times their trade was mainly peaceful land-trade, particularly with their northern neighbours. When Rome conquered their country, the Etruscans continued to ply their trade, seeing that the Romans scorned trafficking and allowed the inhabitants in the conquered territories to live their life as heretofore.

What manner of ideal was the Etruscan's ? The most trustworthy authorities describe it as rational and practical.[254] They were also a religious folk with a

national church.[255]   Is it not curious that the same can
be said of the Florentines, no less than of the Jews and
the Scotch ?

During the Roman sway the Etruscan ethnical layer
had superimposed upon it another of Asiatic origin,
which was probably of the same quality, seeing that the
newcomers wandered into Italy as traffickers.   The
influence of the two elements continued right into the
Middle Ages.   "The number of Greeks or Hither-
Asiatics in Florence," says one writer,[256] "was considerable.   Of 115 tombstones of the pre-Christian period, the
inscriptions on 21 are in Greek, and of 48 epitaphs · of
Christians 9 are in Greek. . . . In one of these it is
recorded that the grave contains a man born in Asia
Minor."   The same authority holds that the Greek inscriptions would seem to point to the conclusion that
traders from Hither-Asia must have settled in Florence.
As late as the 11th century there is evidence pointing to
the same fact.   At baptisms the priest asked whether the
formulas were to be pronounced in Latin or in Greek.

As for the Scotch, if there is any truth in the
hypothesis [257] that the Frisians settled on the eastern
shores of Scotland, are we not justified in asserting that
the Scotch too have possessed their peculiar national
traits from the very earliest period in their history ?
The Frisians, so much is certain, were a clever and
skilful race of traders.[258]   On this basis it is perfectly
easy to trace the peculiar characteristics of the English
to the influence of the Romans, Saxons, and Normans ;
that of the Lowland Scotch to the Frisians.   It is a racial
or blood difference.

One other nation is indebted to the Frisians for its
national bent—the Dutch.   From their earliest history the
folk in the Low Countries were devoted to trade, traffic,
and calculations.   The Frisians, indeed, may be regarded

as the paramount commercial race in the Germanic family, by whose side later the Alemanni took up a similar position. The Alemanni were the ancestors of the Swiss.

As for the Jews, I believe that in my treatise on *The Jews and Modern Capitalism* I have established the fact that the racial characteristics of this gifted people, as we perceive them when they first began to exercise an influence on capitalism (say about the 17th century), were inherent in their blood from the earliest times. Jews were traders from the first.

Summing up our considerations, we arrive at this important conclusion : that the capitalist spirit in Europe was cultivated by a number of races, each with different characteristics of its own, and that of these races the Trading peoples (Etruscans, Frisians, and Jews) may be divided off from those we have termed Heroic.

Now, the original traits of a people are only a starting-point in the consideration of its biological development. In every generation the original traits are influenced anew, and two processes are responsible for the change. The one is selection, the other admixture with other races.

So far as our knowledge goes, it would seem that among the trading people the process of selection left the fittest to survive ; that is to say, those who possessed the trading characteristic in a high degree. Of the Jews it may even be said that among them selection was hardly active at all, for they were from the first a pure trading people. The Florentines, on the other hand, had a trace of Germanic blood, which flowed in the veins of the nobility. So long as the influence of this social group predominated, Florence had the appearance of a military town. But slowly the foreign element was shed, nowhere so soon and so thoroughly as in this city. A large part of the nobility vanished. Did not Dante mourn the decline of

numerous noble families ? What was left was removed
by force. As early as 1292 the people with the true
commercial spirit in them succeeded in establishing a law
that no grandee should be a member of the Senate.
What was the result ? Those of the nobility that
possessed the quality of adaptation had themselves put
down among the commons ; the others, those in whom
we must suppose the seigniorial temperament to have been
strong, whose natures were averse to traffic, emigrated.
The later history of Florence showed that its public life
became more and more democratic, that from the 14th
century on its citizens were all bourgeois.

Some such similar process must have taken place in the
Scotch Lowlands, from which the Celtic nobility were
eliminated before long. Their decline commenced in the
15th century ; it was due to their " eternal want of
pence," and their inability to dispense with them. " The
day had gone by when a following of rudely armed
retainers made a great man of Bell-the-Cat or Tiger Earl.
As things now went, what had been a source of strength
was fast becoming a source of weakness. Retainers had
to be maintained, and their maintenance was a drain on
the lord's resources which his extended wants made ever
more undesirable. . . . A noble lord with broad domains
and a scanty purse was a stranded leviathan, impotent to
put forth his strength in the new conditions in which he
found himself." [259] Those of the nobility that could,
saved themselves by removing to the Highlands. The
result was that the Frisian trading element became predominant in the Lowlands.

The process of selection was the same, if slower, among
the other peoples. Probably there were two stages
among them. First the non-capitalist elements were
eliminated, and then from the residue those that had a
strong tendency to trade. The process went on in so far

as the more gifted in the lowest social grades worked their way up and became capitalist undertakers. They could only do so by skill in negotiating, by economy, and by careful calculation.

So much for selection. Blood-admixture had the same results, and they may already be perceived in the Middle Ages. From the 16th century onward the admixture of blood in countries like France and England had important consequences. To explain these it is necessary to assume that as a general rule, when nobles and commoners intermarried, the blood of the latter was the stronger and prevailed. How else are we to account for a man like Leon Battista Alberti? The Albertis were among the highest and purest of the Germanic nobility in Tuscany, spending their lives in martial undertakings. Many of its branches we know something about; [259A] the Contalbertis may be mentioned as an instance. Leon Battista's own clan was proud and mighty. It sprang from Castello di Catenaia in Val d'Arno; beside their own family estate they were the lords of many others; and they had intermarried with distinguished Germanic noble families. Defeated in a local quarrel, they moved into the town (in the 13th century), where the first of the Albertis joined the Gild of the Giudici, and gradually they became the most famous drapers in Florence. It was the descendant of such a line that wrote a book second to none in its bourgeois sentiments, a book which already breathed the spirit of Benjamin Franklin. How many shopkeeper families must have crossed the noble breed to produce a result like this? In Leon Battista's own case the crossing was certain : he was an illegitimate child and born in Venice. His mother must have been a woman of the middle class sprung from a trading stock.

One other point before we conclude these considerations. Every increase of capitalist variants denoted an extension of the capitalist spirit. But it also denoted its greater intensity, for every additional variant increasingly facilitated the expression of that spirit. In a word, the reaction on each other of the variants with similar traits increased the possibilities of their expression.

It only remains for us now to consider the historical aspect of our problem. We must discover what it was that enabled the original inherent national tendencies to capitalism to grow and expand. I see two groups of such forces, internal and external, if you like to call them so— though the terms are hardly exact, seeing that the internal group is influenced from without and the external can scarcely be conceived without internal, psychological processes. Still, the moral forces press more from within outwardly, and the social circumstances exercise their influence more from without inwards.

The influence of nature I have not considered separately. I refer to the influence of the land, climate, geographical position, mineral wealth. In so far as these must be noted, we shall take cognizance of them under the group of forces we have termed "social circumstances." For example, the effect of particular callings, the exploitation of mineral deposits, the development of technical science, and so forth.

One word more before we leave the debatable problem of biology—a word of comfort to the sceptical. The historical considerations that we are about to enter upon are of value even if the biological arguments have failed to carry conviction. The most devoted advocate of the environment theory will find nothing to object to in them. For those who, like us, believe in latent tendencies, these historical investigations will demonstrate what forces developed them, and how unsuitable variants were shed ; whereas for those who pin their faith to the environment theory they will explain how capitalism came into being (out of nothing apparently). But both sides will agree that the trend of history has resulted in the development of the capitalist spirit ; both, therefore, will attach the utmost importance to the historical factors in the problem.

SECTION II

MORAL FORCES

CHAPTER XVI

PHILOSOPHY

IF the idea of the ethical outlook is so far extended as to
include the religious sanctions of morality, then it may
be said that the highest moral forces that shape our
conduct and our actions are to be found in philosophy
and religion. Hence both are not without influence on
the soul of man in so far as his economic activities are
concerned. Hence both must have counted for something in the growth and development of the capitalist
spirit.

To assert that philosophy is one of the fountains from
which the capitalist spirit drew inspiration may at first
sound like a bad joke. Yet such is the case. There can
be no doubt that philosophy has done its share to help
capitalism grow. But the minds of capitalist undertakers
were influenced by the degenerate children of a noble
mother. The philosophy of common sense, utilitarianism
in all its aspects—in reality nothing more than a systema-
tized middle-class outlook on life—is it not on this that
the many authorities with whose views we have become
acquainted rely ? And who more so than Alberti and

Franklin, the one at the beginning of the early capitalist epoch, the other at the end ? Both are thorough-going Utilitarians. Be good and you will be prosperous—such is the essence of their doctrines. By "good" they meant economical. To be good, therefore, was to economize in body and soul. Hence the supreme importance of frugality in their philosophy. They said in effect, Ask yourself what is most profitable for you, and your life will be virtuous ; if it is virtuous, it will be happy. But how discover what is profitable ? Listen to the voice of Reason. Reason is the great teacher in life. Reason and self-control will enable us to achieve whatever we resolve. Accordingly, to rationalize and economize life is the first duty of a wise man.[260] "Vicious actions," writes Benjamin Franklin, "are not hurtful because they are forbidden, but forbidden because they are hurtful. . . . It was therefore every one's interest to be virtuous who wished to be happy even in this world ; and I should from this circumstance . . . have endeavoured to convince young persons that no qualities are so likely to make a poor man's fortune as those of probity and integrity."

What was the origin of these views ? The men who preached them, the one a draper and the other a printer, could hardly have invented them. Possibly in the case of Franklin we may associate them with the empirical schools of philosophy, then coming to the fore in England, in which the law of virtue was so important a factor. In Alberti and others of his type the philosophy of the ancients is manifest, more particularly of the later classical period. There is little doubt that this philosophy was one of the sources from which the capitalist spirit received nurture. There is, indeed, evidence of a direct connection between the economic conceptions current in Italy in the early capitalist epoch and those of the ancient world. The doctrines of the mediæval church were a bond of this sort, but I am excluding that. There is no need to refer to it, for did not every man of the early Renaissance pride himself on his knowledge of the classical authors and on his efforts to make their opinions his own ?[261] Take any of the Italian writers on economic questions in those days, those who first worked out capitalist ideas systematically, and you will find that they were well versed in classical literature. In Alberti's Family Books there are frequent references to Homer, Demosthenes, and Xenophon, to Virgil, Cicero, and Livy, to Plutarch, Plato, and Aristotle, to Varro, Columella, Cato, and Pliny. Another merchant of the period, Giovanni Ruccellai, supports his rules for trade by quotations from Seneca, Ovid, Aristotle, Cicero, Solomon, Cato, and Plato.[262] As for writers on agriculture, it goes without saying that they all based their treatises on those of the Roman *scriptores rei rusticæ*. Moreover, the frequency of the references would go to show that the views of the old writers and those of the Florentine political economists coincided.

But the latter did not just take over the philosophical systems of the former in their entirety, and develop their own views logically from them. The Italian gentlemen were no philosophers. They were practical men, men of affairs, and having read widely they mingled their reading with their experience, and so arrived at their conclusions for the conduct of life.

Among the principal ideas of the later classical philosophy none appealed to them as much as that of a moral, natural law (a cardinal doctrine of the Stoics also), according to which Reason governs appetites. The thought is a noble one ; it lay at the root of the exalted view of life taught by the Stoics. But the Italian economists, by giving it a utilitarian interpretation, turned a noble ideal into a commonplace one. They urged that the greatest happiness flowed from the rationalization of life, from making life practical. Life should be disciplined and methodical, so Alberti and his kind taught ; and there is no doubt that the doctrine was eminently helpful to the growth of capitalism. In every case they backed up their admonitions by appeals to the ancients. Alberti never tired of preaching self-control, and is for ever quoting the classical writers in support.[263]

The Stoic philosophy, moreover, is capable of being turned into a commonplace, utilitarian, rationalistic system, if its teachings are taken by themselves and out of their context and applied to life. Our drapers were acquainted with those teachings, and I can well imagine how many wise saws they found among them which coloured their outlook. I can well imagine Alberti or Ruccellai turning to the marvellous *Meditations of Marcus Aurelius*, and specially noting many a passage in them.* Many of the maxims of the Imperial philosopher read as though they were translations of passages from Alberti's Family Book or Penn's *Fruits of Solitude*, or Franklin's writings.

This philosophy of life must have been specially popular with our Florentine friends for yet another reason. They found in it excellent excuses for their acquisitiveness. Thus, Seneca's disquisition on the meaning and use of wealth is copied almost word for word by Alberti. A few of the passages will be illuminating (*De tranquillitate animi*, 21–23) : —

> The wise man does not hold himself unworthy of accepting the gifts of Fortune. He does not love riches, but he is not averse to them. He does not give them a place in his heart, but in his home. And when he has them he does not despise them but holds them fast.

---

* [See, *e.g.*, i. 3 ; i. 8 ; ii. 16 ; iv. 13 ; v. 1 ; vii. 74 ; ix. 7 ; x. 31 ; xii. 20.]

Of course, when a wise man has means he is able to cultivate his mind to better effect than when he is poor. . . . Riches offer great opportunities for moderation, generosity, care, pomp, and wise spending. (Alberti, careful of the pennies, did not take quite so broad a view. Generosity with him had a practical end, either to get a reputation for open-handedness or to acquire new friends.) Riches bring joy, much like a fair breeze on a voyage, or a fine day, or a ray of sunshine on a wintry landscape. . . . Some things are valued but slightly ; others much. Among the latter every one will vote riches . . . . Cease then proscribing money to the philosopher. Has any one condemned wisdom to poverty ? A philosopher indeed may possess great riches. They have made no man the poorer ; they are not blood-stained ; they have been gotten without injustice and ignoble courses.

These ideas about wealth were common in the ancient world. The reader will probably recall Cicero's dictum that " Money is to be sought after, not for itself but for the advantages it is able to bestow." Was not this the prevailing sentiment throughout the early capitalist age ? Acquire as much as you can, so it was said, but do so honestly. And when you have wealth, do not make a fetish of it. Remember, it is a means to an end, and not the end itself.

Still more popular must those writings of the ancients have been wherein practical rules for managing affairs were ready at hand. These could at once be adopted in one's own business, and though, strictly speaking, the maxims in question hardly come under the heading of philosophy, I should like to deal with them here. To the best of my judgment Xenophon's *Œconomicus* in Greek, and the agricultural writers (Columella above the rest) in Latin literature, must have exercised very great influence on the development of capitalist thought. Xenophon was more widely read and more highly esteemed than Aristotle.

Let us glance at a passage or two from the *Œconomicus.*

My conduct is always right and proper and my aim is to secure, by fair means, strength, health, honourable citizenship, the good opinion of my friends, success in war and riches. Riches enable you to honour the Gods and your friends in due fashion, to be of assistance to the latter in time of need, and to contribute something to the beauty and splendour of your native city.[264]

Alberti copied this almost word for word. So too the following :—

If you spend money extravagantly, out of all proportion to your income, it is not surprising to find want in place of superfluity.[265]

No less attractive to Alberti was Xenophon's advice to the good housewife to see to it that orderliness is the first rule in her domain. "Order is the most useful and beautiful thing in life." It keeps women from frivolity, flirtation, and vanity ; the careful housewife does not paint her face ; and more to the same effect.

The Roman writers on farm management were equally popular. They, too, are full of wise saws to enable the farmer to carry on his business profitably and successfully.[266] Acquisitiveness and rational conduct are surprisingly developed in these writings.[267] Above all else they preach the value of time.[268]

Side by side with these formal treatises on domestic or agricultural economy, our Italian drapers must have found many a quotation from the poets and the historians in praise of middle-class virtues, more especially industry and frugality. Many such dicta were particularly effective because of their crisp expression, making them into popular proverbs. One of them Alberti actually quotes. An old saw, he says, repeated in his own day, was that " Idleness is the source of all evil." There were many others. Let us conclude with one from Lucretius, who writes : " The greatest riches come from saving." [269]

CHAPTER XVII

THE INFLUENCE OF RELIGION ON THE AGE OF
EARLY CAPITALISM

1. THE CATHOLICS.

WE have observed that the economic outlook of the
Florentine drapers was influenced in many respects by
the more or less philosophical ideas of the ancient writers.
But let us be careful not to rate that influence too highly,
for it was overshadowed by that of religion, and at first
of Roman Catholicism. The origins of capitalism made
their appearance at a time when the Church held sway
over men's minds in all their activities, and therefore
social and economic activities were subject to its regulations. This extensive power of the Church continued
until the 15th century, and every man was subject to it,
even the advanced spirits who attempted to think for
themselves, who read the Greek and Latin classics, and
sought to fashion their life in accordance with ancient
ideals. For even these people with but few exceptions
wished to be orthodox, and took over from the heathen
world only so much as was compatible with the Catholic
faith within them. We see it in the case of Alberti, who
protests his orthodoxy again and again, and admonishes
his disciples above all else to serve God (as Mother
Church had taught him). " Whoso does not fear God,
whoso has driven religion from his heart, must be

accounted wicked in all things. Children should first and foremost be filled with the greatest awe of God, for the observance of His laws is a wonderful help against all manner of evils." [270] Accordingly, Alberti established all his maxims on the basis of God's commandments. And even when he adopts a wise saw from the heathen writers he at once connects it with God's will. Thus in preaching industry he clinches his argument by the assertion that " It was not God's purpose that any living thing should be idle. Consequently man should be active ever." [271]

If the advanced spirits were thus under the influence of the Church, how much more the masses. It is now a recognized fact that in the 14th century Italy was still orthodox ; scepticism did not begin to be rampant until the 15th.[272]

Now, it is of supreme interest to note that religious zeal was nowhere so hot and strong as in Florence, the Bethlehem of the capitalist spirit (of Christian origin). Tuscany was the citadel of clericalism in the early Middle Ages. The history of the individual churches in this province was more closely intertwined with that of the towns than anywhere else ; monasticism was exceedingly active and widespread ; the orders that were established in other parts took on a new lease of life when they came to Tuscany, and the population prided itself on its intolerance of schismatics and the purity of its faith.[273] Pretty well all authorities on the history of Florence are agreed that its democracy of craftsmen and traders were faithful children of the Church.[274]

As for the later period, it is not a far-fetched assumption that the living faith of the great mass of the Catholics in all lands must have continued, especially after it had been strengthened by the Reformation, until the end of the period of early capitalism. The industrialists and

merchants of the 18th century were as pious as those of
the 14th, and lived in the fear of the Lord.   Their religion impregnated their business.   Many an expression of
opinion found in merchants' memoirs must have sprung
from an honest religious conviction.   " A merchant's life
and conduct should be above suspicion," so we read
in one such production.   " Dishonesty never thrives,
whereas the possessions of a God-fearing and righteous
man take root and have the blessing of Heaven showered
upon them, even unto the third and fourth generation."
Sentiments such as these were frequent.   Profit is God's
gift ; so are children.   " From God we obtain our all.
He it is who sends blessings on our enterprises and brings
them to fruition "—so wrote a French woollen-draper of
the 18th century.   The same man commenced his *Livre
de Raison* with the words : " In the name of the Father,
the Son, and the Holy Ghost.   Blessed and exalted be the
Trinity in all Eternity." 275   One cannot help feeling
that they came from his heart.   It was no empty phrase
in those days when men looked to God to bless their
business.   To-day it would be nothing short of blasphemy.

Finally, we must not forget how mighty a weapon
the Catholic Church possessed in the confessional.   The
Lateran Council of 1215 had imposed it as a duty on
the faithful to go to confession at least once a year.
It is not difficult to perceive how the soul and the
will-power   could   be   influenced,   and   consequently
the life of the individual.   We must suppose that
the business man discussed with his father-confessor the
principles that governed his economic activities.   Do we
not know that numerous treatises (known under the
name of *Summæ theologicæ*) were written, advising the
clergy how to guide their flocks in all that affects life,
even to the minutest detail ?   Economic activities were
naturally also considered, and rules were laid down for

their regulation and direction. These books are one of the most illuminating sources for a right understanding of what the Church taught should exist, and at the same time, reading between the lines, for what actually did exist. We shall recur to these books later.

2. THE PROTESTANTS.

It is a matter of common knowledge that in all Protestant countries there was an exceedingly strong religious fervour during the two centuries that followed the Reformation. There is therefore no need to enlarge upon it. But one thing I should like to point out. It was in Scotland that this religious feeling reached its height, in the land where, as we have already seen, the capitalist spirit took on enormous proportions towards the end of the 17th century. It is difficult to imagine the fervour, nay, the violence, of religious sentiment in Scotland in the 17th century. Buckle has painted it in its true colours in the fourth chapter of the second volume of his standard work, *The History of Civilization in England.* What does he tell us? That in all activities of life religion was the dominant force. The Scotch attended church most zealously, and their subservience to their preachers was almost servile. The clergy interfered in the most intimate affairs and the elders almost dragooned the congregation into orthodoxy. Whatever came from the pulpit was regarded as a voice from God. A system such as this was bound to breed superstition, and superstition there was. Evil spirits, with Satan at their head, were believed to swarm on the earth, attempting to terrorize man. Indeed, the fear of the Evil One became an obsession, and the preaching of the clergy, detailing the punishments of hell, only fanned the flame into fiercer heat. God

Almighty Himself, in the minds of the masses, became Vengeance personified. But then the God of Calvin and John Knox was a fearful Being, striking awe into the heart of man. This conception of Him resulted in the widespread desire so to order life as to bring it into complete accord with the doctrines of the Church. That is the important thing for us to observe, considering as we are the influence of religion on the soul of man, more especially so far as his economic activities are called into question. There can be little doubt that in the 17th century religious influences on life in Protestant, or at least in Calvinist, countries were much deeper than ever they had been before. Religion became a sort of madness, depriving man of his common sense. Think of the doctrine of predestination and how it made the Calvinists into religious fanatics. Yet the simple logic of common sense says that if my salvation and happiness have nothing to do with my will and actions, why should I not arrange my life as I wish, seeing that my fate is already determined beforehand? But you could not reason with men out of their minds.

The views of the clergy as to the good life were embodied in stout tractates, called in England *Directories*, which every Calvinist preacher of any significance thought it necessary to publish. They may be looked upon as the Protestant prototypes of the *Summæ theologicæ*, and in both economic ethics occupies no small space.

3. THE JEWS.

In considering the influence of religion on the development of the capitalist spirit, it is self-evident that the Jewish religion will have to receive special attention. To begin with, let it be stated that in the age of early capitalism religion was an exceedingly powerful influence in all walks of life among the Jews as well; nay, more among the Jews than among other peoples. So much may be asserted without fear of contradiction. I have attempted to demonstrate this fully in my book on *The Jews and Modern Capitalism*, and I would refer the reader to its pages for the details.[276] Here I shall merely summarize the more important and unquestioned conclusions arrived at therein.

Religion for the Jew was not an affair of Sabbaths and holydays; it entered into his everyday life and regulated the minutest action. The influence of his religion on the Jew is therefore apparent. Indeed, all human actions were sanctified by religion. In every course of conduct the Jew asked himself whether it would tend to the glory of God, or to the profanation of His name. And Jewish law regulated not only the relationship between God and man, but also every possible relationship between man and the natural world. Jewish law, it must be remembered, is as much a part of the Jewish religious system as are Jewish ethics. For the law is from God; it is morally right. Moral laws and Divine ordinances are inseparable terms in the Jewish outlook.

No other people have taken so great a care that the tenets of their faith shall be generally known among them. Jewish education is proverbial for its excellence. Even divine service is to a large extent instruction in religion. Passages from Holy Writ are publicly read and explained, in accordance with a cycle whereby the whole of the *Torah* [Pentateuch] is gone through in the course of the year. Moreover, the duty of *Torah* study is inculcated in the Jew as a prime necessity.

Nor has any other people walked so steadfastly in the ways of God, or so scrupulously observed the ordinances of religion. The Jews have been called the most irreligious of all peoples. I will not now consider whether justly or not. But they are certainly the most God-fearing people in all the earth. They always lived in fear and trembling of the Divine wrath. And in the course of history this fear of God was seconded by other forces in making the Jews more scrupulous than ever in the observation of their religious practices. First and foremost must be placed the tragedy of their national existence. The destruction of the Jewish state brought with it as one result that the Scribes and Pharisees, the men who kept alive the tradition of Ezra, who before must have had some moral influence, now became the chief authority of the people, and directed it into grooves of their own choosing. When their national sanctuary was razed to the ground, when their state came to an end, the Jews flocked round the Pharisees and the *Torah*, " the portable fatherland," as Heine called it. The Rabbis thus established their authority, and the fate of the Jews in the Middle Ages only helped to strengthen it, so much so that it became a yoke, of which, from time to time, the Jews themselves complained. The more the Jews were excluded (or excluded themselves) from the nations among whom they dwelt, the greater became the influence of the Rabbis. Which is only another way of saying that the Jews were more and more submissive to the Law. But the Law was observed for its own sake too. In the midst of the cruel persecutions and humiliations that were the lot of the Jews in every land, what could give them hope, what help them to maintain their self-respect, what make life worth living, so much as the loving obser-vance of religious precepts? These were contained in the *Talmud*, and *in* the *Talmud* and *for* the *Talmud* the Jews throughout the centuries lived and had their being.

Internal and external causes thus combined to make the Jews strictly religious. Nor must it be imagined that this was true only of the masses. On the contrary, the wealthy and the intelligent were equally orthodox, the very people among whom the capitalist spirit took root and throve. The Rabbis, too, gave decisions and advice on the conduct of life, perhaps more so than the Catholic and Protestant clergy ; and, like these, they collected their opinions in the large volumes of *Responsa* literature, which in their turn became the sources on which later decisions were based. And so, like the *Directories* and the *Summæ theologicæ*, these collections contain a very large amount of advice on economic affairs.

CHAPTER XVIII

CATHOLICISM

RELIGIOUS systems and churches are able to influence economic life in different ways, particularly by their power of directing the mind to this goal or that. Sometimes their influence may be direct, sometimes very roundabout. It may check certain tendencies or give them an impetus. It is not surprising therefore that the history of the capitalist spirit should be inextricably bound up with the history of churches and religious systems.

In the following chapters I shall attempt to show how the great religions helped capitalism forward, and only incidentally touch upon the checks and stumbling-blocks for which they were responsible.

The capitalist spirit received a set-back at the hands of Catholicism in Spain. There religious interests developed to the exclusion of all others. The reason for this is plain, and historians have not overlooked it. The history of the Iberian Peninsula for a thousand years and more was the story of the struggle between Christianity and Islam. The Mahometan domination resulted in giving the Spanish Christians one great aim in life—the expulsion of the Moors. " While the other peoples of Europe turned their gaze to the new intellectual and economic problems of the day, the Spaniards, so long as a single Moorish banner flapped in the breeze, had no thought for aught else but its removal." Lafuente speaks of " an everlasting and constant crusade against the infidels." It is said that no less than 3,700 battles were waged against the Moors before they were finally expelled. But even after that the ideal of Christian chivalry predominated in Spain, so much so that it characterized all the Spanish colonial enterprises and coloured the home policy of the crown. Feudalism and fanaticism intertwined to form a special outlook on life, which maintained itself as long as it could, but was wholly out of place in the modern period of history. The national hero of Spain is probably the most un-capitalist type in the annals of the world. Who does not know him—the last knight-errant, the kindly and attractive Don Quixote?

Whether Catholicism stood in the way of the capitalist spirit in Ireland it is not easy to say. But certain it is that in all other countries its influence was most beneficial to capitalist growth, which it assisted and accelerated. Such was the case in an especial degree in Italy, which played the first role in the history of early capitalism. Let us see how Catholicism achieved this end.

There is no doubt that the popes and their financial policies contributed much to the establishment of capitalism, and thus to the expansion of the capitalist spirit. But I do not intend considering that side of the problem, which I have already dealt with in another connection, and which other scholars have elaborated with great skill.[277] Moreover, the facts are generally well known. The system of papal taxation, which extended to the whole of the then known world (especially from the 13th century on), called into existence an upper class of powerful international bankers, who acted like yeast on the capitalist dough.

What is of far greater significance, and what I propose to review, is the influence exercised by the

Catholic Church on the capitalist spirit by reason of its doctrines.

Of course, not all the doctrines of Catholicism will come into our survey. To consider them all would be to make our labour much more difficult than it need be. It would also distract us from the root of the matter, which is the influence of religion in any period on the mind of man in his capacity of economic agent. Religious and metaphysical hair-splitting are quite unnecessary for the solution of the problem ; all that is needed is just to view the practical rules of everyday life and common religious exercises. There is no need for our purpose, so it seems to me, to go into the philosophical and theological depths of the problem. Deep ploughing is not always a necessity of successful tillage. If, therefore, I remain on the surface of things, it is because I believe that the causes and their effects will be best apparent there.

The doctrines of the Catholic Church were embodied in mediæval scholasticism as formulated by Thomas Aquinas. Ever since the 14th century this religious system has been recognized as official by the Church of Rome. Its main characteristic [278] is that it unites the two currents of thought found in Christianity from its very beginning—the Pauline and Augustinian doctrines of love and the legalism of the Law. Thomas Aquinas did away with the opposition between the Law and the Gospels, and his theory of legal ethics is what we must turn to.

The fundamental idea of the ethical system is the rationalization of life. Reason, everlasting and divine, that governs nature and the universe—Reason must regulate the world by the senses and control the passions and appetites. " Sin in human affairs is what is contrary to the dictates of reason," says Aquinas. Or again, " the more necessary a thing is, the more should reference be had to the demands of Reason." The sexual passion is most necessary for the common good ; consequently it should most stringently be held in sway, in accordance with the dictates of reason.[279] Virtue is nought else but the maintenance of the equilibrium in all things,[280] as reason demands ; its essence consists in making the desires of the senses subservient to reason, so that no passions out of all accord with reason may spring up.[281]

In the natural world with its appetites and desires a moral, rational world is built up of the Biblical Laws. This new world, born of freedom, Aquinas puts on an equality with the decalogue,[282] although elements of Hellenistic philosophy formed part and parcel of it in later times. The goal set by Aquinas for all men is to live in accord with reason. What means to that end does he suggest ? The fear of God. The fear of God sets a man thinking ; it forces him to review his conduct ; it makes a rational being of him.[283]

Now bear in mind that the very idea of rationalizing life was in itself a great impetus to the growth of capitalism. Acquisitiveness and economic rationalism are in reality the result of applying to economic life the rule of religion. Before capitalism could develop it was needful to root up natural man with all his passions, to replace the primitive and original outlook by specifically rationalist habits of mind, to turn topsy-turvey all the values of life. The *homo capitalisticus*, that artificial and artistic creation, was the result. Whatever other forces may have helped the growth of economic rationalism, there can be no doubt that one of its mightiest supports came from the fact that rationalism was inculcated by the Church, which desired to influence the whole of life in the same direction as the capitalist spirit influenced economic activities. Even were we to suppose that economic interests were not without influence on ecclesiastical ethics (a problem we shall touch upon in due course), the view would still hold good that economic rationalism was bound to profit by forming part of such a thoroughly rationalist body of rules, supported moreover by the all-embracing power of the Church.

The influence of religious doctrines on the economic outlook must have been immense, seeing that they affected the mind in just such ways as were beneficial to capitalism. Take the behest of Christian ethics that the erotic appetite should be held in check.[284] No one perceived more than St. Thomas that middle-class virtues would thrive only where the sexual life of man was controlled. He knew only too well that extravagance, the deadly sin of the bourgeois outlook, went as a rule hand in hand with an advanced attitude towards love. Extravagance in other things usually meant extravagance in voluptuousness.[285] He knew also that luxury and debauchery are twin sisters. Accordingly, he taught that whoso lived in purity and moderation was hardly likely to be subject to the sin of prodigality, and besides would manage his affairs economically. What bearing had this on capitalism? The abstemious liver was sure to make an energetic undertaker.

Moderation of appetite was thus the foundation for a larger structure. To begin with, if you ordered your passions aright you would the more easily be able to order aright the whole of life and be economical in material things. Reason and order in worldly affairs was a cardinal doctrine in Christian ethics.

But above all else the Schoolmen praised economy, which they termed *liberalitas*. Liberalitas represents the right middle policy which avoids the two extremes of avarice and prodigality ; it denotes a proper balancing of income and expenditure ; [286] it teaches the art of using the goods of the world [288] aright ; [287] it inculcates the true love of money and opulence.[289] The prodigal loves money too little, the miser too much.[290] In Aquinas's condemnation of too great an expenditure,[291] especially when it tends to make you live beyond your means,[292] there is implied the duty of saving ; and his dwelling upon the evil consequences of extravagance [293] implies a recommendation of the bourgeois economy based on income, and a condemnation of the seigniorial economy based on expenditure.

But extravagance is not the only enemy of middle-class virtues condemned by Christian ethics and accounted sinful. There are others, chief among them being idleness, which is the beginning of all evil. The idler commits a sin because he wastes time which is exceedingly precious ; [294] he is lower than the beasts, for even brute creation is industrious ; in nature nothing idles.[295] Particularly eloquent in his plea for filling up every minute is St. Antonine of Florence, who brushes aside the excuse of idlers that they are intent on divine contemplation, that they follow Mary rather than Martha. Narrow is the gate of those who can see God, he says, and few be they who enter in thereby. Consequently the great mass of people must be active and busy.

Honesty no less than industry and frugality was also taught by the Schoolmen, more especially commercial honesty, which, as we have seen, forms a good part of the capitalist spirit. Commercial honesty owes much to the teaching of the Church. Within the bounds of the city, where your neighbour's eye might be looking, or the gild brethren watching, you could not help being honest in your business. But when markets extended beyond the city, what but the conscience of the tradesman could keep him straight ? That was where the Church came in, for it was its business to stir up the individual conscience.

It did so by condemning all manner of cheating as one of the mortal sins.[296] How great the influence of the Church was in this respect appears from a remark of Alberti's, who ascribes the success of his family not only to business acumen but also to their commercial honesty, for which God Almighty had rewarded them.[297]

From a careful study of the writings of the Schoolmen, and more especially of the wonderful works of Thomas Aquinas, who for grandeur may be worthily compared with Dante and Michael Angelo, the impression is borne in upon the mind that their intention was not merely to instruct their contemporaries in the ways of middle-class respectability and honesty, but also to make them straightforward, courageous, wise, and energetic men. Else why do they constantly attach so much importance to energy and freshness ? Nothing moves their ire more than intellectual or moral laziness, that *acidia* which was considered good form in 13th-century Italy, and of which Petrarch has so much to say. The Schoolmen condemned it as a deadly sin. Indeed, much of their moral teaching reads like a course of " soul-training." What are the two cardinal virtues ? Wisdom and strength, the sources of intellectual and moral energy.

Wisdom is an intellectual virtue and includes many others [298] which are secondary to it — remembering, understanding, insight, common-sense thought, willingness to learn from others, foresight, circumspection, and caution. And what are the opposites of wisdom, that a man should avoid ? Imprudence, rashness, inconsideration, and negligence.

St. Antonine [299] of Florence was especially concerned with the intellectual fault of *acidia*, which may be best translated " moral laziness." In his view moral laziness leads to negligence, idleness, unreliability, stupidity, time-wasting, and imprudence. And luxury is the mother of this brood—luxury with its pleasure-seeking in general and its erotic licence in particular. Perfect wisdom is only the controlling of sensual passion.[300]

Imagine how valuable this training was from the point of view of capitalism. The Church fathers certainly did not think of the capitalist undertaker, but he more than any other profited much by the practice of these virtues of intellectual energy. They are the very qualities needed for success as an undertaker, and here was the Church backing them up with all its authority. If the subject of a prize-essay were, " How would you make the lusty feudal lord and the stupid, lazy craftsman respectively into a capitalist undertaker ? " there could be no better way of answering the question than by quoting the ethics of the Schoolmen.

I am aware that my view of the influence of the Church's teaching on capitalism is opposed to the prevailing one. Not only has the latter not observed that the ethics of Thomas Aquinas are very favourably disposed to the capitalist spirit, but it has also been suggested that numerous maxims and prescriptions in it show that scholasticism was actually opposed to the new type of man who came into being in the capitalist age. A renewed study of the sources has convinced me that the accepted views are incorrect. The opinions of the Schoolmen, especially of the later ones, concerning wealth and its acquisition, and more particularly their views on usury, far from being a hindrance to the growth of the capitalist spirit, were in reality an impetus of no small weight.

Nor is there anything remarkable about that. For what manner of people were the Schoolmen ? It is a mistake to think of them as mild bookworms, unlearned in the ways of the world, abstruse thinkers of the cloisters and the study, engaged in hair-splitting and endless repetitions concerning unrealities. Many of the lesser lights do indeed fit into this picture. But the great minds never. I have already indicated what I think of the writings of Aquinas. I want to add in this place that it is an error to regard St. Thomas as a mediæval writer. The century in which he lived and wrote was for the country where he was active the beginning of the modern era. But even if Thomas Aquinas be placed in pre-capitalist times, the men who wrote on Christian ethics after him were certainly children of an age of capitalist development. Take Antonine of Florence, who was born in 1389 and died in 1459 ; take his contemporary, Bernard of Siena ; take the commentator on Aquinas, Cardinal Cajetan, who died in 1489 ; take Chrysostom Javellus and many more besides. These men were neither without knowledge of the world nor were they unworldly. They understood the inwardness of the economic revolution that had been effected in their day, and had no inclination to sacrifice themselves to the " steam-roller." As a matter of fact, these later Schoolmen had more sympathy for and understanding of capitalism than the 17th-century zealot preachers of Puritanism. How much practical knowledge is to be found in the *Summa* of St. Antonine ! It is the work of one of the most wideawake men of his time, who walked through the streets of Florence with his eyes open, who was acquainted with the thousand and one business tricks of his fellow-citizens, who was not unlearned in transport insurance nor in the nature of bills of exchange, who knew all about the silk industry and wool-making.

What, then, was the attitude of these men to the new economic order and its spirit ?

Let us first turn to the teachings of the Schoolmen

in regard to poverty and wealth. The old Christian
ideal of poverty which the early Fathers valued so much,
and which the first sectaries not only preached but
practised, appears in the later Schoolmen to have vanished
altogether. It is of little moment whether the pious
Christian be poor or rich ; what is of consequence is
what use he makes of his poverty or his riches. The
wise man does not flee from opulence or from poverty
as such ; he discountenances and avoids the misuse of
either.[301] And if you weigh up the advantages and
disadvantages of wealth with those of poverty, those of
the former overbalance those of the latter.[302] In any
event, whether you are rich or poor it is God's doing,[303]
and in either case He is fulfilling His beneficent purpose.
The poor is being taught contentment, the rich is given
a sign of grace or is provided with the means of nobly
applying his possessions.[304] The noble use is what
matters, and the good Christian should not therefore
think too much of his riches or misuse them for a sinful
end. If he does not do this, if he utilizes his wealth in a
godly way, then the term " sinful " which may sometimes
be applied to riches is not appropriate.[305] The end of
riches is not, of course, more riches ; it has only one end,
and that is to minister to man's wants and through man
to God. God is the ultimate, man the immediate goal.

To be wealthy was always looked upon by the
Schoolmen as an act of God. But what of becoming
wealthy, what of acquiring wealth ? On this point the
views did not always accord. St. Thomas holds the
static conception of society, that which characterized
social conditions in the pre-capitalist era. Every man
had his niche wherein he stayed to the end of his
days. He had his calling and his status, and the income
in accord with that. All change, all development, all
progress were inward processes and were conceivable only

as regards man's relation to the Deity. Consequently the amount of wealth of every person was a fixed quantity. He was as rich as his status required.

But such a view could not possibly be maintained in the revolutionary 14th and 15th centuries. Indeed, it was something of a problem for the father-confessors. For if you followed it to its logical conclusion, it meant that no one should rise above his station, that no one should obtain riches, and so be able to live the life of the social grade above him. Accordingly, once a peasant always a peasant, once a craftsman always a craftsman—" which is absurd," as Cardinal Cajetan concludes in his criticism of Aquinas's opinions. Clearly, he holds, every man ought to have the possibility of working himself up and becoming richer than he was. And these are his reasons. If any one has special gifts which enable him to rise beyond his station, he ought also to be allowed to acquire the means appropriate for the higher status. This version of the matter opened wide the doors for the capitalist undertakers, the men who stood out from the crowd by virtue of their greater capacities, " who could justly claim to have dominion over the rest, although they were not lords," the men who had a keen eye for business and other large enterprises. These could acquire gain and accumulate capital as much as they wanted with the full approval of Mother Church.[306]

As much as they wanted ? There were limitations, of course. Their acquisitions had to be made in accordance with reason, and the means they adopted for reaching their goal had to be such as were not in conflict with morality. But what was not in accordance with reason ? To get gain for its own sake, to heap up riches for the riches themselves, to climb upward for the sake of the climbing—all this was worthy of punishment. It was also foolish, seeing that no limit was set to any of the three.[307] Equally reprehensible was it to pay no heed to morality in business, or to act in a way contrary to the general good, or to stop your ears to the voice of conscience. Whoso did such things as these was endangering his soul's welfare for the sake of filthy lucre.[308] In a word, unscrupulous and unbounded acquisitiveness has always been condemned by Catholic teachers of morality down almost to this very day. By so doing they lent their support to the conceptions of the old-fashioned bourgeois, which prevailed to the end of the period of early capitalism, but which, it must be added, was not averse to profits honestly gotten. It was not so much the quantity of profit that the Church teachers were concerned with as the mental attitude of the capitalist undertaker. What they wanted to prevent, and no doubt succeeded in preventing, was the utter transvaluation of all values, such as that which characterizes our own age.

A warm sympathetic understanding of the expansion of economic life in their age and country rings true in all that the later Italian Schoolmen wrote touching economic questions. In other words, capitalism appealed to them. It was on that account that they clung to the teaching of the canon law concerning usury. For what did the prohibition of usury mean to the Catholic moralists of the 15th and 16th centuries? Expressed in modern terms it denoted : Don't prevent money from becoming capital.

At first sight this may seem paradoxical. Yet the more carefully I study the sources the more convinced I become that the prohibition of usury gave a mighty impetus to the expansion of the capitalist spirit. I am surprised that no one has noticed this before. Possibly one reason is that the specialists who have hitherto devoted themselves to scholastic philosophy were not economists and lacked that knowledge of affairs which Bernard of Siena and Antonine of Florence both possessed.

The conception of capital in St. Thomas's writings is in the germinating stage. But even he differentiates between borrowing for unproductive purposes (the simple loan) and borrowing for productive objects (capital), and goes so far as to say that while to receive payment for the first is wrong, to receive payment for the second is perfectly legitimate.[309] Antonine of Florence and Bernard of Siena appear to understand the essence of capitalism in its completeness. Indeed, they use the term " capital," and what they have to say about it political economy has learned afresh from Karl Marx. Incidentally it may be noted that Antonine, with a fullness of knowledge, indicated the importance of a speedy turnover for increasing profits.[310] But we are more interested in his clear demarcation between the investment of capital (*ratio capitalis*) and the simple loan of money (*ratio mutui*).[311] In the second case money is barren, in the first it is productive, " possessing in that capacity not merely the character of money or of a commodity, but something more—the power of creation, which we term 'capital.'"[312]

What is the attitude of the Church authorities to interest and profit ? Payment for simple lending they forbade, but a share of the surplus which capital created they allowed in all cases, whether it flowed from commerce or from the work of a middleman [313] or from transport insurance [314] or from a joint-stock,[315] or in any other way.[316] Only one condition is postulated : the capitalist must himself participate in the undertaking. If he remains in the background, if he will not adventure his money, if he lacks the spirit of enterprise, let him have no profit. It is clear from this that before a man might receive interest he had to be prepared to bear the losses as well as provide the initial capital. Hence a joint-stock company had to limit its liabilities ; bank deposits could not yield interest ; [317] you were not allowed to lend a craftsman a sum of money at a fixed rate (seeing that you eliminated risk) ; [318] a partnership might be entered into only if all the partners agreed to share the losses.[319]

It is clear that these pious men were anxious to spur on enterprise. What they rewarded was industry, the mother of all profit. Money in itself was just barren dross. Only when industry—undertaking—is applied to it does it become fruitful, and then only the surplus is lawful.[320] The Schoolmen hated nothing so much as idleness, and their theory of interest bears witness to the fact. For if a man lends out money at interest without himself being an undertaker of some sort, he is an idler, who may not therefore receive his reward in the form of interest, even if the money borrowed is productive capital. This holds good so long as others and not the lender apply it productively. A passage in Antonine's writings is characteristic. It is there pointed out that the *nobili* who will not work, but put their money in other people's businesses without also sharing their risks, are receiving usury pure and simple.[321]

We can understand why the later Schoolmen hated professional money-lending, which is one of the deadly foes of capitalist undertaking. Avarice in their view was one of the most heinous sins, and avarice, remember, is not only not the same thing as the acquisition of profit but its very opposite. The avaricious man is a usurer, whom St. Antonine pictured in such bold outlines—how he gleefully surveys his treasure, how he trembles in his shoes at the thought of thieves and robbers, how he counts and recounts the golden coin evening after evening, how horrible visions make his flesh creep at night, and how he is on the look-out by day for some one to draw into his net. The significance of the last touch will become apparent if we call to mind how much money-lending there was in those days in the shape of consumptive credit, so necessary in a feudal society to make ends meet.

Note further that avarice breeds idleness. "The avaricious soul of the usurer kills all energy within him, so that he is unable to find profit in lawful and useful callings. He becomes idle, slack, and slothful, and is thus forced to have recourse to unlawful practices in order to maintain himself." [322]

The doctrine of lawful profit and that of the intellectual virtues thus coalesce. The burden of both is the same : energetic undertaking is a delight unto the Lord, but an extravagant nobility, stay-at-home slackers, and idle usurers are an abomination unto His soul.

CHAPTER XIX

PROTESTANTISM

PROTESTANTISM has been all along the line a foe to capitalism, and more especially to the capitalist economic outlook. How could it be otherwise? Capitalism is something worldly, something for this life on earth, and the more man's gaze is directed to the joys of existence here below, the more devotees will capitalism enrol. But for that very reason it will be hated and condemned of all who regard our life here as only a preparation for life hereafter. The increasing intensity of religious feelings necessarily results in an increasing indifference to economic activities, and an increasing indifference to economic activities means a weakening and dissolution of the capitalist spirit. This actually happened at the Reformation. The reform movement gave a fillip to the inner life, and intensified the craving for metaphysics in men. Consequently capitalism was prejudiced in proportion as the reform doctrines spread.

In Lutheranism this tendency was strengthened by Luther's own devotion to the economic conditions that prevailed in the early Middle Ages with the self-supporting peasant and craftsman. That is why Luther's philosophy is far behind that of the Schoolmen. It may be said with certainty that in those countries where Lutheranism triumphed the influence of religion on economic affairs, in so far as it was effective, made not for the growth, but most decidedly for the retardation, of capitalist tendencies. But other forms of Protestantism, and Calvinism in particular, were no different in this respect. In Calvinist lands the Church was distinctly hostile to capitalism, and the assumption is not far-fetched that the new faith was on the whole more harmful than helpful to the growth of the capitalist spirit.

This view, I know, is contrary to that generally prevailing, which holds that Calvinism, especially in its Anglo-Scottish guise of Puritanism, aided capitalist development, if, indeed, it did not give it birth. It remains for me therefore to demonstrate the anti-capitalist direction of Calvinist-Puritanical ethics. I shall limit my consideration to English and Scotch sources, seeing that it is commonly accepted that Puritanism helped capitalism in Great Britain more than anywhere else.

At the outset let us note that the early Christian ideal of poverty came to the fore once again in Puritan ethics. Riches and their acquisition were regarded in much the same fashion as the Gospels speak of them, and the aversion to earthly goods was more marked than in scholasticism. In principle, the Puritans and the Schoolmen were agreed. For both, riches and poverty were of no consequence whatever for the soul's salvation. But whereas we observed a certain inclination on the part of the Schoolmen to riches, among the Puritans the consensus of opinion is more sympathetic to poverty. In other words, reason in both schools is indifferent to poverty and wealth alike, but the feelings of the doctors sway them in opposite directions. The Schoolmen were for wealth, the Puritans for poverty. Hence it is that the condemnation of riches in Baxter's *Directory* occupies ever so much more space than in the *Summæ theologicæ* of the Catholic writers. Let us hear Baxter on the subject.

How little do the wealth and honours of the world concern a soul that is going into another world, and knows not but it may be this night. Then keep the wealth, or take it with thee, if thou canst.

Labour to feel thy greatest wants, which worldly wealth will not supply.

Thou art dead in sin and polluted and captivated by the flesh, and money will sooner increase thy bondage than deliver thee.

Will honest poverty or overloved wealth be sweeter at last?

Remember that riches do make it much harder for a man to be saved. Remember the apostle's word (I Tim. vi. 10): "The love of money is the root of all evil." Do you believe that here lieth the danger of your souls? And yet can you so love and choose and seek it?

Worldliness makes the Word unprofitable, and keepeth men from believing and repenting and coming home to God and minding seriously the everlasting world. What so much hindereth the conversion of sinners as the love and cares of earthly things? They cannot serve God and Mammon.

In a word, as ye have heard, "the love of money is the root of all evil," and the love of the Father is not in the lovers of the world.

Remember that riches are no part of your felicity. Yea, remember that riches are not the smallest temptation and danger to your souls. . . . It is not for nothing that Christ giveth so many terrible warnings about riches, and so describeth the folly, the danger, and the misery of the worldly-rich . . . and telleth you how hardly the rich are saved.[323]

Baxter summarizes the evil consequences of the love of money under ten headings, viz. it draws the heart away from God; it stops the ear to His word; it makes impossible holy meditation and conference; it steals the time needful for preparing for death; it generates spite between neighbours and wars between nations; it is the source of all unrighteousness and oppression; it destroys charity and good works; it disordereth and profaneth families; it is the very price that the devil gives for souls; and it distracts from communion with God.

If wealth is thus frowned upon, how much more its acquisition, especially by means of capitalist undertaking.

Here, too, the Gospel provides a watchword : " Take no thought for the morrow."

He that is greedy of gain troubleth his own house, but he that hateth gifts shall live. Do you not know that a godly man contented with his daily bread hath a far sweeter and quieter life and death than a self-troubling worldling ?

If Christ did scrape and care for riches, then so do thou ; if He thought it the happiest life, do you think so too. But if He contemned it, do thou contemn it.

If you had believed that the gain of holy wisdom had been better than the gaining of gold, as Solomon saith (Prov. iii. 14), you would have laid out much of that time in labouring to understand the Scriptures, and preparing for your endless life.

Piercing sorrows here and damnation hereafter are a very dear price to give for money.

Take heed lest the success and prosperity of your affairs do too much please you.[324]

I have hitherto quoted Baxter because he is the typical representative of the Puritan moral teachers. All of them, however, were inimical to acquisitiveness ; all of them are everlastingly asking, Why care for earthly goods ? Why take thought for to-morrow ? The words are almost identical with those of Baxter.

When men are not content with food and raiment but would still heap up more, it is just with God to leave them not so much as bread ; and to suffer men to have an evil eye upon them, even so long as they have meat.

Ye may have things necessary here — food and raiment ; and if ye seek more, if ye will be rich, and will have superfluities, then ye shall fall into many temptations, snares, and hurtful lusts which shall drown you in perdition.

And certainly to crave and be desirous of more than what is competent for the maintenance and support of our lives is both inconsistent with that dependance and subjection we owe to God, and doth also bespeak a great deal of vanity, folly, and inconsiderateness.

Why should men rack their heads with cares how to provide for to-morrow, while they know not if they shall then need anything ?[325]

Men are loth to lend their ears to the Word, when they abound in prosperity.

Such is the weakness even of godly men that they can hardly live in a prosperous condition and not be overtaken with some security, carnal confidence, or other miscarriage.[326]

It was only to be expected that this condemnation of all earthly goods was paralleled by a strong recommendation to turn the mind to God. Every moment spent not in the service of God is lost. Every hour spent in prayer, in attention to sermons, in holy ceremonies, is fruitful of treasures that cannot be compared with money. Time is only wasted with " excess of worldly cares and business." Men so occupied are full of mundane thoughts from early morn till late at night. The world leaves them no time for earnest communion, and robs them of precious moments which belong to God and their immortal souls—moments for prayer, reading, or conference on holy matters.[327]

For many a year life was moulded in accordance with views such as these, especially in Scotland, the stronghold of Puritanism. Which means that the greater part of men's waking hours were spent in church or in preparation for the Church services. Markets were forbidden to be held, certainly in the 17th century, on Saturdays, Sundays, and Mondays. There were week-day services, morning and evening, in all the churches ; sermons were delivered twice and even three times a week ; in the year 1650 an address was given every afternoon. In 1653 a weekly programme was instituted for religious exercises. For Wednesdays, fasting and eight hours' prayer and preaching ; for Saturdays, two or three sermons ; for Sundays, twelve hours' service in church ; for Mondays, three or four sermons.[328]

To flee from the world—that was the ideal of every word, of every action of the pious Puritan of those days.

There had been nothing like it since the early Christian sects. Nevertheless, Puritanism did not altogether suppress the capitalist spirit. Indeed, certain of its aspects unconsciously facilitated its growth. Puritanism served the interests of its arch-enemy, capitalism, in that it took up and developed the ethical principles of scholasticism passionately and with a singleness of purpose.

Puritanism re-echoed the old watchwords : Rationalize life ; keep the passions under control ; let reason dominate the natural inclinations. " Take nothing and do nothing merely because the sense or appetite would have it, but because you have reason so to do." [329] These words of Baxter appear again and again insistently. Once more the master-sin is sensuality, flesh-pleasing or voluptuousness. Isaac Barrow's treatise *Of Industry* sums up the fundamental teaching of Puritanism. " We should govern and regulate according to very strict and severe laws all the faculties of our soul, all the members of our body, all internal motions and all external actions proceeding from us ; we should check our inclinations, curb our appetites and compose our passions ; we should guard our hearts from vain thoughts and bad desires ; we should bridle our tongues from evil and from idle discourses ; we should order our steps in the straight way of righteousness, not deflecting to the right hand or to the left." [330]

Conduct of this kind was held to lead to grace, and every individual had to keep close watch on himself if he would retain that grace. So the habit was formed of fashioning the whole of life on the basis of reason, in accordance with the will of God. Not that the average man ever gave the theory of it a thought. Sufficient for him that the minister proclaimed God's desire for a particular conduct of life, which to the pious was just the sum total of a number of behests. These he obeyed according to the measure of the fear of God within him. He was no different in this respect from the good Catholic, who had likewise to plague himself with self-control. If anything, the Puritan was stricter in his observance. Now, as the doctrines of scholasticism and Puritanism were identical in their terms, the sternness of the Puritan can be accounted for only by the deeper religious feelings of the 17th-century man.

It is curious how the single virtues are recommended to the faithful by the Puritan preachers and the Catholic doctors in exactly the same way, word for word. Life was to be ordered aright, so both demanded ; and the middle-class virtues which each proclaimed were identical.

First as to industry : " By industry we understand a serious and steady application of mind, joined with a rigorous exercise of our active faculties in prosecution of any reasonable, honest, useful design in order to the accomplishment or attainment of some considerable good ; as, for instance, a merchant is industrious, who continueth intent and active in driving on his trade for acquiring wealth." [331] Industry is desired of God. All gifts, of course, come from Him, but His will is that we should attain them by work. We are therefore to be industrious. That is the burden of Isaac Barrow's dissertation, which quotes the Old Testament freely. "Shall we alone be idle, while all things are so busy ? We may easily observe every creature about us incessantly working toward the end for which it was designed, indefatigably exercising the powers with which it is endowed ; diligently observing the law of its creation. . . ." [332] Is not this the repetition of what St. Antonine wrote ? And this likewise ? " Idleness is indeed the nursery of sins, which as naturally grow up therein as weeds in a neglected field or insects in a standing puddle : ' Idleness teaches much evil ' (Eccles. xxxiii. 27)." 333

Next, employ your time usefully ; games, gaming, hunting, and masked balls are evil things and should be avoided.334

Thirdly, in both codes sensuality and drunkenness are of the Devil, and are deadly sins. Possibly there was greater control of these things in the Puritan countries in the 17th century than in the Italian cities in the 15th. We are told, for example, of an elaborate and refined spying system in Scotland.335 Perhaps, too, the demands of religion were more insistent among the Puritans.than among the Schoolmen. In particular the sexual life of individuals was more closely watched in Puritan than in Catholic countries. Purity among the Anglo-Saxons became prudery. It is not too much to say that Puritanism is responsible for the humbug and hypocrisy in sexual matters in old England no less than in New England across the Atlantic. " We separate the sexes," boasts an American Quaker merchant of the 18th century to a French colleague, " for when they are together they melt away like snow in the sun." 336

Fourth in order comes economy, a master virtue with the Schoolmen and the Puritans alike. In 17th-century Scotland the preachers reintroduced sumptuary laws, insisting that there should be strict economy in clothing, in house-room, and at celebrations of weddings and the like.337 Is it not well-known that Quakers drove economy to excess, applying it even to words, gestures, and the names of the days of the week ? 338

But all Protestant sects took an extremist view of economy, so much so that we are perhaps on the track of one—the only one—point of divergence in the social ethics of the Puritans and the Schoolmen. It can be best expressed by saying that Puritanism utterly crushed the least sign of any artistic longing for sensuous magnificence and grandeur. Far otherwise was the outlook of scholasticism. Its beauty was that it sprang from a deeply artistic temperament. Even yet we may perceive in it the heavenly spirit of the Augustinian outlook on life. Recall St. Thomas's words about the glorious harmony of the world and of man, a harmony worthy of beautiful expression, even as Dionysius pointed out, who said : "God as the source of harmony in the universe is robed in beauty." So the body's comeliness is in the harmony of its members, and the harmony of conduct worthy of reason is the beauty of the soul. St. Augustine, indeed, calls honesty a " spiritual beauty."

All this sense of the artistic expresses itself in the recognition as a virtue of high rank of something which finds no place whatever in any of the systems of Protestant ethics. I refer to what the Schoolmen called *magnificentia*, which denoted the striving to accomplish what is great and glorious. In the first place, you think of the Church and public life. But you are by no means to exclude a love of the ornate from your own life, whether it be for special occasions, as, for example, a wedding-feast, or for constant enjoyment, as, for example, your home. And of course in works of art this love of beauty and magnificence must most certainly express itself.[339]

The Protestants had lost all sense of beauty ; *magnificentia* found no place in their ethical and religious system, well-suited as it was to their cold, drab, whitewashed, pictureless kirks,[340] that took the place of the noble Gothic piles with their "storied windows richly dight casting a dim religious light." Indeed, in Puritan ethics the very opposite of *magnificentia*, miserliness, became one of the cardinal virtues. The Schoolmen, on the other hand, had condemned it as a deadly sin. " A man is termed a miser when he is small-minded in doing things.

. . . He who loves pomp and magnificence first thinks out his plan and then considers the great expense, which for the sake of the result he does not shrink from. The miser, however, first reflects how much a thing will cost before he decides upon it, his object all the time being to spend as little as possible." [341]

Nevertheless, to change parsimony into miserliness was one of the chief services rendered to capitalism by Puritan and Quaker ethics, unless it be held that the removal of the ban on interest was a greater service. This I myself doubt. We have already observed that the mediæval prohibition of interest was really a blessing in disguise for the capitalist spirit. Consequently the attitude of the later moralists to interest and usury was of little moment.

But there are a number of things for which Puritanism was certainly not responsible. First and foremost, it had nothing to do with middle-class virtues as such, seeing that when Puritanism arose these had been in existence for several centuries. Does not Alberti know them all to perfection? If any religious system is to be made responsible for them, it must be Catholicism. Protestantism merely took over what the Schoolmen had created.

Nor do I think Puritanism accountable for the boundless development of acquisitiveness, and the senseless desire to make money anyhow, which characterizes the capitalist spirit at its zenith. Puritan preachers were totally averse to all money-getting. In so far as they did reckon with natural acquisitiveness and the desire for riches, there was always the condition, implied or expressed, that riches were not to be regarded as an end in themselves. Wealth could be justified only when it was spent in ways pleasing to God, and so long as it did not endanger the salvation of the undertaker. Here again we meet with the precisely similar language of the Schoolmen. Baxter is not opposed to riches, but they must only be used for doing good—" in the service of God, in beneficence to our neighbour, in advancing public good." Or again, " Riches may enable us to relieve our needy brethren and promote good works for Church and state." Once more, " That you make not riches your chief end : riches for our fleshly ends must not ultimately be intended or sought. But—in subordination to higher things they may. Then your end must be, that you may be better provided to do God service, and may do the more good with what you have. You may labour to be rich for God, though not for the flesh and sin." 342

In the third place, unscrupulous money-getting cannot be laid at the door of Puritanism. Like scholasticism it preached the need for honourable ways in business. " What a man compasseth by honest industry that he is apt highly to prize." 343 Moreover, Puritanism clung to the doctrine of " just price " current among the Schoolmen. And what does " just price " mean but the subjection of the market to the laws of righteousness and the cheapening of wares ? Free competition Puritanism condemned utterly. " It is a false rule of them that think their commodity is worth as much as any one will give. But it is taken for granted in the market that every man will get as much as he can have and that ' Caveat emptor ' is ' the only security.' It is not so among Christians, nor infidels who profess either truth or common honesty." 344

Finally, I doubt very much whether Puritanism was the cause of the great undertakings that appeared later in Puritan countries. Puritanism hardly encouraged far-sighted and adventurous enterprises ; shopkeeping was the most it could achieve. Your Scotchman is a Puritan. But to regard as Puritans men like Cecil Rhodes and the really great undertakers who came to the fore in England

and America in the 19th century, that is hardly warranted by the facts. It would be but a narrow conception of the capitalist spirit thus to see its various manifestations springing from Puritanism. The truth is that our latter-day " merchant adventurers " are all made of very different stuff ; their progenitors were the Raleighs, the Cavendishes, the Drakes, the Fuggers, and the rest of them, who, born before Puritanism became a force, were immune from the abstruse stuff which a ghost like Mr. Baxter crammed into the *Christian Dictionary.*

It cannot be denied, of course, that there were some great capitalist undertakers among the Puritans. But whether they owed their greatness to Puritan ethics is doubtful. It was more probably much more due to their racial qualities or to fortune's guiding hand, as we shall have occasion to consider in due course. One factor, and only one, may have helped the capitalist spirit, and that was the subjection of the undertaker to the laws of Puritan ethics. But deep this influence could never have been.

CHAPTER XX

JUDAISM

FOR a detailed consideration of the influences of Judaism on economic life, especially on the development of the capitalist spirit, I would refer the reader to my book, *The Jews and Modern Capitalism*.

On the whole, my views on the subject have undergone little change since I wrote that book, despite the criticism levelled against it, particularly by learned Rabbis. There is only one point to which I should like to reply. It has been suggested that I have overlooked certain aspects of Judaism ; for example, its mystical elements. Without going into the merits of the question, I need only add that my business was to lay bare the relationship of Judaism and capitalism. To this end there was no necessity for me to include in my survey of the problem such elements of Judaism as had no influence whatever on the capitalist spirit. Jewish mysticism was therefore not mentioned, just as in my consideration of the scholastic ethics I leave out of account its Pauline and Augustinian doctrines of love, though these are part and parcel of official Catholicism.

This particular criticism thus falls to the ground. Nevertheless, there is one important point on which I must revise my opinions.

When I wrote the book on the Jews and modern capitalism I had not made a study of the ethics of Aquinas.

Accordingly, many doctrines of Judaism (for example, the conditional recognition of wealth, or the behest to rationalize the whole of life), seemed to me specifically and uniquely Jewish, and I contrasted them with the Christian views prevalent in the pre-Puritan age. That was an error. Those portions of Judaism which were of great significance for our problem were by no means unique. They certainly were not in their entirety part of early Christianity, but as certainly they found a place in scholastic morality. There is nothing surprising in this, inasmuch as the Schoolmen looked upon Jewish moral laws as the kernel of the divine law of nature. Truth to tell, Judaism, Catholicism, and Puritanism all expressed themselves alike on those points which are vital for our problem.

Nevertheless, there are elements in Judaism that differentiate it from the two other religious systems (always bearing in mind that I am referring to those parts of it only which had any bearing on capitalism). What is especially peculiar to Judaism is that it perfected and carried to their logical conclusions all those teachings that were beneficial to the capitalist spirit.

Take its attitude to riches. It is a shade more favourable than even that of the Schoolmen. Nor is this surprising. Judaism found support for its views in the Old Testament, wherein riches and prosperity in ninety-nine cases out of a hundred were not classed as an evil; whereas Christian moralists had to get over the New Testament ideal of poverty. Judaism never formulated a poverty ideal.

As for the rationalization of life, it is preached much more thoroughly, and was given a more comprehensive connotation, in Judaism than in Catholicism. The Jewish attitude was closely akin to the Puritan. More especially was this the case in the subjugation of the sexual appetite.

This assuredly occupied an important place in Scholasticism too, but in Judaism and Puritanism it was a sterner demand, turning self-control in both into a caricature that made you shiver.

Similarly, Judaism and Puritanism have in common their suppression of every artistic taste, which, as we have seen, Aquinas allows and makes much of. In fact, the second commandment seems to have been quite disregarded by the Schoolmen ; in Judaism, on the other hand, its influence was immense.

Jewish ethics require a place apart, so far as their influence on the modern spirit goes, for yet another reason. They received form and shape at a time when Christianity moved in such different channels. While Christianity was yet held in bond by the Essene ideal of poverty, Judaism did not reject riches ; while the former was filled with Pauline and Augustinian spirit of love, the latter preached a rabid and extremist nationalism. Thus all those ethical regulations that were favourable to the development of the capitalist spirit were influential in Judaism a thousand years longer than in Christianity. Moreover, in the course of a long period of history the process of selection was at work among the Jews, eliminating the units too weak for capitalism and allowing the strong capitalist types to survive. Accordingly, when the capitalist epoch in modern history commenced, the Jews, thanks to their religion, had undergone a more thorough and longer training for it than any Christian people. Had other things been equal the Jews would in this way have had an enormous advantage over non-Jews.

In one respect, however, Judaism was able to exercise an almost revolutionary influence : in its attitude to the stranger. Jewish ethics, Janus-like, was given two aspects. One was applicable for intercourse with Jews, the other for intercourse with non-Jews. All early peoples had this double-barrelled morality, with one code of conduct towards the tribesmen and another towards the stranger. But the fate of the Jews through long centuries perpetuated this twofold code, and until quite recently gave their commercial principles a peculiar tendency.

This special law for the stranger the reader will find elaborated in my *Jews and Modern Capitalism.** Here we need only refer to its consequences. In the first place, intercourse with strangers was bereft of all considerations, and commercial morality (if I may put it so) became elastic ; in the second, the differential treatment of non-Jews in Jewish commercial law resulted in the complete transformation of the idea of commerce and industry, generally in the direction of more freedom. We have called the Jews the Fathers of Free Trade and therefore of capitalism. They were prepared for this rôle by the free-trading spirit of their commercial and industrial law. This received an enormous impetus towards a policy of *laissez-faire* by its attitude towards strangers. And if free trade and industrial freedom were in accordance with Jewish law, they were in accordance with the will of God. Think what a mighty motive power this was in economic life !

* [See especially pp. 242–48.]

CHAPTER XXI

MORAL INFLUENCES AND THE CAPITALIST SPIRIT

In the preceding chapter we have been occupied, without prejudice, not to say naïvely, with the influence of moral forces on the growth of the capitalist spirit. But with what justice? For we have yet to satisfy ourselves that the influence was a real one. The preceding pages have by no means proved this. What they did show was that in numerous instances there is a parallelism between certain aspects of the capitalist spirit and certain teachings of philosophy and religion.

It may be objected that the parallelism is not necessarily due to interaction between the two groups. It is quite well possible to imagine that the capitalist spirit drew its nurture from other sources which happened to give it the same colouring as ethical teaching might have done. Or, an even more damaging objection may be urged, one that is to be expected considering the prevailing trend of thought in some quarters. It is admitted that ethics and the capitalist spirit have interacted, but the interaction was the very opposite of that which we have assumed. The capitalist spirit was not shaped by philosophy and religion, but, on the contrary, these reflected the prevailing economic conditions. A consideration of the question is essential, but we shall be brief.

Think as you like of the genius of the founder of a religion, this much is clear—that before any religion can

strike root certain conditions must exist. Economic
conditions are of the number, but they are not the only
ones. Biological and ethnological factors play a very
important part too. In a word, the totality of a people's
life—its blood and its social state—determines whether or
no any religion (or indeed any philosophical system, for
the same to a less degree holds good of that too) is
accepted, and the totality of its life likewise explains the
development of the adopted religion through the ages.
This is what is meant when we say that a people has a
certain disposition for some religion. " As well expect
seed to bring forth fruit from a flinty rock as a philosophical religion of love to be accepted by ignorant and
wild savages."

This disposition in a people will be influenced more
and more by economic conditions the nearer we approach
our own times, seeing that economic life, anyhow in the
modern history of Western Europe, has dominated man
to a greater and greater degree. Consequently, the
more recent a religion is, the more likely is economic
life to have a strong influence upon it.

This in my view is a fundamental dictum, and we
shall best see its truth by comparing the influence of
economic life on the different systems of Christianity in
their respective epochs.

To ascribe any influence whatever to economic conditions on the Augustinian doctrines is clearly to subvert
facts. They had none. But when we come to scholasticism, the influence of economic life is somewhat
marked. I am inclined to think that the development
of scholastic ethics in the 14th and 15th centuries was
very much affected by the economic development of the
period. On the whole, however, we may take it that
Catholicism, even in the later Middle Ages, continued to
draw on its earliest founts, and not on those of its own

time or place. As we have already seen, it was a composite of religious experience, the wisdom of every-day
life, the maxims of later antiquity and the morality of
the Jews.

Still more marked is the influence of economic life on
Calvinism. The somewhat advanced capitalist system of
its age was not without results on this species of Protestantism. Economic conditions forced from Puritanism
the admission that the bourgeois mode of life was not
opposed to the state of Grace. The true nature of
Puritanism was absolutely inimical to capitalism. The
Puritan preachers of the 16th and 17th centuries would
have been very much inclined to consign the whole
business of Mammon-service to the depths of the sea, and
to have replaced it by the subsistence economic order of
the early Middle Ages with its small peasants and craftsmen. Such a social system was more in accord with
their other-worldly teaching. But it was too late. It
was impossible for them to do what Luther had
succeeded in doing in the economically backward
Germany of his day—ignore capitalism altogether.
With heavy hearts, no doubt, they had to reckon with
it, and they sought as best they could to bring it into
accord with their religious views. How much it
entered into these is manifest in their mode of present-
ing their doctrines. Many a time and oft they utilize
pictures and comparisons from economic activities.
Thus, one writer urges that when the " Saint " takes
stock of his sins, let him think of them as capital and
interest, so that " the sanctification of life may become as
it were a business." Baxter himself, in explaining God's
invisibility, remarks that just as by correspondence one
man may carry on profitable business with another whom
he has never seen, so too it is possible by means of
"holy intercourse " with the invisible Deity to obtain " a

precious pearl." Commercial similes such as these were characteristic of Puritanism, which in effect suggested that man should bargain for his salvation.345

But there was nothing new in this ; these ideas were to be found in Judaism in abundance, as I have shown in my book on the Jews and capitalism. The probability is that the Puritan preachers found the similes and metaphors they used in the writings of their Jewish colleagues. That they adopted them only shows that capitalism was already firmly rooted in their day, seeing that Jewish theological thought was most suited to capitalist conditions. Had the Puritan preachers lived in the manorial or gild stage of social development, it would have been absurd if, in order to drive home this message, they had referred by way of illustration to book-keeping, capital, or interest.

However (and this is the important thing), once a religion (or a philosophical system) has become accepted, there can be no doubt that its teachings, surrounded with a divine halo as they often are, cannot but influence the whole of life, and therefore also of economic activities. It would indeed be passing strange were not the mental and moral outlook of the economic agent conditioned by systematic and reiterated instruction in a special ethical code.

But this influence depends for its effectiveness on two considerations, one personal, the other external.

The personal consideration is simple enough. If ethical dogmas are to have any practical influence on economic conduct they must be real forces in the life of men. The best ethical teaching in the world would be useless if no one believed in it and carried it out. This condition certainly held good in the age of early capitalism. The real, living interest in philosophy during the period of the Renaissance and the deep religiosity

prevalent in all lands until the 18th century are generally
admitted facts.

The other and external condition was likewise fulfilled
in the early capitalist age, in that capitalism was then but
slightly developed. For as long as any economic order is
in process of growth, as long as it depends on the untrammelled decisions of individuals, the influence of ethical
teaching must necessarily be strongly marked upon it,
much more so than when every branch of economic
activity has become specialized, the processes almost automatic, and the individual economic agent held in the
system as in a vice.

We are thus led to this conclusion. .During the age of
early capitalism both considerations held, and therefore,
no matter what view we may entertain as to the origin of
religion and philosophy, there can be no doubt that both,
once they were established, contributed their quota to the
development of the capitalist spirit. In the parallelism
between the two, therefore, the moral forces were the
cause, the particular economic conduct the effect.

What precisely did the moral forces achieve for the
capitalist spirit ? I fancy we might point to three
things.

1. They produced a frame of mind, as we may term it,
favourable to capitalism. They helped the evolution of a
conception of life that was in accordance with reason, and
demanded order and method for its realization. The
philosophy of the later ancient world and the three
prevailing religious systems all shared in that.

2. They contributed to the cultivation of middle-class
virtues, beloved and recommended alike by the sages of
philosophy and the saints of religion.

3. They put a brake on the acquisition of wealth and
hemmed in economic activities.

Briefly expressed, it may be said that capitalism, down

to the end of this period, was under the restraining influences of Christian ethics. If you do not see that, you have not grasped the true nature of early capitalism.

But even during this period the old landmarks were being removed. Jewish ethics, as we have seen in considering its attitude to strangers, knew nothing of the ordinances that regulated and circumscribed the economic activities of Christians. The Jews, then, could take the open road in the direction of unrestricted and unscrupulous competition, and they did so quite early. But it was not until capitalism was full blown that unrestricted and unscrupulous competition became bone of its bone and flesh of its flesh. When this occurred religion, at any rate in Protestant countries, had undoubtedly lost its former domination, while equally undoubted was the increasing influence of Judaism. So that we may say that full-blown capitalism also owed something to moral forces—to the Christian religions, that they were no longer active ; to the Jewish, that it was.

But let us not overestimate the influence of moral forces on the economic life of the era wherein capitalism reached its most perfect form. Moral forces could not possibly have been responsible for the whole of capitalist development. Some share in it they certainly had, but we must be clear in our minds as to its limitations.

1. Observe that as long as ethical values were current, i.e. as long as men were religious (in the broadest connotation of the term), moral laws helped to shape the capitalist spirit under certain conditions.

2. But even so long as men continued to be religious, the capitalist spirit drew upon other sources also for its nutrition. Were this not the case, similar religious systems would have produced a capitalist spirit of exactly the same tenor. But this never hap-

pened : compare Spain and Italy. Nor could the same capitalist spirit have sprung from different religious systems : compare Italy, Germany, and America.

A little thought will suffice to make it clear that moral forces were not alone in shaping the capitalist spirit. Are not some of its aspects, are not many of the forms in which it expressed itself, quite beyond the possibility of being shaped ? Economic methods, for instance, cannot spring from moral behests.[346] And is not the capitalist spirit a composite conception to which numerous qualities of mind and heart have contributed ? Only some of these are subject to moral influences ; these alone, therefore, may be shaped or trained or educated. We called them virtues—intellectual and moral virtues—and both depend on the way intellect and will have been trained. They may be acquired by obedience to certain ethical teaching, though it is as well to remember incidentally that some natures acquire them more readily than others because of their peculiar " disposition." Anyhow, the influence of moral forces is limited to these virtues alone.

But there are other factors in the capitalist spirit of which some cannot at all be acquired, because they are natural gifts or talents, while others again depend on technical skill.

You are either born with talents or you are not. The makings of the daring capitalist undertaker, the brilliant speculator, or the wonderful calculator are in the blood. No moral force in the world can make a genius out of a good-for-nothing fellow or a calculator out of a dreamer. Of course, talents may be trained and perfected ; they may even be added to. But in either case there is no question of the influence of moral forces.

As for technical skill, I refer to such things as the capacity of controlling a business, or organizing ability in general. These may be learned, but moral forces have nothing to do with them. After all, it is clear enough that the most morally perfect man will be a bad capitalist undertaker if his book-keeping is on a wrong system or his calculations have grievous errors in them.

The truth is that all the abilities of the capitalist depend on three things—on the sum total of technical skill in existence, on the personal capacity of each one to learn them, and on the will-power in the learning process. Only the last has a point of contact with moral forces ; the other two are wholly independent of them. Technical improvements depend on the inventing capacity, which people either have or not ; how quickly and perfectly any one may learn to utilize them and work them depends on his native ability, which, as we know, varies in each individual. The average of this ability may be raised in the course of generations by a process of selection. But moral forces have nothing to do with that.

It is evident, then, that many elements of the capitalist spirit are wholly independent of the influence of moral forces, even though these may still hold sway over men's minds. But what if they have lost this power, as has certainly been the case among Christians ever since the period of early capitalism came to an end ? What if in the interval the capitalist spirit has evolved through revolutionary changes ; changes that were only possible by rejecting the doctrines of Christian morality, Protestant and Catholic alike ; changes that resulted from breaking through the bounds which both Catholicism and Protestantism set to economic activities ; changes that were in accord with only one ethical system—the Jewish ? It would really be too much to ascribe the characteristics of modern man in his economic life to the influence of Jewish ethics, though truth to tell that influence was not by any means slight.

There is no alternative but to discover other forces which contributed to the shaping of perfect capitalism. Other forces must, as a matter of fact, always have existed. In the early capitalist period they stood side by side with the moral forces ; in the period of perfected capitalism they took their place. These other forces resulted from the existing social conditions—the consideration of which has been reserved for the next section.

SECTION III

THE SOCIAL CONDITIONS

CHAPTER XXII

THE STATE

In the next chapters I propose to point to the external, i.e. social, circumstances that have had a directing influence on the psychological development of modern man regarded as an " economic animal." But obviously I shall on the one hand have to limit myself to a fairly comprehensive general survey of the mass of complex causes, and, on the other, to bring into relief a few points which appear to me to be of special importance. To do more would mean writing the economic history of the last five hundred years; it might even mean writing the whole history of civilization during that period, seeing that the problem in which we are specially interested has a more or less close connection with almost every aspect of that history.

The first in the mass of complex causes that I mention is the state. And I do so not only because of the tremendous influence exercised by the state on the development of the spirit of capitalism (more especially in its earliest stages), but also because the state, like a husk which encloses the kernel, contains within itself a large number of other complex causes.

To begin with, I want to indicate how the state helped the capitalistic spirit to grow. But before doing this let me mention in what way the state has also hindered capitalism.

There can be no doubt that the theory of bullionism driven to excess may be a stumbling-block to enterprise, and may eventually even crush it altogether. If taxes are very heavy, if they reduce profits either by being too much of a burden to the employing class or by raising wages make competition with foreign lands impossible, it is obvious that the desire to invest capital will be weakened. The economic decline of Spain since the 17th century, and the speedy disappearance of Dutch industry in the 18th century, have both been attributed to the great pressure of taxation. Similarly (though to be sure to a lesser extent) a wrong commercial or industrial policy may set bounds to enterprise ; and an extremist social programme in a state might have the same effect, though there is no actual case on record up to the present.

But the capitalist spirit has been hemmed by the growth of the modern state in another direction. I refer to national debts, where the complaint about a wrong policy was scarcely apposite. In another place 347 I have adduced figures to show what enormous sums have flowed into the coffers of states since the Middle Ages, more especially for warlike undertakings. This loss of life-blood deprived the body economic of a good deal of its strength, despite the fact that the spending of the sums collected increased production. For not only was instrumental capital lessened, but enterprise received little encouragement ; at any rate, when money could be invested in profitable public loans its development was not so fast as it might have been. Directly the moneyed classes, instead of putting their money into capitalist undertakings, begin to buy government securities, they at once sink into what may be termed a state of economic lethargy. This was a general complaint in the 17th and 18th centuries in England, France, and Holland on the part of those who were well disposed to capitalism. Money that might have been used to create thriving trade and industry found its way, it was said, into the public treasuries, which paid a high rate of interest for it.[348]

One of the most effective methods of killing the spirit of enterprise manifested itself in France, where, as we have already seen, the traffic in offices under the crown became a marked characteristic of public life throughout many centuries. The form this evil took was different from that of the public debt ; but the effect was the same. The rich became comfortable and interested themselves no longer in capitalistic enterprise. We have here a specially good example of the interdependence of the different forces which influenced the capitalist spirit. The French national spirit, little gifted as it was for capitalism (probably, as we have seen, because of its Celtic origin), had recourse to the selling of government posts as a method of utilizing money best suited to its nature. This in its turn had a clogging influence on enterprise, with the result that any capitalist qualities that may have existed in France were starved. And so on in an everlasting circle.

The same effects may ensue from the attitude of the state to the different social groups within it. Suppose it favours the nobility, which neither knows nor cares for commerce ; suppose it raises to the highest social grade the most successful elements of the middle class. Will it be possible to say with certainty what is cause and what effect ; or whether the lack of interest in capitalist affairs was due to the ennobling of simple burghers or the ennobling merely the outward recognition of an internal atrophy ?

But when all is said, the advantages that the capitalist

spirit enjoyed at the hands of the state in all manner
of ways more than compensated for these obstacles.

In the first place, the state wished to help capitalism
forward, and so adopted a number of regulations in its
favour. Indeed, as we already know, the state was itself
one of the earliest of capitalist undertakers and invariably
continued to be one of the largest. In this way it set
an example to private enterprise; it showed the way in
all matters of capitalist organization, and it was educative
in questions of commercial morality. But it also exerted
an influence in the transvaluation of social values. By
itself engaging in business the state removed the prejudice
against " low callings " which prevailed in the pre-
capitalist era ; it raised the *artes sordidæ* to the position
of being activities fit for gentlemen.

But greater still was the indirect influence of the state,
chiefly because of its particular economic policy. Let it
not be forgotten that capitalist interests in the era of
early capitalism were favoured tremendously by the
mercantile system. In accordance with the doctrines of
mercantilism the state, as it were, almost led the private
citizen by the hand in order to direct his activities into
the channels of capitalist undertaking. It pushed him
into capitalism ; it held out good reasons for his
remaining there. This picture of physical force is
actually to be found in a cameralist writer of the 18th
century, who holds " that the lower orders will not give
up their old ways until they are dragged by the nose and
the arms to their new advantages."349 In the same
way Colbert's efforts to stir up his lazy countrymen are
positively touching.350 As for England, behind ever so
many undertakings in the 16th and 17th centuries we
see the monarch as the direct moving force, for he was
financially interested in them. The Drakes and the
Raleighs were urged, in long interviews, to set out on

new expeditions. The idea that Raleigh should sail to
Guiana emanated from the impecunious James I,351 and
in the reign of his successor we find the King's agents up
and down the country making profitable contracts with
industrial undertakers.352

Nor must we leave unmentioned the system of privileges by which the mercantile state favoured such
capitalist interests as already existed, nursed those that
were about to take root, and planted new ones. The
real meaning of these state privileges (using the word
in its widest connotation) is best brought out in a letter
of Henry II of France, dated June 13, 1558, in which
he expresses the hope that his privileges and benevolence
may act as a spur to honest and industrious handicrafts-
men to undertake profitable enterprises.353 In every
case the underlying idea was the same—to stir up the
spirit of enterprise by the inducement of material or
other advantages. The privileges took different forms.
Sometimes they were monopolies, negative privileges as
it were, in that a monopoly for producing a particular
article was granted, or a monopoly of trade, or again a
monopoly in the means of communication. Sometimes
they meted out special commercial advantages to their
holders ; sometimes, too, they were direct bounties. In
his *Dictionnaire* Savary gives a list of some of the
inducements held out to spur on new undertakings :
you were made a peer, or you were naturalized, or you
were excused custom dues, or had a loan made to you
without interest, or you received a pension or a grant
of land. " All manner of inventions were assisted by
privileges and protection ; the King's treasury was on
the look-out for all those who had made any invention
in order to give them a reward." What is this but state
assistance and support for the " projects " of which we
have already discoursed ?

Similarly, by the break-up of the mercantile system and the introduction of economic liberty in the 19th century, the state also cultivated the spirit of enterprise —to a limited extent, it is true, seeing that it already flourished at the time. More effective in the impetus it gave to the capitalist spirit was the stress laid on education in all its branches. We have already observed how the establishment of educational institutions was to be regarded as a sign that the capitalist spirit in one form or another was in existence ; here it is our business to lay stress on their importance as a nursery of that spirit. From the arithmetic schools, founded in Florence as early as the 14th century, to the commercial colleges of our own day, the institutions which were established by public bodies to spread the sort of knowledge useful to the trader have all become centres where the capitalist spirit throve. Did they not all teach the art of calculating and the rules for carrying on commerce ?

I am of opinion, however, that some of the effects of state action which were hardly contemplated were of more significance for the growth of capitalism than those which the state of set purpose tried to achieve. The very non-existence of the state (if I may put it so) was in many cases of tremendous advantage to capitalism. What I mean is that the peculiar conditions in a state, which for a time were unfavourable to the rise of a great political entity, formed a splendid environment for the speedy growth and development of the capitalist spirit. Take Switzerland, or Germany before 1870. The Swiss and the Germans had no mighty state to back them up and win markets for them ; consequently, in their economic activities they had to rely on themselves to a great degree. They had to accommodate themselves to the needs of customers ; if they wanted to capture trade they were forced to do so by their skill in selling and the excellence of their commodities. Hence their wits were sharpened and their backs adjusted to any burden. All this meant the development of the capitalist spirit, more especially of its commercial elements. We have already seen some special characteristics of the German bourgeois spirit, clearly distinguishing it from the English, and one reason for the difference will be found in the lack of German unity, which prevented it from obtaining assured colonial markets, and forced its merchants and captains of industry to win respect abroad, to carve out for themselves "a place in the sun" without the help of a navy.354

But if the "non-existence" of the state was effective in forwarding the capitalist spirit, much more so was its existence. The state may be regarded as one of the basic forms of enterprise, showing the way to the other great capitalist undertakings in the organization of its officials, in the extensiveness of its aim, and in the persistence of its efforts. Organizing ability was thus encouraged and developed.

Some branches of state activity influenced the growth of the capitalist spirit in a special degree. The first and foremost of these was the army. It may be said that the rise of the professional military class—in the Middle Ages the feudal army, in modern times the paid army—was one of those social phenomena which had far-reaching results. For what was its significance? Specialization had set in, and the demand was no longer for a complete man, struggling for his existence, no longer for a man who possessed both military and economic capacities, but only for half a man—that is to say, for one who devoted himself to military or to economic affairs. The result of such differentiation was obvious. Those virtues which we have termed "middle-class" had a better chance of growth, and the trading spirit, freed from any admixture

of military elements, was able to develop apace. For an
effective illustration look at the Florentines. The
burghers of the famous Italian Republic as early as
the 13th century engaged hired soldiers for their
defence. How different would the Florentine commercial spirit have been if the good citizens had had, like
German peasants, to bear arms themselves in defence
of hearth and home. Indeed, so keen an observer as
Alberti traces the conspicuous trading ability of his fellow-
citizens to the very fact that in his native town there was
no occasion to exercise the soldier's craft. This being
the case, he avers, men sought for themselves honoured
positions in the state by accumulating gold, and they got
gold by trading.355

If the Florentines furnish one illustration of the general
statement, the Jews supply another. The Jews may be
taken as the most perfect type of a trading people. But
how did they become such? Surely no small reason was
that Fate for 2,000 years deprived them of any need of
cultivating warlike activities. The warlike natures among
them thus gradually disappeared.

The growth of modern armies has brought two forces
to the fore—discipline on the one hand, and organizing
talent on the other. The influence of standing armies
on the capitalist spirit, so far as these two forces are
concerned, is plain enough.356

Look at the military virtues as they have grown up
since the 17th century. Are they not all essentially
those of capitalism? Nor must we forget that before
ever organization began to play its very important rôle
in modern capitalist undertakings, it was already a mighty
force in the management of armies. It is no accident,
therefore, that in the countries with a perfected military
system we find a great development of those capitalist
qualities that owe their existence to efficient military drill.

Take Germany. To-day, when capitalist enterprise is more and more extended, when it takes on more and more the appearance of a disposition of mighty armies in the field, it is only natural that Germans should profit by their military training. Unprejudiced foreigners admit the superiority of German capitalist undertakers in this respect. Here, for instance, is the view of an Englishman whose capacity for observation no one will deny. It is no exaggeration to say, he writes, that military service has an influence greater than any other on German industry. Employers and employed have both been through the training, they have both learned in the same school that order and discipline are needful for any organized ·powers, be they military or industrial.357

Finally, biological qualities and historic destiny both had an influence on the problem before us. Little did the guiding spirits of the time think, when modern states first began to have strong standing armies, that one element in the population would come to the fore as a result. I refer to the Jews. In my book on the relation between the Jews and capitalism I have shown in detail how this people, from the 17th century onward, furnished the ruling princes with the necessary money for carrying on wars, either by personal loans or by acting as agents on the stock exchanges (to the growth of which they contributed so much). Besides this, the Jews became army contractors, whereby not only was their wealth increased, but their social position also improved. It is not too much to say, therefore, that the growth of modern armies was responsible in no small measure for the emancipation of the Jews, and as the Jews were mightily concerned in extending the capitalist spirit, the latter may thus indirectly be traced, in this connection also, to the growth of standing armies.

Next in importance to the military factor we must consider the finances of the state in their influence on the growth of capitalism. Once more the Jews are the pivot. The princes of modern times were wise enough to utilize for their needs the services of Jewish financiers. The special treatment accorded to these men resulted in increasing Jewish influence. Now, whatever increased Jewish influence—and be this noted once for all—that also extended the spirit of capitalism in its highest form ; whether it was through the increase of Jewish undertakers or the influence of Christian undertakers by the Jewish spirit, or, again, by the impregnation of this spirit through the whole of economic life, or, finally, by the survival of those fittest for the new commercial enterprises.

The financial system of states was not without effects in other directions too. In its earlier stages its very forms contributed something to the growth of capitalism. We have it on record that the financial methods of the Italian republics are, in many respects, quite modern. There is little doubt now but that commercial bookkeeping first came to be used in connection with the finances of Genoa ; and we may assume that the need for exact statistical information must have arisen among those who were responsible for the finances of this thriving community. " A power such as that of Venice, resting as it did on so complicated a foundation, its activities and interests extending in very many directions, can scarcely be conceived without a thorough survey of the whole, without constant calculations as to strength and burdens, increases and declines. We may regard Venice, and Florence with it, as the cradle of modern statistics." [358] What influence a summary of social life in terms of figures may have had, we can well imagine. Calculations and qualitative manipulations, both factors of great significance in modern capitalism, must certainly have been cultivated.

In short, public finance furnished the first instance of "applied housekeeping" on a large scale, just as the modern state was the first great "undertaking." In both, therefore, capitalist ideas must have found a model.

As for the public debts, we have in them the first instance of contracts on a large scale which affected larger groups than the clan or the social class, and which therefore looked to other moral forces for their recognition than were to be found in primitive communities. "Social" sanctions had to be created; all those forces on which capitalist intercourse rests—commercial morality, confidence and credit, acceptances in advance over a long period of time with the intention of honouring them. Nowhere did these forces show themselves so early, nowhere was there as much opportunity for their exercise, as in the arrangements for the public debts of rising states and cities.

But the public indebtedness had other influences also on the capitalist spirit. Speculation was early associated with it; we need only recall the South Sea Bubble in England or the John Law fiasco in France. These may have been swindles; nevertheless, they were not without lessons for joint-stock enterprise in later times; and both would have been inconceivable without the peculiar and extensive growth of national debts.

Side by side with the army and the finances of the state we must place as the third great factor the state's ecclesiastical policy. Here once more we meet the Jews. For in a large point of view Jewish emancipation is part of ecclesiastical policy, and the importance of the Jews in the development of capitalism we have already seen. But in speaking of the ecclesiastical policy of modern states as an influence on the speedy growth of the capitalist spirit,

I have something very different in view. I refer to the
creation by the state, chiefly through the institution of a
national church, of the conception of the heretic or non-
conformist as a social or political category. Do we not
find two sorts of citizens in modern states—full citizens
and semi-citizens, according to the religion they profess?
The former belong to the national church and enjoy
full privileges of citizenship ; the latter subscribe to
the doctrines of other churches and are subject to civil
disabilities. The Jews were " semi-citizens " in this sense
pretty well everywhere down to the 18th century, and
in some countries even beyond that date. In Catholic
countries the Protestants, in Protestant countries the
Catholics, were in the same class. In Great Britain the
Presbyterians, the Quakers, and the rest were the nonconformists ; in the Presbyterian New England states
those who professed High Church doctrines.

This sort of heresy, quite apart from its particular
tenets, must be looked upon as an abundant well-spring of
capitalism. The reason is clear : it brought economic
interests to the fore and gave commercial ability a special
chance. Is it not obvious that the dissenters, excluded as
they were from public life, could not but throw all their
energies into economic activities? Only from this source
could they hope to derive the means for winning for
themselves respected positions in the body politic. What
wonder, then, that in this " excluded " class money was
valued more highly, other things being equal, than among
the rest of the population? For these people money was
the sole means to power.

On the other hand, it followed from their peculiar
position as dissenters that their economic activities were
hampered by all manner of difficulties. Hence there was
a tendency for their economic capacities to be highly
developed. For they could hope for commercial success

only from the most scrupulous conscientiousness, the most careful calculations, and the utmost endeavours to meet the needs of their customers. What says Benoit of the Huguenots? "Persecuted and suspected as they were, they were able to maintain their position only by wise conduct and honesty."

Now, in the first stages of capitalism, capitalist enterprise offered the greatest profits ; it held out the promise of wealth, and therefore of distinction. Consequently, it was only to be expected that the dissenters should throw themselves heart and soul into capitalist undertakings, and accordingly, in those critical times, say from the 16th to the 18th centuries, they were the foremost bankers, merchants, and manufacturers. In a word, they dominated trade. Contemporary observers were not blind to this tendency. The Spaniards asserted that heresy was good for trade. And in England, this is what was written by a man so gifted with insight as William Petty :—

Moreover, it is to be observed that trade doth not (as some think) best flourish under popular governments, but rather that trade is most vigorously carried on, in every state and government, by the Heterodox part of the same, and such as profess opinions different from what are publicly established : (that is to say) in India, where the Mahometan religion is authorized, there the Banians are the most considerable merchants. In the Turkish Empire the Jews and Christians. At Venice, Naples, Leghorn, Genoa, and Lisbon, Jews and non-Papist merchant-strangers ; but to be short, in that part of Europe where the Roman Catholic religion now hath or lately hath had establishment, there three-quarters of the whole Trade is in the hands of such as have separated from the Church, (that is to say) the inhabitants of England, Scotland, and Ireland, as also those of the United Provinces, with Denmark, Sweden, and Norway . . . do at this present time possess three-quarters of the trade of the world. And even in France itself the Huguenots are proportionately far the greater traders. . . . From whence it follows that trade is not fixed to any species of religion as such, but rather, as before hath been said, to the Heterodox part of the whole.[359]

Petty's opinion was by no means an isolated one; we meet with very many similar views as to the great significance of the nonconformists in the development of English commerce and industry. "They (the nonconformists) are not excluded from the nobility and among the gentry they are not a few; but none are of more importance than they in the trading part of the people and those that live by industry, upon whose hands the business of the nation lies much." [360]

The facts certainly go to support all these writers. Consider, for example, the economic history of France, about which we have a mass of information in the reports which the Intendants sent to the King after the Revocation of the Edict of Nantes.[361] It would appear that the greatest part of the capitalist industries and oversea trade of France were in the hands of the Reformers. They owned the ironworks of Sedan, the paper-mills of Auvergne and elsewhere, and the tanning establishments in Touraine, which competed so hotly with English tanning. In Normandy, Maine, and Brittany they had the controlling influence in the linen-weaving factories; the silk industry of Tours and Lyons was under their control, so was the woollen trade of Provence and the lace-making of Paris. The wine trade of Guienne was wholly theirs; in two provinces, de Brouage and d'Oléron, a dozen families held the salt monopoly; and in Sancerre the Intendant reports that "their numbers, their wealth, and their prestige are far superior to those of the Catholics." In foreign trade, likewise, they were superior. They traded mostly with Holland and England, and the Dutch and the English preferred to trade with them because—such is the opinion of Benoit— they had more confidence in them than in the Catholics. It was not otherwise in finance. We come across many Reformers in France who are bankers; and where they received the necessary permission they became farmers of taxes. No wonder Colbert, as is generally known, was much opposed to the edicts which excluded them from the administration of the finances.[362]

The question now presents itself, Are we not in error in deducing the capitalist spirit from nonconformity? Did the nonconformists incline to capitalism because of their nonconformity, or was it not rather because they were dominated by the capitalist spirit that they became nonconformists? Or, indeed, may it not be said that possibly they were nonconformists and capitalists at the same time because their blood inclined them to both? May it not be said that the French Huguenots are descendants of Germanic tribes, and thus tended to capitalism and to a more unfettered religious attitude? It may be so. Nay, I am even inclined to the view that probably nonconformity and capitalism are both the expression of certain biological characteristics, and that nonconformity may be traced to economic causes. To prove the statement is obviously impossible. But suppose the assumption is true ; can there be any doubt but that the social condition produced by nonconformity must have accentuated tendencies already in existence? If certain capitalist capacities are exercised in this way, is there not a speedier and more determined survival of the capitalistically fit? And if such be the case, are we not justified in the view that in every case nonconformity is no insignificant source of the capitalist spirit?

We now proceed a step further. Closely bound up with religious, or, if you will, with political heresy is another social phenomenon, which has exercised even greater influence on the growth of the capitalist spirit than heresy itself. I mean the migrations from one land to another, which were due to religious or political persecutions in the centuries of the early capitalist period. The heretics became emigrants.

But migrations resulted from causes other than religious or political; and therefore the question becomes a large one—so large that it requires a chapter to itself.

CHAPTER XXIII

MIGRATIONS

I can imagine it to be of exceeding great interest to write the history of mankind from the point of view of the stranger and his influence on the trend of events. From the earliest dawn of history we may observe how communities developed in special directions, no less in important than in insignificant things, because of influences from without. Be it religion or technical inventions, good form in conduct or fashions in dress, political revolutions or stock-exchange machinery, the impetus always, or at least in many cases, came from strangers. It is not surprising, therefore, that in the history of the intellectual and religious growth of the bourgeois the stranger should play no small part. Throughout the whole of the Middle Ages in Europe, and to a large extent in the centuries that followed, families left their homes to set up their hearth anew in other lands. The wanderers were, in the majority of cases, economic agents with a strongly marked tendency towards capitalism, and they originated capitalist methods and cultivated them. Accordingly, it will be helpful to trace the interaction of migrations and the history of the capitalist spirit.

First, as to the facts themselves.363 Two sorts of migrations may be distinguished, those of single individuals and those of groups. In the first category must be placed the

removal, of their own free will, of a family, or it may
even be of a few families, from one district or country to
another. Such cases were universal. But we are chiefly
concerned with those instances in which the capitalist
spirit manifested itself, as we must assume it did where
the immigrants were acquainted with a more complex
economic system or were the founders of new industries.
Take as an instance the Lombards and other Italian
merchants, who in the early Middle Ages carried on
business in England, France, and elsewhere. Or, recall
how in the Middle Ages many an industry, more especially
silk-weaving, that was established in any district was introduced by foreigners, and very often on a capitalist basis.
" A new phase in the development of the Venetian silk
industry began with the arrival of traders and silk-workers
from Lucca, whereby the industry reached its zenith.
The commercial element came more and more to the
fore ; the merchants became the organizers of production,
providing the master craftsman with raw materials which
he worked up." So we read in Broglio d'Ajano.[364] We
are told a similar tale about the silk industry in Genoa,
which received an enormous impetus when the Perolerii
began to employ craftsmen from Lucca.[365] In 1341
what was probably the first factory for silk manufacture
was erected by one Bolognino di Barghesano, of Lucca.[366]
Even in Lyons tradition asserts that Italians introduced
the making of silk, and when in the 16th century the
industry was placed on a capitalist basis, the initiative
thereto came once more from aliens.[367] It was the same
in Switzerland, where the silk industry was introduced by
the Pelligari in 1685.[368] In Austria likewise we hear
the same tale.[369]

Silk-making in these instances is but one example ;
there were very many others. Here one industry was
introduced, there another ; here it was by Frenchmen or

Germans, there by Italians or Dutchmen. And always the new establishments came at the moment when the industries in question were about to become capitalistic in their organization.370

Individual migrations, then, were not without influence on the economic development of society. But much more powerful was the effect of the wanderings of large groups from one land to another. From the 16th century onwards migrations of this sort may be distinguished under three heads : (1) Jewish migrations, (2) the migration of persecuted Christians, more especially of Protestants, and (3) the colonizing movement, particularly the settlement in America.

Let us take a brief survey of the facts necessary for the understanding of the importance of the trend of events.

1. Jewish Migrations.371

The Jews have been a wandering race ever since the Babylonian exile. But so far as our problem is concerned, we need only recall their movements from about the end of the 15th century, when some 300,000 Spanish Jews migrated to Navarre, France, Portugal, and the Orient. A goodly number, too, made for England, Holland, and the German cities of Frankfort and Hamburg—and that when Jews were being expelled from Italian towns and those of Southern Germany. Again, from the time of the Cossack massacres in the 17th century, the Jews began to leave Poland, whither they had foregathered from all parts throughout the Middle Ages. This dispersion of Russo-Polish Jews continued, in an almost organized fashion, until at the end of the 19th century the volcano belched forth fresh masses, hundreds of thousands of them, who sought a haven of refuge in the lands of the New World. Possibly the last movement may have affected millions of Jews ; in East Prussia alone, between 1880 and 1905, more than 70,000 left their homes.

We have already had occasion to refer to the vast importance of the Jews in the story of modern capitalism, and to their enormous influence on the shaping of the capitalist spirit. Those who desire further information on the subject are recommended to turn to my book on *The Jews and Modern Capitalism.*

2. THE MIGRATION OF PERSECUTED CHRISTIANS, MORE ESPECIALLY PROTESTANTS.[372]

From the period of the Reformation these migrations were generally concerned with large masses of people. Pretty well all countries have given and received in the process ; but it is generally agreed that France lost most, and that other lands admitted more French immigrants than the emigrants they lost. A statistical survey is impossible. Nevertheless, it may be asserted that hundreds of thousands changed their place of abode in Europe because they would not change their faith. One estimate [373] of the number of Protestants who left France after the Revocation of the Edict of Nantes (1685) is between 250,000 and 300,000 (the total French Protestants at the time being about one million souls). Besides, it must be remembered that the migrations had commenced as early as the 16th century, and, furthermore, that France was not the only country from which an exodus took place. But, after all, whether a few hundred thousand people more or less were concerned in the movement is of no great consequence ; our business is to see clearly the significance of these migrations for economic life. This is no difficult task if we direct our attention to the activities of the newcomers in the lands where they settled. What do we find ? Everywhere the immigrants were foremost in building up the capitalist fabric ; more especially, the growth of banking and of industries in all lands owes much to them. To demonstrate this in detail would be to write the economic history of the three centuries from the 16th to the 18th. But the salient points may with advantage be referred to ; they will help the reader to appreciate in some measure how much modern capitalism owes to the refugees fleeing from religious persecution.

Let us turn to Germany, where large numbers of Austrians, Frenchmen, and Scotchmen found a new home. Of these, the Scotch and the French are the important factors in the growth of capitalism. The former came in the 16th and 17th centuries to East Prussia and Posen, where, by the way, among others, the forefathers of Immanuel Kant (Cant) settled. Whether Catholics or Protestants, they had left their native land for their faith's sake, and for the most part were wealthy and intelligent, and rather looked upon as dangerous competitors.374 But they pushed more inland too. Towards the end of the 16th century there were Scotch settlements in Cracow, Bromberg, and Posen, and everywhere they were among the most respected traders. When the 17th century set in, more than half of the merchants in Posen were Scotchmen ; in 1713, eight of them, out of a total of 36, were members of the Merchant Gild there. What they were thought of in Posen is evident from a petition, bearing date 11 August, 1795, of the Posen merchants to the Marquis of Hoym.375 " The city of Posen," they say, " is indebted for its ancient prestige and the magnitude of its commerce to those of its inhabitants who had emigrated from Scotland."

Refugees from the Palatinate and Holland—they were Reformers and Mennonites—established the silk industry of Crefeld, which from its earliest beginnings was capitalistically organized. Members of the refugee family of von der Leyen, who came to Germany in 1688, may be regarded as its founders ; in 1768 the Crefeld house of von der Leyen Brothers employed 2,800 silk-weavers.[376] Dutchmen also—and Jews—were the foremost bankers in Frankfort on the Main.

As for the French immigrants, their influence on German economic life in the 17th and 18th centuries is well known. Many an industry and many a branch of commerce owes its foundation to their activities. What were their main settlements ? [377] In the Duchy of Saxony, Frankfort, Hamburg, Brunswick, Cassel, and, most important of all, Brandenburg and Prussia generally. It is estimated [378] that under Frederick William I and, Frederick III no less than 25,000 Frenchmen were received into Prussia, of whom 10,000 came to Berlin. Everywhere they introduced the domestic system of industry, more particularly in the silk and wool industries of Halle, Berlin, and Magdeburg. In the last-named cities in 1687 André Valentin, of Nimes, and Pierre Claparède, of Montpellier, employed 100 weavers and 400 female spinners. Nor were these capitalistically organized industries the only ones which were introduced by the French. The making of stockings and of hats (in 1782 the first hat factory, with 37 employees, was opened in Berlin by a Frenchman) ; [379] leather goods and gloves ; paper and playing cards ; linoleum and mirrors,[380] are some other manufactures of French origin.[381] Indeed, in the year 1808, of the 386 members of the Drapers and Mercers' Gild in Berlin, no less than 81 had French names.[382]

It is the same story in Holland. Ever since the revolt of the seven provinces Holland became a haven of refuge for all manner of folk. *La Grande Arche des fugitifs* Bayle calls it,[383] and the religious motive was by no means decisive.   The Low Countries offered a welcome to all who could be of commercial advantage to them ; Heathens, Jews and Christians, Catholics and Protestants, all were alike received.[384]   Thirty thousand Englishmen migrated to Holland in the reign of Mary Tudor ; numerous Germans arrived in the time of the Thirty Years War ;   Walloons, Flemings and Brabanters fled thither from the Spanish Netherlands in the 16th century ; the Jews, as we have already seen, came even earlier still —on their expulsion from Spain ; and lastly, in the 17th century, large masses of French Protestants, to the number probably of between 55,000 and 75,000.[385]

The newcomers, here as elsewhere, contributed no small part to the general economic revival which took place ; in other words, to the rise and growth of capitalism. Jewish influence on the stock exchange and on speculation receives detailed treatment in my book, *The Jews and Modern Capitalism* ;   the Amsterdam Stock Exchange was almost completely dominated by Jews in the 17th and 18th centuries.[386]   But the other immigrants also were very soon to the fore in trade and industry.   The French more especially ; among them may be mentioned Balthazar de Moncheron, "genial and energetic," who founded trading companies, and his brother Melchior, a merchant of great standing.[387]   It was as the fathers of capitalist industries that the French was best known. One 17th-century writer is of opinion that more than twenty different branches of industry were introduced into Holland by French refugees.[388]   And what of the rise of Amsterdam ?   Another contemporary writer[389] ascribes it to the influence of the aliens.   Leiden and Haarlem likewise profited by their settlements.[390]   The principal new industries, here as elsewhere, were silk, hat-making, the manufacture of paper, and printing.[391] That the tendency to capitalist organization was always due to the influence of foreigners is clear enough. Until the 17th century the old mediæval handicraft system existed in full vigour. But in the second half of that century the towns entered into contracts with foreigners for the erection of factories. In 1666, for example, the city fathers of Haarlem entered into agreement with an Englishman that he should start a mirror factory there ; and in 1678 they arranged with J. Becher for a silk-weaving establishment.392

That alien immigration had much to do with the growth of capitalism in England is less well known ; but the fact is none the less true. Consider the influence on English economic life of the Italians who swarmed in this country in the 14th century. No less an authority than Cunningham is of opinion that the earliest organizations of capitalists were modelled on Italian originals.393 Consider further the deep furrows marked on English economic development by the Dutch and French immigrants in the 16th and 17th centuries. The newcomers must have been pretty numerous. In 1560 the Spanish ambassador reported that 10,000 Flemish refugees had found shelter in England ; for 1563 the number he gives is 30,000. Possibly he was exaggerating ; but that he was not very far from the actual state of the case is proved by official statistics. In 1568 the Lord Mayor of London's census of aliens in the capital showed a total of 6,704, of whom 5,225 were from the Low Countries. In 1571 there were 32,925 Dutchmen and Walloons in Norwich ; in 1587 they formed the larger part of the population there—4,679.394 Indeed, some authorities declare that the history of English industry commences with these Dutchmen. But numerous as these were, the total of the French settlers is said to have been even greater. Eighty thousand is the estimate, of whom about half, it is alleged, must have continued their journey to America. But those who remained in England were the wealthier sort, including the rich Huguenots.395

The capacity of the new settlers for capitalist organization began to be exercised in all directions in industry and commerce, and much of their activity was excellent pioneer work. What trades were affected ? Again it was silk, lace-making also ; carpet-weaving and hat-making. Before this hats were imported from Flanders ; but already in 1552 immigrants established a factory for felt and " thrummed " hats. A German, Spillmann by name, introduced the making of paper in 1598·; we learn from one of Thomas Churchyard's poems that he employed 600 workpeople. Glass-making is another instance. In 1566 a patent for twenty-one years was granted to Anthony Been and John Care, both Dutchmen, for the erecting of a glass-blowing factory " in order to make glass of the French, Dutch, and Burgundian sort." In 1670 Venetians erected a large plate-glass factory. Wire-drawing is said to have been introduced by Dutchmen. In 1577 English dyers were taught the use of indigo dyes by Pero Vaz Devora, a Portuguese ; in the 17th century a Fleming, Kepler by name, introduced the famous scarlet dye ; Bauer, another Fleming, perfected wool-dyeing in 1667. And so in numerous other instances. Alien immigrants were responsible for calico-printing (1690), the making of fine cambrics, the cotton industry, clocks (Dutch clocks) ; the water supply of London was planned by an Italian, Genelli ; a company of German undertakers carried on copper-mining ; Sheffield cutlery first became famous through Flemish craftsmen. The list might be considerably lengthened ; but enough has been mentioned.396

3. COLONIZING MOVEMENTS, PARTICULARLY THE SETTLEMENTS IN AMERICA.

The stream of emigration from Europe to America during the last two centuries far surpasses in magnitude and extent the migrations we have just considered. With the close of the 18th century some hundreds of thousands at least must already have left Europe for ever to seek their fortunes in the New World ; of Germans alone there were probably between 80,000 and 100,000. But the stream reached its maximum volume from the 'thirties of the last century onward. Thus, from 1820 to 1870 the statistics of American immigration show a total of 7,553,865 persons. Great Britain and Germany sent some two-thirds of these (3,857,850 and 2,368,483 respectively) ; France comes next (with 245,812) ; then Sweden and Norway (153,928), followed by China (109,502), and other countries. But in the subsequent decades the total was greater still ; nearly 12 million immigrants arrived in the United States between 1871 and 1900. We may say, therefore, that in the 19th century Europe sent America some 20 millions of people.[397] The origin of the mass of the wanderers in the last generation differed considerably from what it was in the past. Britains and Germans are no longer the mainstay of the arrivals, but Italians, Slavs, and Jews. This latest migratory stream, however, does not affect the problem we are considering.

It remains for us to prove that the "spirit" of the inhabitants of the New World (and we may regard them as typical of all colonial countries) is capitalist in its essence. That the Americans are filled with the most perfect expression of that spirit we already know. We know, too, that in its present aspect this spirit dominated the American in his economic activities at a time when

Europe was acquainted with only its earlier forms. Read the reports of competent observers of the third, fourth, and fifth decades of the 19th century—their name is legion [398]—and you will find a picture of the typical American of those days little different from that of his descendants of to-day. Greed of gain, devotion to work to a degree which might even be regarded as folly, the chase of profit irrespective of all other considerations, the highest degree of economic rationalism ; in short, the characteristic features of a highly developed capitalist system—you will find them all in the United States before the Civil War.

We come, then, to the general question. Is it not a fact that the " stranger," the immigrant, was possessed of a specially developed capitalist spirit, and this quite apart from his environment, and, to a lesser degree, his religion or his nationality ? We see it in the old states of Europe no less than in the new settlements beyond ; in Jews and Gentiles alike ; in Protestants and Catholics (the French in Louisiana were, by the middle of the 19th century, not a whit behind the Anglo-Saxons of the New England states in this respect).[399] The assumption therefore forces itself upon us that this particular social condition —migration or change of habitat—was responsible for the unfolding of the capitalist spirit. Let us attempt to show how.

What is it that leads to emigration ? It seems to me that the answer to this question will throw much light on the influence of migrations. In the first place, every one of these movements of the population represents a process of selection. The capitalist variants emigrate—that is to say, those who are already fully developed, in the capitalist sense, or those who possess the necessary qualities for development. In other words, those who resolved to leave home—particularly in early times, when to change your abode was no easy matter, to say nothing of planting new colonies —those who resolved to leave home must have been the most active, the strongest-willed, the most enterprising, the coolest, the most calculating, the least sentimental natures ; and this quite apart from the particular consideration that forced them to emigrate, whether religious, political, or merely economic. Oppression at home, as we have already seen, was the best school of capitalist training. But even among those who were oppressed there was a process of selection. Those migrated who would no longer by adaptation and abject submission keep their heads above water in their own country. The wanderers therefore represented the strongest among the oppressed ; for not all the oppressed would decide to leave home. The great majority of the Huguenots—four-fifths of them, it is said—remained in France ; and very many Jews continued to live in Russian Poland for centuries before beginning to move.

It may be, too, that, regarded as a complete whole, those races that exhibited capitalist variants in a high degree were essentially of a wandering disposition. Think of the Etruscans (that is, the Lombards), the Jews, and the Scotch, other Germanic races from whom the French Huguenots were sprung, the Alemanni (that is, the Swiss), and others. The mere dispersion of these gifted popular groups was a powerful influence for the extensive development of the capitalist spirit, for each of them acted like yeast in the dough. Obversely, when any country lost these capitalistically gifted individuals it suffered of necessity an economic decline. Think of Spain or France.

But what we want to discover most of all is the particular reason why a sojourn in a new land should tend to broaden and intensify the capitalist spirit.

If we are content to find it in a single cause it would

be the breach with all old ways of life and all old social relationships. Indeed, the psychology of the stranger in a new land may easily be explained by reference to this one supreme fact. His clan, his country, his people, his state, no matter how deeply he was rooted in them, have now ceased to be realities for him. His first aim is to make profit. How could it be otherwise? There is nothing else open to him. In the old country he was excluded from playing his part in public life; in the colony of his choice there is no public life to speak of. Neither can he devote himself to a life of comfortable, slothful ease; the new lands have little comfort. Nor is the newcomer moved by sentiment. His environment means nothing to him. At best he regards it as a means to an end—to make a living. All this must surely be of great consequence for the rise of a mental outlook that cares only for gain; and who will deny that colonial activity generates it? " Our rivulets and streams turn mill wheels and bring rafts into the valleys, as they do in Scotland. But not one ballad, not a single song reminds us that on their banks men and women live who experience the happiness of love and the pangs of separation; that under each roof in the valleys life's joys and sorrows come and go." [400] This plaint of an American of the old days expresses my meaning; it has been noted again and again, particularly by those who visited America at the beginning of the 19th century. The only relationship between the Yankee and his environment is one of practical usefulness. The soil, as one of them says, is not regarded as " the mother of men, the hearth of the Gods, the abiding resting-place of the past generations, but only as a means to get rich." There is nothing of " the poetry of the place " anywhere to check commercial devastations. The spire of his village is for the American like any other spire; in his eyes the newest and most gaudily painted is the most beautiful. A waterfall for him merely represents so much motive power. "What a mighty volume of water!" is, as we are assured, the usual cry of an American on seeing Niagara for the first time, and his highest praise of it is that it surpasses all other waterfalls in the world in its horse-power.

Nor has the immigrant or colonial settler a sense of the present or the past. He has only a future. Before long the possession of money becomes his one aim and ambition, for it is clear to him that by its means alone will he be able to shape that future. But how can he amass money? Surely by enterprise. His being where he is proves that he has capacities, that he can take risks; is it remarkable, then, that sooner or later his unbridled acquisitiveness will turn him into a restless capitalist undertaker? Here again we have cause and effect. He undervalues the present; he overvalues the future. Hence his activities are such as they are. Is it too much to say that even to-day American civilization has something of the unfinished about it, something that seems as yet to be in the making, something that turns from the present to the future?

Another characteristic of the newcomer everywhere is that there are no bounds to his enterprise. He is not held in check by personal considerations; in all his dealings he comes into contact only with strangers like himself. As we have already had occasion to point out, the first profitable trade was carried on with strangers; your own kith and kin received assistance from you. You lent out money at interest only to the stranger, as Antonio remarked to Shylock, for from the stranger you could demand more than you lent.

Nor is the stranger held in check by considerations other than personal ones. He has no traditions to respect; he is not bound by the policy of an old business. He begins with a clean slate ; he has no local connections that bind him to any one spot. Is not every locality in a new country as good as every other ? You therefore decide upon the one that promises most profit. As Roscher says, a man who has risked his all and left his home to cross the ocean in search of his fortune will not be likely to shrink from a small speculation if this means a change of abode. A little travelling more or less can make no difference.

So it comes about that the feverish searching after novelties manifested itself in the American character quite early. " If to live means constant movement and the coming and going of thoughts and feelings in quick succession, then the people here live a hundred lives. All is circulation, movement, and vibrating life. If one attempt fails another follows on its heels, and before ever one undertaking has been completed the next has already been entered upon " (Chevalier). The enterprising impulse leads to speculation ; and here again early observers have noticed the national trait. " Everybody speculates and no commodity escapes from the speculating rage. It is not tulip speculation this time, but speculations in cottons, real estate, banks, and railways."

One characteristic of the stranger's activity, be he a settler in a new or an old land, follows of necessity. I refer to the determination to apply the utmost rational effort in the field of economic and technical activity. The stranger must carry through plans with success because of necessity, or because he cannot withstand the desire to secure his future. On the other hand, he is able to do it more easily than other folk because he is not hampered by tradition. This explains clearly enough why alien immigrants, as we have seen, furthered commercial and industrial progress wherever they came. Similarly we may thus account for the well-known fact that nowhere are technical inventions so plentiful as in America, that railway construction and the making of machinery proceed much more rapidly there than anywhere else in the world. It all comes from the peculiar conditions of the problem, conditions that have been termed colonial—great distances, dear labour, and the will to progress. The state of mind that will have, nay, must have progress is that of the stranger, untrammelled by the past and gazing towards the future.

Yet results such as these are not achieved by strangers merely because they happen to be strangers. Place a negro in a new environment; will he build railways and invent labour-saving machines? Hardly. There must be a certain fitness; it must be in the blood. In short, other forces beside that of being merely a stranger in a strange land are bound to co-operate before the total result can be fully accounted for. There must be a process of selection, making the best types available, and the ethical and moral factor, too, counts for much. Nevertheless, the migrations themselves were a very powerful element in the growth of capitalism. The others we shall study in the next chapter.

CHAPTER XXIV

THE PRECIOUS METALS AND THEIR DISCOVERY

An increase in the gold supply is a necessary condition for the development of the capitalist spirit ; at the same time it is also a direct agent in the process.

1. You must have a minimum of metallic currency before the capitalist spirit can appear. In other words, a money economy is the environment in which capitalism first shows its head. When a money economy becomes general, gold gradually obtains its all-embracing influence, and when it reaches this stage, gold is highly valued. Once this comes about, the result is, as we have already seen, to turn greed of gold into desire for money, and to place all economic activities on a new basis—that of gain. In the history of Europe, anyhow in the history of certain countries (Italy, for instance), the absolute supremacy of gold was undoubtedly established by about the middle of the 14th century. We can thus understand why it was that money-making became the passion we have shown it to be (cf. p. 34).

A remarkable piece of evidence for those days is to be found in a fine passage in one of Petrarch's letters. I shall quote a translation of it here as additional testimony to what has already been said, first because it is probably the best that has ever been written about the power of gold, and secondly, because to my knowledge no economic

historian appears to have observed the passage. Here
it is :—

We, dear friend, now have everything made of gold—lances and
shields, chains and coronets ; gold binds and holds us ; gold makes us
rich or poor, happy or miserable. Gold enslaves the free and frees the
slaves : it acquits evildoers and punishes the innocent ; it gives speech
to the dumb and makes the eloquent speechless. . . . It turns slaves
into princes, and princes into slaves ; makes brave men cowards
and gives the coward self-reliance ; arms the defenceless and disarms
the warrior ; tames bold leaders and crushes whole peoples down ;
creates strong armies and wages long wars in a few hours' space ; dictates and maintains peace ; dries up rivers and surveys countries ; connects oceans and removes mountains ; throws open the entrance to
cloisters ; attacks cities ; captures fortresses and destroys stout
ramparts. As Cicero hath it, no place is so strong but that an ass laden
with gold will find a way in. Gold forges bonds of friendship ; brings
partnerships about ; even makes honourable marriages. You ask how ?
By making the noble-hearted, the powerful, the learned, the hand-
some, and—it may surprise you to hear it—even the saintly its masters.
So it comes to pass that those who are rich are called good citizens and
their word is trusted. But there is little confidence in the poor, seeing that they have no money. There is much truth in the verses of
the satirist who said, "The good repute you may command is measured
by your cash in hand." Finally—I say so unwillingly, but truth compels
me—gold is not merely powerful, it is almost all-powerful, and everything under the heavens above is subject to its domination. Piety and
chastity and faith all serve gold ; in short, all virtue and all renown
recognize it as their overlord. Why, marry, even over our immortal
souls the glittering metal exercises sway. Gold holds Kings and
Popes in bond ; it appeases mortals, and, as some assert, the Gods also.
Nothing withstands its power ; nothing is beyond its reach.[401]

Now, a money economy accustoms people to look at
the world in a purely quantitative way. When the habit
of applying money as a canon or rule for all things has
grown for years and centuries, the natural attitude of
mind which regards the inherent and qualitative differences in things, dies out. Arithmetical valuations—
weight, mass, etc.—come to be taken as a matter of course

in everyday life. A money economy, therefore, is in reality the preparatory school of the capitalist spirit ; therein the minds of men were trained for a capitalist view of the universe.

The universal adoption of money (in the form of metals, and mostly of precious metals) gave an impetus to that factor in the capitalist spirit which we have termed calculation. In the independent family economy, or even in the social system a stage more advanced, to calculate was uncommonly difficult, if not altogether impossible. Before you can reckon you must have numbers, and you cannot have numbers before you have some sort of size or quantity. It is only when you can express values in terms of money that you may speak of measurable quantities.

Furthermore, without a money economy the modern state would have been inconceivable ; and how the modern state has advanced the capitalist spirit we have already seen. Without a money economy there would have been no St. Antonine of Florence. And so on, *ad infinitum.* Without a money economy there would, in a word, have been no capitalism, that is, no sphere of influence for the capitalist spirit.

It must not be forgotten that a money economy was conditioned by, and its extension dependent on, a sufficient supply of the commodity from which money is made being available. In practice this meant a sufficient quantity of the precious metals.

2. An increase in the quantity of money in circulation usually accompanies increased private possessions ; that is to say, large amounts of money tend to accumulate in certain spots. As a result, the expansion of the capitalist spirit receives an impetus. For increased private possessions heighten the desire for money, and the desire for money is the mother of the capitalist spirit.

It would seem to be an innate characteristic of the human soul that the more we possess the more we desire. At all times and among all peoples has the tendency been observed. *Crescit amor nummi, quantum ipsa pecunia crescit* [As money increases the love of money increases with it], says Juvenal (*Satires* 14), and *Crescentem sequitur cura pecuniam maiorumque fames* [Increase of wealth increases love of money and the desire for more] are the words of Horace (Lib. 3, c. 16). Or, as Montaigne puts it, *C'est plutôt l'abondance qui produit l'avarice* [More often than not superfluity brings forth greed]. But have we not all seen the same thing in our everyday life ? And does not history bear witness to its truth ? Where in the Middle Ages do we first find greed of gold and the chase of profits ? Among those who were the first to accumulate large quantities of money—the clergy and the Jews.

This simple psychological phenomenon certainly lays bare one of the roots of that endless profit-hunting which characterizes modern economic activities. We will note others in due course.

Now, observe that it is not merely our own possessions that stir up in our hearts the desire for more. The sight of other people's money, the very thought of large quantities of cash, may have exactly the same result. When men brood on these things it makes them mad ; they develop that mentally excited state which, as we have already observed, is a striking feature of all great speculative periods. We see the glitter of the yellow metal, we hear its clink, and it whips up our blood to madness, confuses our senses, fills us with a wild longing to possess as much as possible of it ourselves. Read Zola's *L'Argent* and you will see there the picture of it all, with the " music of money " that is heard through all business, that music that is " like the voice of the elves in fairyland."

The influence on the soul of the conception of large masses of gold is partially effected by pure sensual impressions. We are bewitched through our eyes and our ears. Sometimes, however, the same end is achieved by such abstractions as huge figures; for example, tremendous profits, enormous wealth, an extraordinarily large turnover, and the like. In short, exhibit large sums of money anywhere and our pulses beat more quickly.

3. Closely akin to this effect is another, which is likewise due to the large accumulation of gold in any land. I refer to speculation—the offspring of the mad union between the greed of gold and the spirit of enterprise. An increase in the different kinds of money may facilitate speculation in diverse ways. To begin with, we know that the mere existence of large supplies of the precious metals in any country intensifies the already existing propensities of capitalist undertakers. Colbert must have had some sort of vague idea of this when he wrote, " When money is in the land, there is a universal wish to profit by it, whereby it is set in motion." [402] Or it may call forth the desire in capitalist undertakers themselves to participate in gold production. That was certainly the result in Spain and Portugal, the two nations concerned when America was discovered. A reliable authority on the subject tells us that " about that time (1530) innumerable offers of colonial enterprises were made to the India Council, for, once more rumours were current of the discovery of another gold-bearing reef in the heart of South America, and all the adventurous spirits were wildly excited in consequence." [403]

These results were important enough, but I want to lay stress on another. Increase the money in any country, and indirectly you produce a period of expanding trade and a general boom. Europe passed through such an epoch of prosperity for the first time towards the end of the 17th and the beginning of the 18th centuries. There have been others since.

The results of that first trade-boom—we may call it the age of speculation or of company promotion—I have already tried to describe in an earlier chapter. I attempted more especially to demonstrate how at that time a new aspect of the capitalist spirit manifested itself in speculation, since then a necessarily component part of capitalism. Here I am anxious to point out that the mania for speculation and company promotion, which was a direct result of the rapid and immense accumulation of bullion, appeared in France and England, the two countries most concerned.

France in the 17th century was filled with silver and gold by reason of its foreign trade. We have no reliable statistics for the extent of this trade, but indications are available of its immensity. Between 1716 and 1720, the period be it noted of the greatest bubbles and swindles, France exported 30 million francs' worth of goods more than it imported.[404] The lion's share of available cash was due to Spanish-American trade, and the surplus from this quarter was utilized in paying debts to other countries. When the French East India Company was criticized for taking money out of the land, Seignelay [405] defended its action by informing the King that the Indian imports were paid for in Spanish silver. Many ships there were that carried more than 300 million francs on board. Tiepolo,[406] the Venetian ambassador, bears testimony to the great profitableness of the Spanish-American trade, and English writers calculated that from this source alone France obtained some hundreds of millions, and so would be enabled to continue the war. Indeed, the weightiest criticism of the Whigs by the Tories was that they had done nothing to undermine that trade.[407]

Another source whence money flowed into France was Holland. In the 17th century Holland simply abounded in ready cash. In 1684, for instance, money was so plentiful that the city of Amsterdam reduced the rate of interest on its loans from 3½ to 3 per cent.[408] For the large supplies of cash Holland was indebted to the French refugees,[409] and, doubtless, also to the Jews. But the trade with Spain, as all authorities agree,[410] must have produced by far the largest portion.

From Holland France drew a good deal of money all through the period in which Franco-Dutch trade continued. In 1658 French exports to Holland were valued at 72 million francs, of which 52 millions were for manufactured articles.[411] These goods were paid for mostly in cash; indeed, it was calculated that in those times France received from Holland more than 30 million gulden annually.[412]

But the sums of money that flowed into England towards the end of the 17th and the beginning of the 18th centuries must have been larger still. They came from three sources. The French immigrants brought their fortunes with them, and if those who settled in Holland were rich, those who came here were richer.[413] Then there were the Jews, who were likewise wealthy. Some had come from Portugal, in the suite of Catherine of Braganza; others from Holland with William of Orange.[414] Thirdly, English export trade was so far above the import trade that in the first decades of the 18th century it yielded an annual surplus of between two and three millions.[415] Four tributaries fed this stream. The Dutch trade was one.[416] The second was the trade with Spain. In the 17th century Englishmen had managed to obtain a number of commercial privileges in Spain;[417] and in the Assiento Treaty of the Utrecht settlement England reserved the

right of sending to Spanish America a ship of 500 tons
(later 650 tons) of English goods to compete freely at
the fairs of Porto Bello and Vera Cruz.[418]   The third
channel of commerce was with Portugal.   By the middle
of the 17th century, when the wave of prosperity
commenced in Portugal, England entered into close
relations with that country.   In 1642 a commercial
treaty was signed which gave the English a more favoured
position than the Dutch in trading with Portuguese
Colonies.   Then came Charles II's marriage with Catherine
of Braganza ; and by the Methuen Treaty, concluded
in 1703, no less a sum than 50,000 pounds sterling was
said to flow every week from Portugal into England.[419]
The figure is probably not too high, for a Portuguese
authority is of opinion that in the first year of the
treaty England exported foods to Portugal to the value
of 13 million crusados (1 crusados equals about two shill-
ings).[420]   Finally there was the stream of commerce with
Brazil, whither a large part of the exports from England
to Portugal were re-exported.   But there was a fair
amount of direct trade too, more especially in English
woollen goods, which were much favoured by the rich
Brazilians.[421]

These facts, it seems to me, showing as they do that
England and France, when the 17th century ended
and the 18th began, were simply flooded with cash,
are of very great significance, and should not be overlooked in forming a proper estimate of economic activities
in those days.   I have already pointed out that reliable
contemporary authorities described the period as " an age
of projecting "—quite generally, and apart from the South
Sea and the Law bubbles which burst towards the end
of it.   The evidence we have adduced goes to prove that
the contemporary views were correct.   Did we not see
how much money flowed into France and England ?

And is the conclusion not justifiable that these vast sums both produced and nourished the speculating fever? We have here standing out with perfect clearness a most important fact in economic history. Increase the available quantity of money in a country and you prepare the ground for a development of the capitalist spirit.

Where did all the money come from? The answer to this question takes us a step further. But it has already been given in the course of our considerations. It was American silver and Brazilian gold that fructified the economic life of England and France.

Holland gathered the bullion of the New World in its markets. From there it was carried directly (by emigration) and indirectly (by trade) to England and France. Commercial intercourse between these two countries and the source of supply only added to the stores already obtained.

This was the case in the 16th century; in the course of the .17th the system became perfected. Spain and Portugal were merely canals through which the precious metals of their colonies were distributed.[422] To obtain some idea of the quantities produced, let me give a few figures, generally accepted as reliable. Silver came from Mexico, Peru, and Bolivia. The rich mines of Guanaxuato and Potosi were first opened about the middle of the 16th century, and the output increased from an average of some 30,067,000 ounces, between 1521 and 1544, to 103,900,000 ounces, between 1545 and 1560. In the 17th century the supply varied between 100,000,000 and 140,000,000 ounces. In that century Brazilian gold was discovered, and the silver age of capitalism ended, to give place to the age of gold. Between 1701 and 1720 Brazil yielded gold to the value of $7\frac{1}{2}$ millions sterling.

Here we have the key to the proper appreciation of

the economic life of Europe from 1680 to 1720. We
may now realize the connection between the expansion
of the capitalist spirit and the supply of the precious
metals. In this particular instance, to be sure the most
important one, I have attempted to show the facts in
some detail. But the generalization holds good universally. German commercial enterprise in the 16th century
was not unconnected with silver-mining in Schwaz and
Joachimstal ; the feverish speculation of the 'fifties in the
last century may be similarly traced to the Californian
gold-mines. There is no need for figures in proof of
these facts ; those already given are typical. Besides,
they are of further importance because they bring to
light the underlying causes for the first appearance of
speculation on a large scale.

Let it be noted that, despite the title of this chapter,
we treated of an increase in the supply of money first,
and then went on to discuss the increase in the supply
of the precious metals. The reason is obvious. Money
is the medium through which gold and silver can influence economic activities. We see this in the early
capitalist period, that is, in the 15th and 16th centuries,
to say nothing of the Italian city states before the 15th
century. About their supply of metallic currency we
know hardly anything ; we can only assume that the
precious metals, which made the rise and progress of
capitalism possible, they must have obtained from
Germany (silver), and from the Byzantine Empire and
North Africa (gold).

But, when all is said, it is obvious that modern
economic activities and the people who participate in
them cannot be wholly explained by a reference to the
discoveries of gold and silver. These could have had
only a limited influence. Nay, more, in order to effect
even this influence many other conditions were necessary.

And they were operative in Western Europe all through the centuries with which we are concerned. Had they not been in existence, the results of the opening of the gold and silver mines in America might have been very different. Spain and Portugal bear witness to that.[423]

On the other hand, even if all the other circumstances necessary for the evolution of the capitalist spirit had been present, without the American supplies of the precious metals the capitalist spirit might have grown into something very different from what it actually is. Just think of it. If the miners on the Cordilleras and in the Brazilian valleys had not chanced upon gold and silver veins—quite by accident too—the modern business man might never have come into existence.

But we must proceed with the unravelling of the threads. Two other factors were potent in shaping the capitalist spirit—technical inventions and economic activities themselves. The two combined had mighty consequences. We must, however, consider them singly, and the next chapter proceeds to do so.

CHAPTER XXV

THE INFLUENCE OF TECHNICAL INVENTIONS

Is it possible to picture to one's mind that peculiar economic animal, the modern commercial man, without reference to the technical inventions and improvements of the last five centuries, particularly those that have facilitated production and transport? We think not. But what is meant by technical improvements? In the widest sense, any applied knowledge to achieve a given end; in the narrower sense, the utilization of instruments either for manufacturing goods or for moving from place to place commodities, persons, or news.

Such being the case, are we justified in placing technical inventions among the social factors that have helped to mould the capitalist spirit? Surely technical inventions are due to individual knowledge. That criticism is just; but it must be remembered that the first condition for the growth of technical knowledge is an organized social system. Another objection must also be met. We talk of the effects of technical inventions on the capitalist spirit. But may it not be asserted that technical inventions are themselves the offspring of the capitalist spirit? How, then, can they be looked upon as its generator?

In the first place, every technical invention is not necessarily due to capitalist enterprise. Many advances in technical science are due to pure accident, and even those that are sought after often take on a shape least expected.

But suppose that indeed every mechanical invention be due to the influence of the capitalist spirit, would not each invention, in its turn, help to shape the capitalist spirit in its further growth ? We see this over and over again : cause and effect combine as influences in its development.

The effects on the capitalist spirit exercised by technical improvements may be of two kinds, those that are direct, which we shall call primary, and those that are indirect or secondary.

The very existence of an invention is due to enterprise. Inherently, therefore, all inventions exercise a primary influence on capitalism. Carry your mind back to 1484, before the discovery of the nautical astrolabe. No ship could venture on the ocean, for it had no means of directing its course aright. Oversea voyages were therefore impossible. But as soon as this difficulty was overcome, think what opportunities were opened out to enterprising spirits.

Take another instance. Before the water-pump was invented in the 16th century, a limit was set to mining, seeing that man could not control the water in mines. But when it became possible to extend the working of old mines and to open any number of new ones, what an impetus must have been given to capitalists, who had only been waiting for their opportunity. Indeed, we can see how in the 16th century the gradual introduction of the water-pump into mines was followed by the participation of moneyed men in mining ; in other words, how the mining industry was placed on a capitalist basis.

The same process manifests itself from century to century. Every invention that renders production on a large scale possible and makes the process of manufacture more roundabout, results in the stirring up of latent powers of enterprise. Inventions give the conditions necessary for capitalist undertakings, but they also force their pace. The more complex and extended production and transport become, the more capitalist spirits are tempted to master the new conditions. " Undertakers to the fore " is the cry whenever a new invention is patented. Consequently technical advance acts as a selective force among those who are engaged in economic activities ; it trains the capitalist undertaker, from whom more and more is expected, the more the latest inventions make it necessary to have a complexer organization if the best results of technical science are to be attained.

We may go so far as to regard it as a law, certainly applicable to modern inventions, that the work of the capitalist undertaker in modern times goes on increasing. For every new mechanical appliance means the use of a greater number of instruments of production ; means also, in the great majority of cases, the lengthening of the processes of production.

Look at our big industries of to-day—those which manufacture tools for production ; which make machinery and the materials for machines. Undertaking on the largest possible scale is called for in these branches of manufacture—machine-making, iron-founding, coal-mining. It is obvious that those countries which, by reason of their natural resources, are best fitted for the growth of industries of this kind, are also splendid nurseries of the capitalist spirit. Accordingly, the coal and iron fields of Germany, England, and America have not been without influence on the expansion of modern enterprise. The same holds good for those countries that are blessed with an abundant water supply. Directly the water can be utilized as a motive power, say to generate electricity, an army of undertakers will rush to the spot. Incidentally, it is apparent why the capitalist spirit takes on different aspects in different countries. But certain it is that if any land is rich in coal and iron it will possess a more developed capitalism than its less favoured neighbours.

One other fact must not be lost sight of. Technical improvements in our day have developed beyond the dreams of man. They have liberated applied science from the organized, living forces of nature, so that it can now utilize the energy which the sun has stored up deep down in the earth. Applied science no longer looks to men of flesh and blood or to the fields and woods for aid in making progress ; it relies on dead matter and mechanical power for its achievement. What is the result ? Technical improvements know no bounds ; they make possible what was inconceivable before ; they pile up Pelion on Ossa and create the universe anew.

We cannot here enter into a consideration of the reasons why technical improvements in modern times have achieved these marvellous things. 424 It must suffice merely to draw attention to the results, with which, indeed, every man is more or less acquainted. But the important fact is the bearing of these bound-less possibilities on the growth of the capitalist spirit. Obviously they must have been a most potent factor in its development. The limitless expansion of capitalist enterprise to-day can be explained only by reference to the undreamed-of possibilities of technical science. You would not have the hustle and the hurry and the scurry of a modern capitalist undertaking if technical science were not able to perform marvels. In order to master this giant, man in his economic activities had to have recourse to organization, and the desire to hold him in complete control kindled a fire in the breasts of our big captains of industry which is consuming them, and with them the rest of us.

Nor must we forget the many-sidedness of technical knowledge. Every day produces something new, and so creates the need for a new form of organization. That only expands the possibilities of the capitalist spirit. Take a small illustration. In one industry technical knowledge remains at a standstill for a decade or so, and you go on employing the same methods in your factory year after year. In another, technical science revolutionizes the processes of manufacture every few years, and if you are to keep pace with them you must introduce more modern organization. Often enough the new organization demands the foundation of an entirely new enterprise, and so technical improvements may be responsible for the setting up of a new factory or the starting of a new business. In many cases the enterprise owes its origin to the younger and more sanguine brother of the capitalist spirit—speculation. Hence, we may say that technical improvements are often responsible for speculative activity. Look at the history of the last few centuries and you will find that in the wake of epoch-making inventions, or in a period when inventions were particularly numerous, speculation became exceedingly active. Take the case of that wonderful age towards the end of the 17th century, to which I have already referred more than once, when speculation was for the first time at fever heat. But technical inventions were also very numerous ; and indeed it was no less an age of projecting than one of inventing. Inventions were just beginning to appear, and therefore even those of minor importance were able to produce speculation on a large scale. Later on, and more particularly in our own time, technical improvements became so commonplace that only the very important ones had sufficient magnetic power to call forth new enterprises. But their effects were all the more powerful. I need only mention by way of illustration two remarkable periods of speculation in the 19th century, one about the middle, in connection with railways, and the other towards the end of it, when there were numerous inventions for utilizing electricity.

All this goes to show that as technical knowledge advances it influences the will-power of modern man in his economic activities. But it does more. It also influences, nay, often enough revolutionizes, his thoughts.

To begin with, it gives that thought a goal and a purpose ; which is another way of saying that it stirs and develops rationalism in him ; and rational thinking, as we know, is an element of the capitalist spirit. The influence of technical improvements on the growth of economic rationalism in every age has already been noticed by many writers. Every new invention, as one authority puts it,[425] brings man into contact with reality, and by so doing crushes the traditional habits in his character, which, as we have noted above, are rooted deep in his being. So long as the inventions appear at rare intervals, their power to influence man's natural conservatism will not be great. It will be merely, as it were, a scratch on the surface, and before long all trace of it will have vanished. But as soon as inventions come thick and fast, as has been the case since the opening of the modern era, then their effect is more lasting. Constant changes in technical processes cannot but influence the state of mind of those concerned with them. But when the changes are themselves due, as is the case with inventions in our own day, to organized scientific thinking, their influence on the psychology of men is even stronger and more lasting.

All earlier technical advances,[426] remarkable though they were, were empiric in character ; they sprang from the personal experience of generations of masters, handed down from one man to another. Those engaged in an industry knew all the " tricks of the trade," and contented themselves with them. The experience which had accumulated in the past was preserved for the future.

But from the 17th century onward natural science began to make its influence felt in supplanting the gathered experience of ages as the soil from which inventions sprang up. Henceforth new methods came to be used, not because one man who had acquired them by way of experience showed the way, but because any one interested could learn the underlying technical laws and be assured of success if he conformed to them. Before, men worked according to rule of thumb ; now they looked to laws, the explanation and application of which was the work of rational thinking.

The contrast between the old and new methods of work is paralleled by that between domestic handicrafts and industries on a capitalist basis ; and the parallel is by no means accidental. In either case it is a contrast between empiricism and rationalism, or rule-of-thumb and scientific knowledge. Now, when in two such closely related spheres as technical knowledge and economic activities there is so great a similarity in development as that noted above, the inference is surely not far-fetched that the one has had an influence on the other. We may say, then, that economic rationalism owes much of its growth and expansion to technical rationalism.

As a matter of fact, we are not altogether without evidence on this point. Do we not all know that nowadays every business is organized in accordance with the demands of technical science? And does not every director of a business constantly study the technical side of the processes of production? The employment of technical specialists in business, as we have already noted (p. 143), is only in accordance with the demands of economic rationalism. All in all, the needs of technical science call for the very highest economic organization.

Thought in economic activities, then, becomes more definite and conscious, in other words, more rational; and modern technical science has tended to make it so. But it has also helped to make it more exact and punctual, by providing the necessary machinery for measuring quantities, more especially for measuring time.

Clocks have played a very important part in the mental history of the business man. Pendulum clocks are said to have been invented in the 10th century; while the first clock worked by wheels was that made by Heinrich von Wick, in Paris, in 1364, for King Charles V. During the 14th century nearly all the large towns in Italy had clocks that could strike twenty-four hours.427 Watches were first invented by Peter Hele in 1510. Writing about them in 1511, John Cocläus says, "He made small clocks of iron, which contained many wheels; they indicated and struck forty hours, and could be carried in the bosom or the purse." 428 In 1690, second hands were introduced by John Floyer as a more exact means of examining the pulse-beat—an instance, by the way, of an invention not due to economic needs. Now, the exact measurement of time became possible only when the necessary instruments were available, just as exact calculations in terms of money became possible only when technical progress was able to provide a reliable currency.

Punctual business likewise owes much to the gradual perfection of technical processes. Exact calculations as to the delivery of goods presuppose a reliable system of production; and it is not too much to say that modern means of transport have made modern commerce into a sort of huge automatic machine. Calculations of all kinds, therefore, were to a large extent made possible by technical progress. So was the hustle of the modern business man. Would all this haste be conceivable without railways, telegraphs, and telephones? There are, of course, other reasons also for the breathlessness of modern business, as we shall see; but ultimately it is due to technical progress, which intensifies it and makes it universal.

Technical progress can also be held accountable for the particular way in which the modern business man looks at the world. Everything for him is purely quantitative. No doubt this is due largely to the habit of appraising all things in terms of money. But it is not to be forgotten that what specially characterizes modern science is the same tendency of laying stress on quantity to the neglect of quality. The words of Kant are significant. Only when you can express any natural phenomenon by a mathematical formula are you entitled to speak of a law of nature.

Here, too, it would seem that we have alighted on a parallel development, that between the capitalist spirit of to-day and the scientific spirit as seen in technical advancement. The parallelism might be carried a good deal further.[429] But it would not be easy to show, in a general way, the influence of scientific on economic thought, and therefore I will not attempt it in this place. I want rather to direct the reader's observation to another psychological phenomenon, wherein once more we may see the interdependence of the capitalist spirit and the progress of technology.

Is it not a fact that the centres of interest in life to-day are very different from what they used to be? The cause of the change may be traced to the mighty progress in technical science, and its effect on the mental outlook of modern man must be admitted to be stupendous. That interest in problems of technical science is to-day very much to the fore can be easily understood. The remarkable achievements in the field of applied science have appealed to people's inquisitive faculty, have drawn all eyes on to themselves, and have given our age its cause for pride. And no wonder, when it is recalled that technical progress is the one sphere where we may fearlessly reckon up our gains and losses! The crowd, which always worships success, is quite naturally enthusiastic about those spheres of thought where our greatest achievements have been won, the more so as they are so easy of appreciation. It cannot be gainsaid that most people to-day (and this is specially true of our youth) are more interested in the progress of wireless telegraphy and aviation than in the problem of original sin or the Sorrows of Werther.

Nor is this all. Technical progress must also be held responsible for another characteristic of our age—that we value material things far too highly. We have grown rich quickly ; we have come to regard peace as a certainty ; and technical progress has shielded us from dread plagues and cholera. Is it surprising, then, that all idealistic tendencies have been pushed into the background by man's lower instincts—undisturbed enjoyment of pleasures and the craving for creature comforts? We are like a herd of cattle peacefully grazing in the meadow.

The overestimation of material things has had this result on the capitalist undertaker, that it has spurred him on to obtain the means of becoming rich. In other words, it has stirred up his acquisitiveness. The pursuit of the dollars is not so imaginary as some millionaire philosophers, writing from their high tower of princely wealth, would have us believe. On the contrary, it is one of the mightiest motive powers in our modern economy ; and the intense greed of gain, generated as we have just observed, in part at least, by the progress of technical science, is one element in the composition of the soul of the modern business man. That this profit-chasing is now bereft of any shame that attached to it of old ; that we no longer think it dishonourable for any one to engage in dollar-hunting ; that we mix freely with people of whom we know that to make money is their sole aim in life—all this has only tended to cultivate this aspect of the capitalist spirit still more, and the impetus came from the new trend of things produced by advances in technical knowledge.

Another effect of our keen appreciation of technical improvements and our overvaluation of their results has been to intensify the love of profit in the capitalist under-taker in yet another way. It has heightened his interest in the technical side of business and manufacture. We have already noted it as a characteristic of modern eco-nomic activities that man is constantly making things, almost senselessly increasing them ; and that the only explanation of the phenomenon (if, indeed, there is an explanation at all) is to be found in a certain childish pleasure in technical perfection. And can we conceive of such delight except in a technical age ? Can we conceive it possible, except in such an age, that an undertaker should think it of any consequence whether or no he makes ever so many machines or electric lamps or adver-tisement posters or aeroplanes ? How can we explain his satisfaction in the mere production of these things, except that a sort of enthusiasm for producing is a driving power within him ?

This enthusiasm for mere producing is akin to the zeal for " progress " which fills the soul of many an under-taker, and is responsible in America for the childish smugness of the intellectual life of the country. Every traveller cannot help noticing it. You associate it with children, with colonials, with those devoted to technical progress. For if the senseless idea of "progress" means anything, it means undreamed-of possibilities in the realm of technical science. You cannot say that Kant stands for progress as compared with Plato, or Bentham as compared with Buddha. But you can most certainly say so when you compare the steam-engine of to-day with that of Watt's!

The transvaluation of values in modern times is also apparent in the habit of regarding the means to any end as the end itself. Here again, no doubt, money is to blame. But not money alone, for the responsibility is shared by technical science. Technical progress has brought it about that we care far too much to note how a thing is made and how it works, no matter whether it serves a noble end or not. The means (machinery), say, for controlling a whole transport system, or producing a newspaper, are now so wonderful that they take our breath away, and engage our interest to such an extent that we no longer think of the purpose they were intended to serve. We are astounded at the sight of the latest sample of a linotype machine, forgetting all the while that it is printing some journalistic " rag " or other. We feel a shudder down our backs as we watch a flying-machine ascend into the air, but never once do we realize that its only purpose for the present is to add an exciting item to a music-hall programme, or, at best, to enrich a few mechanics. And so on in all things. Here, at any rate, is one explanation of the meaningless transvaluation of values in modern life and the futility of capitalist endeavour.

One other point. We have already seen that the bourgeois spirit of our age is utterly careless of man's fate. We noted how man is no longer the central fact of economic activities and economic thought. It is only the procedure that matters—production, transport, price formation. In a word, *Fiat productio et pereat homo.* How are we to account for this tendency, if not by tracing it to the changes which technical progress has brought about ? Technology has liberated the work of production from the control of man. Before, we needed the living organism to regulate production ; we now direct it by mechanical means.

The natural world, with its fullness of life, has been shattered to atoms ; on its ruins an artificial world of dead matter has been erected by human ingenuity. And this is true for the economic sphere as for that of technical science. Technical improvements have had the effect of changing the face of the globe, and our whole view of the universe has changed in consequence. The more technical science tended to make man of less and less importance in the process of production, the more he was thrown into the background, not only so far as economic activities were concerned, but also in the whole sphere of human thought and action.

There are numerous indirect influences exercised by technical progress on the growth of the capitalist spirit, by the creation of circumstances favourable for its development. I propose to deal with two such cases ; the reader will easily think of others.

In the preceding chapter we saw how the abundance of the gold and silver mines gave an impetus, in the 16th and 17th centuries, to the rise of feverish speculation. But we must not forget that the extraction of the precious metals was only made possible by advances in technical knowledge. Indeed, we may go so far as to assert that without technical science America might never have been settled. But I am thinking rather of the epoch-making improvements in mining, by the aid of which Europe was able to enjoy an abundance of silver in the 16th century. I recall such inventions as the pumping-engine,

or the still more important process of extracting the
silver from the ore by the aid of quicksilver—the
amalgam process—which dates from about 1557. Once
that was known, it was possible, at no great cost, to
extract the pure silver on the rugged slopes of the
Cordilleras, where it was found ; and the new process
so cheapened the expenses of production that silver-
mining became exceedingly profitable.

This is one illustration of the indirect effects of
technical progress on the growth of capitalism. The
other that I have in mind made possible the rapid growth
of population in the 19th century. This was due not
so much to an increase in the actual number of births
as rather to a decrease in the number of deaths. And
was not this decrease due to two causes, both the results
of advances in technical knowledge ? The one was
improved hygienic methods, better precautions against
epidemics, and the progress of applied medicine ; the
other was a more perfected manufacturing and transport
system, which enabled more people to be fed, and so to
be kept alive. Now, the increase in population had,
in its turn, consequences for the development of the
capitalist spirit. On the one hand, a growing population
necessarily leads to emigration ; on the other hand, it
expands capitalist enterprise to its utmost capacity. With
the effects on capitalism of emigration we have already
dealt. As for the expansion of enterprise, is it not
obvious that the more people there are in a country the
greater must competition be ? With a large population
there is an increasing necessity for individuals to be
economically active. With a large population it becomes
more and more difficult merely to live on your income,
merely to be a gentleman at large. The members of
a numerous family look very differently on the need of
earning their livings than do the members of a small one.

Where the children are many, the parents' fortune is necessarily divided into smaller shares than when the children are few. In the first case, therefore, there is greater call than in the second for the children to engage in some occupation, if they are to remain on the social level of their parents. An increasing population very soon creates a definite attitude of parents towards the economic independence of their children. Parents are more concerned with putting their children to a profitable trade than with leaving them sufficient to live upon without having to work.

The increased growth of the population in the 19th century, due chiefly to biological or social causes, has varied in different countries ; and the variations will not be unconnected with the greater or smaller intensity of the capitalist spirit in each.

CHAPTER XXVI

THE INFLUENCE OF PRE-CAPITALIST CALLINGS

THE last set of influences on the capitalist spirit that I shall deal with are the most obvious. A little reflection will show that there were some callings in the pre-capitalist period which were training grounds of capitalism.

First and foremost we must mention trade and commerce, where the seeds of capitalism took root quite early. Trade necessarily taught men the habit of thinking in quantities. The producer in the pre-capitalist age, whether a peasant or craftsman, was dominated, as we have seen, by the idea of quality; the trader, on the other hand, cared less for the quality of his wares, principally because he stood in no personal relation to them. Peasant and craftsman alike had a keen personal interest in the commodities they made; the articles were, in a sense, a part of themselves, an expression of their individuality. The trader was differently situated; his interest in his merchandise was purely objective. He knew little of the travail and care expended on the making of commodities; they reached him in their final form ready for sale, and he was able to look at them from one point of view only—that of their value in exchange. Now, value is represented by a quantity; accordingly, we see a second reason for his quantitative interest. The trader thinks in terms of money, and in the money value all conceptions of quality melt away. In face of this, may it not be said that the trader's calling, like the capitalist's generally, is concerned with money only ; that all his thought is influenced by questions of money ; and that therefore he must of necessity be a calculator ? Of course, in the early stages of trade the calculations were of a primitive kind. But primitive or not, it was calculation, and the trader's calling provided the necessary opportunities for its development.

This holds good of commerce as a whole, and though its various branches and kinds influenced the soul of man in somewhat varying degrees, the direction in every case was towards capitalism.

Look at foreign commerce, the traffic that extends beyond the borders of the state. Its significance for capitalism is much akin to that of the emigration of peoples, for, like the latter, it tends to create a rational outlook on life and rational action. Is not the merchant forced to adapt himself to strange manners and customs ? Does he not strive to choose the right place and to adopt the best methods for his activities ? One powerful aid to rationalist thinking is an acquaintance with foreign tongues; and the knowledge of languages comes easily from international trade. All these results of foreign commerce may arise when a central establishment appoints agents in foreign parts. The agents soon take on a more rational life, and before long infect their principals, to whom they send reports, and with whom, often enough, they come into personal contact. The disintegrating influence of commerce on a system of life dominated by tradition became stronger still when branches of one family of traders scattered themselves in all directions. The effect in such cases was the same as that produced by emigration on a large scale. The best instance of such a policy is furnished by Jewish trading families with whom it was almost a maxim to distribute themselves in different commercial

centres.430   But the Jews did not stand alone in this
policy ; many a Christian family did likewise.   There
were Albertis, for example, at the dawn of the 15th
century, in Italy, England, Flanders, Spain, France,
Catalonia, Rhodes, and Barbary.431

Nor was this all.   Foreign commerce aided the growth
of the capitalist spirit by cultivating commercial morality,
a specifically capitalist virtue.   No doubt religious teaching gave a solid foundation to the confidence of traders in
one another.   As in so many cases, therefore, we see once
more that an element of the capitalist spirit owes its
appearance to more than one contributory influence.   In
this instance it is ethical teaching and business interest.
Gustav Freytag was perfectly right when he observed 432
" that the merchant cannot carry on his calling without a
tremendous amount of confidence in others ; both in those
he himself employs and knows and those who are strangers
to him ; both in Christians and in heathens.   Honesty is a
necessity of commercial intercourse, and even if too great
a confidence results in loss, nevertheless commercial credit
is one of the bases of human intercourse."   The more
frequent the intercourse the surer confidence becomes.   In
the process of time the trader realizes that it is not to his
interest to be dishonest.   He may lose his customers ; he
may have to waste a good deal of his time ; and the
ensuing loss would in all probability hardly compensate
him for his ill-gotten profits.   It is only natural, therefore, to find a gradual development of commercial
morality ; and the go-ahead grocers of the 15th no less
than those of the 18th century knew from practical experience that honesty was the best policy.   The realization
of the soundness of this maxim as making for self-interest
must have slowly gained ground with the expansion of
foreign trade ; and when teachers of morality gave it
their support it only sank deeper into men's consciousness.

One other difference is to be noted, that between inland and oversea trade. The latter continues for a long time to have a dash of adventurous freebooting about it. Oversea trade therefore produced the dare-devil merchant who will take risks. Inland trade, on the other hand, rather lays stress on bargaining and calculating, and produced the careful merchant who cautiously balances gains and losses, and guards himself by amply-worded contracts. Inland woollen trade made the Florentines into the clever merchants they were. Indeed, inland trade (as a rule) rather than bold, enterprising oversea trade, cultivated the bourgeois virtues. That is why I cannot conceive of a book on holy economy appearing in the 15th century anywhere else than in the centre of the woollen trade. Consider further the classical types of successful traders, the Florentines, the Scotch, and the Jews. None of them adventured on the sea ; it was not in their blood to do so. From the very first they were inland traders.

A very special rôle in the history of the capitalist spirit was played by money-lending. We have already brought to the notice of our readers that the worldly-wise and energy-loving Schoolmen of the later Middle Ages regarded money-lending as an activity hostile to capitalism—and rightly so ; and that they condemned it as sinful. Nevertheless, money-lending had a very wholesome influence on certain tendencies in the capitalist system. Because I look at the problem from another point of view than did St. Antonine of Florence, I can account for the fact that one reason why the Jews were so eminently prepared for capitalism was that they had been money-lenders from the days of Solomon, while in the Middle Ages it was a calling which they practically monopolized. I am convinced that my view on the subject is correct. Money-lending was one of the well-springs of the capitalist spirit, much more so than trade, especially in an age when production was on a natural basis and quality a prime factor in it. And why? Money-lending knows nothing of quality; its all-embracing concern is with quantities only. In money-lending everything depends on contract, the substance of which relates to what service is to be rendered, and how much payment for it to be made; to prospectiveness and delivery. Money-lending as such has nothing to do with producing for consumption; it does not call for any use of technical appliances; it is an intellectual economic procedure, no more and no less. Indeed, we can scarcely talk of economic activity in reference to money-lending, for there is no physical exertion entailed; and as it is only an intellectual process, its success alone has any meaning. All in all, money-lending is a most fruitful field for the development of the calculating spirit; we can conceive of the money-lender as sitting at his desk with pencil and paper making calculations all day long. Money-lending enables you to earn money without having to work in the sweat of your brow; enables you to make other people work for you, and that without any recourse to force.

What the professional money-lender lacks is, as Antonine saw long ago, the spirit of enterprise. He won't take risks. But should a money-lender, nevertheless, be able to adventure much, he may easily turn into a capitalist undertaker on a large scale. Specific commercial activities are closely intertwined with lending and borrowing. It is easy to see, therefore, that money-lending may develop into capitalist money-dealing—that is to say, into banking; or it may grow into capitalist production—as in the case of the " clothiers." Florence was the centre of the woollen trade no less than of banking.

But Florence was more than that. To appreciate why

the city on the Arno became the citadel of early capitalism
we must recall that it was *par excellence* the city of gilds
and of gild influence. An historic accident, the quarrel
of the imperialists with the anti-imperial party, brought
the gilds some share in the government of the town as
early as the 12th century. " The craft gilds were paid
heavily for the support they lent the Emperor, and the
Podestà and the councillors were in reality dependent on
the new social class that had risen to power."433 In 1193
the foundation was laid for the democratic development
of the city state.

My point, hinted at above, is that the gild influence
in the history of Florence was in part responsible for the
early rise and growth of capitalism there. It may seem
paradoxical to say so, seeing that the gild system is the
mortal enemy of capitalism. It is true, nevertheless.
A very powerful element in the capitalist spirit hails from
the gild-halls. Think of the bourgeois virtues, and
more especially of holy economy. Where was economy
more at home than in the gild-hall ? The practice was
taught by the gilds because necessity forced it on them.
The gild members, if they were not to endanger their
existence, had to be careful of the pennies, had to live
soberly, work hard, be pure and what not. All these
were called Christian virtues, and Christian they certainly
were. Their cultivation, without any pressure from
without, was a good thing ; it spoke well for the self-
discipline of those who practised them. But the grocer
or the weaver had them forced upon him by his society ;
willy-nilly he was brought to the point of view that to
get into debt and to waste time in pleasure-seeking or
love affairs would surely bring him to beggary. Consequently, the gild members everywhere became " respectable
citizens " by force of habit. Long before the Reformation
in England, we are told by a writer whose judgment is

reliable,[434] long before the Puritan spirit was abroad in the land, "the gaiety of the towns was already sobered by the pressure of business." It was the same in Scotland,[435] where the gilds also narrowed the life of the countryside. Your real yeoman was much like a squire who lives and lets live. But the craftsman in the town declined, his life-blood dried up, his outlook was drab; in a word, he became the ancestor of the " respectable citizen "—the bourgeois.

This bourgeois spirit became part and parcel of the capitalist spirit, and even people who could afford to live in a free-and-easy fashion made industry and frugality their ideals. Many reasons will explain this phenomenon. The morality of the philosophers and the Church was one force that made towards the end. Another was a kind of self-righteousness born of jealousy.

It has been asserted [436] that the whole of modern civilization is marked by this self-righteous jealousy, which, as everybody knows, Nietzsche made responsible for the substitution of aristocratic values by that of crowd morality. I believe that something of the same spirit played a part in the history of capitalism. Does it not adequately explain the raising of lower middle-class principles, born as they were of sheer necessity, into general and highly valued ideals of life? What were simply bourgeois virtues became great human virtues. And who preached them? Middle-class men, generally those who had sunk from the upper class, who looked with jealous eyes at the conduct of their superiors, damned this conduct as sinful, and taught the wickedness of the seigniorial life, though deep down in their hearts they admired and desired it. Study carefully the family records of Alberti and say whether this self-righteous jealousy is not their keynote. I have already quoted passages in which the hatred of the "signori," from whose circles Alberti was excluded, is comic, not to say childish. There are very many such. And in every case the condemnation of the aristocratic way of life, of its hunting, its immorality, its nepotism, ends with pharisaical laudation of the writer's own middle-class ideals. There is no doubt that commercial interests, the precepts of philosophy, and the advice of the confessional all contributed to the establishment of a middle-class view of life. But the burning words of scorn that Alberti has for the " signori " whenever he begins to talk about them show that his experience of them must have been pretty unpleasant. But they also show that perhaps the strongest force that made him cling to his middle-class outlook on life was this spirit of self-righteous jealousy.

Throughout all ages this has been the stoutest prop of bourgeois morality. Every respectable citizen, even in our own day, proclaims that the grapes are sour. It is his comfort.

But to return to the gilds. Whenever and wherever these organizations rose to power, so much so that eventually they " called the tune" of the policy of their community, the result always was that their ideals became dominant and universally prized, despite the fact that they first arose merely from the pressure of necessity and that the necessity was made into a virtue. In such cases the gild spirit became the generally accepted one. In Florence we have the best illustration of the tendency. As early as the 15th century Florence was just soaked in the bourgeois spirit, while other cities, say Venice, for example, retained their seigniorial mode of life for a much longer space of time.

CHAPTER XXVII

THE INFLUENCE OF CAPITALISM ITSELF

YEARS ago, when I made the first attempt to study the problem of the capitalist system by going to the heart of the matter and starting out with the capitalist spirit, I was much misunderstood and blamed. I was accused of putting the cart before the horse. How could capitalism be the result of the capitalist spirit? it was asked; surely the spirit was the product of the system. M. Simian took up the defence of my position with great skill in a review which he concluded with these words : " Was not the capitalist spirit as much the offspring of capitalism as capitalism was the offspring of the capitalist spirit ? " 437

Stated in this way the problem is complex; it will receive full and reasoned treatment in the new edition of my *Modern Capitalism*. In this place we are concerned with the first part of the question, Cannot the capitalist spirit be traced to capitalism itself ? And we are concerned with it very much. For if the answer be in the affirmative, then the whole of the preceding twenty-six chapters have been superfluous. The book might in that case be limited to the present chapter alone. It is needful, then, to look all around the problem.

To begin with, the question as stated is not quite clear. Capitalism and capitalist spirit are not necessarily exclusive conceptions. As well inquire whether the soul is the product of the human being or the human being of the soul. Obviously the capitalist spirit is part and parcel of capitalism, using the latter term as equivalent to the capitalist economic organization of society. Without the capitalist spirit you cannot have the capitalist system.

To be clear, therefore, the question must be stated differently. The capitalist spirit must be so conceived that it may be regarded either as a cause or as an effect. To that end it must be contrasted not with the capitalist system as a whole, but with " the capitalist body," if I may use the term. But what is meant by " capitalist body " ? All those component parts of the capitalist economic system which are outside the soul of the capitalist undertaker. I mean all organization—the treatment of others, general business management, internal economies as exemplified by (say) the planning of a factory, a particular method of book-keeping, business relations with other firms, or a special wage system.

Another contrast is also possible, this time between the capitalist spirit and the capitalist order itself. It is possible if you speak historically. For instance, the capitalist spirit of a former age and the capitalist economic order of to-day are distinct entities.

Looked at in this way, the capitalist spirit may in theory certainly be regarded either as a cause or an effect. Hence we may ask, Does the capitalist spirit create the capitalist social organization, or does it itself spring from the latter? This particular wording of the question already points to the answer. Since organization is the work of man, man and his spirit must first exist before organization can be carried out—that is to say, a capitalist social order cannot produce the capitalist spirit. If it could, we should want to know what produced the capitalist order. We might indeed reply, A pre-capitalist spirit. But then, if a pre-capitalist spirit created anything, it would not and could not be a capitalist organization. It might produce something like it, but never the thing itself.

Very different is the aspect of the second alternative. Capitalism may produce the capitalist spirit, and the cause and effect need not be any great distance apart. A manual labourer whose little shop is close to a capitalist undertaking of some sort may be touched by a spark of the capitalist spirit dominant in the latter, which may set his soul afire. Nor need capitalism develop in such a way as only to influence the next generation; in one and the same undertaking the presence of capitalism may bring changes into the mental outlook of those who are carrying on the business.

If this is so, what will be our reasoned judgment on capitalism, regarded as a well-spring of the capitalist spirit? What shall we say of its influences on the present and on the past?

Before dealing with the answer it is imperative to remember that capitalism is not the only source of the capitalist spirit. It goes without saying that at some time in the distant past the capitalist spirit must have been in existence—in embryo, if you like—before any capitalist undertaking could become a reality. Hence that early embryonic capitalist spirit must have been due to other causes. But more than this. Even when capitalism was already in being, other forces were co-operating with it to produce the capitalist spirit and to make it thrive. The truth of this I believe I have proved in the preceding pages. In this chapter I hope to show that the more capitalism developed the more its importance grew as a creator of the capitalist spirit, until at last one day it will possibly be its one and only creator.

Just think. As capitalism grows and develops, something is produced besides services and material goods which, unlike these, does not pass away. I am referring to experiences. Thanks to certain circumstances, some of which we have already considered, ways and means have been found of withdrawing the different experiences from the individual undertakings where they have accumulated and making them available generally, and even handing them down from generation to generation. This mass of experience, whenever it has been utilized, has made possible the perfection of economic rationalism. That it has been utilized at all, that the later capitalist undertaker profited by the experiences of his predecessors, is due to the stress of circumstances in which the undertaker finds himself. On the one hand, his business is to increase his profits ; on the other hand, competition forces the pace for him. He has to arrange his undertaking on the most rational basis possible.

But the inherent energy of economic rationalism itself, driving it to self-expression, is possibly a mightier force still in the perfecting of business methods and enterprise. It is curious to observe the phenomenon, which is in no wise unique. Here we have a system fashioned by man waking to life of its own accord, and influencing the activities of its creator without any reference to his will. How did the process come about ?

As the demand for economic rationalism arose it was satisfied by specialist work. Thousands of people are engaged to-day in thinking out and carrying through the best methods of conducting business. There is a whole hierarchy of them, from the professors of economics to the army of accountants, makers of calculating machines, card-index systems, typewriters, and what not. In many cases, too, the employees of business houses are urged by promises of bonuses to take part in this production of economic rationalism. What is the result ? A large amount of interest is stirred up in the perfection of business methods ; a large store of energy is directed towards that end. And this production is indeed an end in itself for all those who engage in it professionally. Recall what we said about technical improvements. The end no longer interests us ; we forget it in our admiration of the means, and thus the means are more and more perfected for their own sake. It is the same in this case. Here, too, man and his living, palpitating interests are neglected in order to perfect a system. Consequently economic rationalism in our time grows apace by its own momentum ; it thrives on itself, so to say, and man does nothing to help its development.

This thing which has become alive the capitalist under-taker takes into his service without any very great consideration, much as he engages a manager or work-man ; in fact, just as he introduces the latest, the most perfect machinery, so also he utilizes, quite mechanically, the most up-to-date system of carrying on business. As the systems go on improving—improving means becoming more economical—so he automatically goes on changing them. The system pervades the capitalist undertaking like some silent ghost ; " it " calculates, " it " keeps the ledgers, " it " works out prices, " it " determines rates of wages, " it " saves wherever possible, and so on. " It " dominates the undertaker himself ; " it " makes demands on him, " it " forces him to do what it requires. " It " never rests ; " it " is always on the watch, " it " is constantly becoming more and more perfect.   " It " lives a life of its own.

This independence of economic rationalism—its becoming objective, mechanical, automatic—is not without far-reaching consequences on undertaking, and therefore also on the growth of the capitalist spirit. The undertaker has a load taken off his shoulders. He buys automatic rationalism ready made, as it were, and engages salaried assistants to introduce it into his business and see that it is carried through. But even if he attends to this himself, his responsibilities are lessened nevertheless. For does he not achieve the greatest utilities without any thinking on his part? And what follows? While in olden times the intellectual energy of the undertaker was directed to the discovery of the cheapest and quickest means of production, it is now free to be utilized for other purposes. (Notice, in passing, this curious result : that with the last stage in the development of rationalism there appears a sort of traditional method which holds men in bond.) What these purposes are may be described in a word : Acquisition. The capitalist undertaker can now devote all his powers to this end. But there are other forces at work, all of them the result of the development of capitalism, which only heighten this tendency to get gain. The total result is that economic activities are expanded to the uttermost, a characteristic of modern economic life (as we have already noted), and therefore also a characteristic of the soul of the modern business man.

Let us consider how this comes about. In the soul of the modern business man there is a desire to achieve bigger and bigger things, and this forces him to be constantly undertaking more and more. But why? Principally because he wants more profit. Not that profit-chasing is the chiefest motive in his soul. The condition of things forces profit-chasing upon him.[438] All successful capitalist enterprise must necessarily work to provide a surplus. It matters not how the individual capitalist regards the surplus—whether he contents himself with the mere acquisition of gold, or whether he aims at power, or is satisfied so long as he is occupied, or even desires to utilize the surplus in schemes for social reform. In any event he must make profit ; his enterprise must be gainful.

So the undertaker must be on the move. Constant activity is forced upon him, and we may thus see the psychological explanation of the modern tendency to want to attempt absolutely everything, recognizing no limits whatever. Modern technical appliances only aid this tendency, and when it becomes active it receives an impetus from many quarters. Not the least, as we have already noted, is the psychological law that increased wealth produces an increasing desire for more. Another psychological law in this connection is that the greater the problem to be solved, the greater becomes the strength of the capacities and the will-power. This must have dawned on the earliest writers on capitalism, who praise it for this characteristic. The more business the more work, the more work the more profits—so we may sum up a passage in Alberti.439

The psychological tendency, then, is powerful enough in this direction. But the force of outward circumstances co-operates with it ; and from two sources, technical science and business organization.

Technical science in these days passes beyond all natural barriers, and its application, too, becomes an unnatural one. The undertaker must keep pace with all the latest inventions of technical science ; competition and profit-chasing force him to do so. But to keep pace with invention means that he must be ever ready to enlarge his business. Indeed, it has almost become a law of modern technical progress that if inventions are to be utilized the existing instruments of production must be increased and enlarged, and you must work on a grander scale all round. Perhaps the steel-works at Pittsburg are the largest undertaking of their kind in the world. How did their founder explain their expansion? By reference to the demands of technical progress. "We always hoped," said Mr. Carnegie,[440] "that there would be no need to grow. But we always found that to delay expansion would mean to be left behind. In fact, to this very day so fast and thick do the successive inventions come that we have as much to do as ever before."

Any freedom that technical advance may yet leave to the undertaker is certainly requisitioned by the needs of business organization. Here, as in the previous instance, the stress of outward circumstances forces the hands of the undertaker to attempt unlimited possibilities. There is little need to dwell on this phenomenon in an age when all production (except in agriculture) tends to be on a very large scale. But it is interesting to observe the psychology of the individual undertaker in this connection, and fortunately we have ample material for so doing in the autobiography of a capitalist undertaker on a large scale who was active in the early days of modern German capitalistic growth, and who speaks with a candour that throws a flood of light on the soul of the business man of to-day.[441] What does Dr. Strousberg tell us? His earliest intention was to derive so much profit from his various railway enterprises as would enable him to buy a country seat and to retire from business. If an opportunity offered itself, he intended to stand for Parliament and devote the remainder of his life to Parliamentary activity. But did he achieve his heart's desire? He explains why not. To build a railway takes a few years. In any case, you cannot be sure that your line will turn out a financial success. To be on the safe side, therefore, it is as well to build more than one line, so that the good enterprises may compensate for the failures. Besides, the organization necessary for one line may be used for many. The counting-house, the drawing-office, the various other offices will serve, at a small additional cost, for many railway lines. Moreover, even when the lines are ready, the offices must be retained in order to make final settlements with the railway company, the suppliers of raw material, the contractors, and the rest. You must also retain your engineers long after the work is completed. There are bound to be numerous queries to answer in the working of the line, and many other little things to see to. So it came about that Dr. Strousberg entered upon one engagement after another. His railway building brought other work with it, and little by little his original ideal slowly vanished into the distance and he gave himself up completely to his business.

Yet another characteristic of the modern business man, side by side with the impetus within him to undertake immeasurably large things, is his devotion to small affairs. This expresses itself in his intensive activities, forcing him to squeeze as much as possible into every minute, and so make economic life one long rush and bustle. Technical science has facilitated the process, but technical science cannot be held accountable for it. Telephones are in use in the Vatican, railway trains run in Spain, telegraphic messages are not unknown in Turkey. But in all three cases there is little rush or hurry. You get that only when the modern business man comes along, for capitalism has sown the seed of haste in his soul. Every schoolboy knows how capitalism must needs have a quick turnover. This is the secret power that effects such marvels. The velocity of the turnover determines prices and profits. For the more quickly any given amount of capital revolves the more cheaply can commodities be produced and the more speedily does the total profit grow.

Note, however, that the speeding up in the turnover is assisted by the speeding up in machinery, in transport service, and in buying and selling. All three owe much to modern technical progress, which finds out improved methods every day in order to curtail the whole system of economic activities, if need be, by but a few seconds. The speed with which the modern business man does his work is thus forced upon him by capitalism itself, aided by technical science. He must be quick, whether he wants to or not.

But as a matter of fact he does want to—just as much as he wants to be constantly expanding his business. He must needs be engaged in economic activities without cease, he wants to be economically active every minute of his life. This is our last point in the characterization of the soul of the modern business man, and requires a word or two of explanation.

What is to be said of the phenomenon that perfectly healthy, good-natured people, often enough with mental gifts above the average, should care for such a thing as economic activity? Not, mind you, because they regard it as a duty or as a necessary evil, but because they love it, because they have devoted themselves to it with heart and soul, with mind and body!

To solve this puzzle, let us recall what we saw in the colonist's mind. An utter loneliness filled its every niche, and, as a psychological necessity, gave birth to a longing for undertaking something or other, and to wild business enterprise. Outward circumstances force this state of mind on the colonial; all-powerful influences which we have just considered produce the same effect on the capitalist undertaker by their insistent action. Business is his sole preoccupation; is it any wonder that all else within him dries up? Everything about him becomes a wilderness, all life dies, all values disappear; in short, his environment is like that which Nature produces for the colonist. The home of the capitalist undertaker becomes for him, to all intents and purposes, something foreign. Nature, Art, Literature, Politics, friends—all vanish into nothingness. He has no time for them. The colonist at least finds refreshment for his soul in the family circle, but the fire of enterprise in the soul of the modern capitalist undertaker scorches even this last green spot out of his surroundings. He is thus left in the desert, and is in danger of perishing, seeing that all the ordinary values of life have ceased to exist for him. But life is strong within him ; he has the will to live. Accordingly, he must obtain new values, and he finds them in business. And if he is to retain the ground beneath his feet, if he is to make life worth living, he cannot possibly look upon the new values as useless and senseless. It is a curious phenomenon. From the dry sandy wastes of everyday life there ooze forth for the parched soul new springs of comfort. Though his own needs are few, he derives peculiar satisfaction in seeing his profits grow ; and the constant extension and perfecting of his business make his heart glow with pride. David Hume drew attention to the fact long ago : " If the employment you give him be lucrative, especially if the profit be attached to every particular exertion of industry, he has gain so often in his eye that he acquires by degrees a passion for it, and knows no such pleasure as that of seeing the daily increase of his fortune. And that is the reason why trade increases frugality, and why among merchants there is the same overplus of misers above prodigals as among the possessors of land there is the contrary." 442

If, for all that, this satisfaction of the modern capitalist undertaker should yet be incomplete, he will find pleasure in the universal enthusiasm for the technical progress of our age, more especially as he will be able to feel that he himself, by utilizing the results of technical progress, is helping to make history. It is true that economic activities are only the means by which technical ideas are made useful. But in accordance with the great law of our age, the means play the all-important part, and the end, humanity, is completely lost sight of. We have advanced so far that by a wonderful psychological process we praise economic activities for their own sake, and without a murmur. All values in life seem to be topsy-turvey, and yet the truncated system that ensues is able to offer sufficient attraction to men and women of to-day to go on putting forth effort without a word of complaint.

It was not Puritanism that forced the undertaker into the bog of senseless busy-ness, but capitalism ; and he was able to give himself completely up to it only when he lost the last foothold that kept him from sinking in the mire. I mean his religious feelings. For he requires no sense of duty in the thoughtless busy-ness that fills his life, and Time has taught him to create new life-values even in the desert by adding peculiar delights to his particular form of activity.

One result of this is that the intensity of economic life is stretched to its utmost limit. It is influenced not mostly by will-power but by the joy of action. The business of the capitalist undertaker becomes, as it were, his mistress : he dotes upon her with all his heart. Who shall wonder if this course tends to still greater intensity in economic activities ? Who shall wonder if the soul of the modern business man surpasses itself ?

Our task now is done : the soul of the modern business man is a sealed mystery no longer.

CONCLUSION

CHAPTER XXVIII

RETROSPECT AND PROSPECT

I can well imagine that the effect of this book on many readers will be to produce a troubled feeling within them. There has been so much new material and so many new points of view and questions that a certain restlessness may well be expected. Indeed, we cannot be anything but restless when in the consideration of scientific problems we seem to feel the ground slipping from beneath our feet ; and we do so when we lose the comfortable formulas that have hitherto been our guides amid the complexities of existence. In such a case we feel like drowning in the ocean of facts, until we find a new foothold or learn to swim.

Certainly this book had made short work of the prevailing formulas as to the nature and origin of the capitalist spirit. But many readers may be inclined to throw it aside as useless because I have provided no new formula in place of the old.

Are we to say, therefore, that the book is of no value at all ? A wit once said that a good book is one the contents of which may be summed up in a sentence. I confess I cannot do that in this case, except it be to say, The problem of the capitalist spirit—its true nature and its growth—is exceedingly intricate, far more intricate than most people imagined, more even than I myself once thought.

Yet though I am unable to provide any new formula, I shall attempt in these last pages to lessen the feeling of unrest that may have crept into the mind of the reader. I shall attempt to provide him with a sort of sketch-map by the aid of which he may find his way about in the mass of facts before him.

What was the picture we drew of the nature and development of the bourgeois ?

All historic development is the result of the natural capacities of the different national units that have appeared in European history since the break-up of the Roman Empire, and of their peculiar combination. In each group from its earliest history we find two mighty forces at work ; the one is the greed of gold, the other the spirit of enterprise. Very soon the two united, and from the union there sprang up in the home of each nation a number of strong organisms, economic and other, including the modern state itself. With the state the conception of religious dissent made its appearance, and gave a powerful impetus to the growth of the capitalist spirit. But this conception again arose from one other characteristic of the national consciousness among European peoples—their strong religiosity.

The same motive powers forced the different groups to undertake conquests and enterprises abroad in new lands. Here they discovered an undreamed-of abundance of the precious metals, which in their turn spurred on afresh the old greed of gold and the spirit of enterprise. Colonies were planted which, like the home lands, breathed the capitalist spirit.

The spirit of enterprise was first active in the upper classes, and consequently force played a great part in it.

But gradually it also spread among the broad masses, who strove to become rich not by force but by the peaceful methods of trafficking ; and it is clear that economical habits and careful calculations must have helped them in the process.

All peoples witnessed the gradual rise in their midst of the peaceful middle-class traders, who in the course of time became an influential body ; but in some the commercial spirit seemed to be more intense from the very first, and brought the mercantile interests to the fore more speedily. Such folk were the Etruscans, the Frisians, and the Jews ; and their influence increased as the psychology of the capitalist undertaker tended to become more and more that of the middle-class trader.

At first there were parallel streams in the national life of peoples ; gradually these merged into one, so that the capitalist undertaker united within himself the hero, the trader, and the middle-class respectable citizen. But as the stream flowed down to the sea, it was dominated more and more by the middle-class trader, while the heroic element slowly disappeared. Many forces helped to bring this result about ; in particular the rise of the military calling, the influence of morality and religion, both of which helped to maintain the position of the peaceful citizen, and last but not least the intermarrying of the nobility and gentry with " city " elements, which gave the latter the predominance. The truth is that heroic qualities are rare enough, and any institution that desires to become popular and widely accepted must base itself on those instincts and capacities possessed by the masses.

So the capitalist spirit developed apace, and we may distinguish two stages in its growth. The one reached out to about the end of the 18th century ; the other continued from that point of time to our own day. In the first, the early capitalist epoch, the spirit of capitalism was somewhat restricted by custom and morals, particularly as taught by the Christian sects ; and in the second it enjoyed much more liberty.

Now, capitalist enterprise, aiming as it does at profits, contains within itself tendencies that favour the growth of unlimited and unprincipled undertakings. Five factors combined to help the development of these tendencies : (1) Natural Science, born of the Germanic-Romance spirit, which was the mother of modern inventions ; (2) Speculation, born of the Jewish spirit. Modern technical progress allied with modern speculation provided the necessary forms for the limitless efforts of capitalist enterprise. The process was still more accelerated by (3) the general Jewish influence which since the 17th century has made itself felt in the economic life of Europe. From its very nature this influence could not but strive to extend its economic activities without let or hindrance, regardless of all considerations ; and its religion, far from restraining it, gave it free rein. The Jews were the catalytic substance in the rise of modern capitalism. (4) As religious feeling became weaker and weaker among the Christian peoples, the old bonds of morality and tradition that had held capitalism in check in its earliest stages gave way, until (5) they were completely removed when through emigration the most capable business types settled in new lands.

And so capitalism grew and grew and grew. To-day it is like a mighty giant striding through the land, treading down all that stands in its path.

What will its future be ?

Those who believe that the giant Capitalism is destroying both nature and man cannot but hope that he will be captured and put within the bounds that restrained him of old. Some people, indeed, expected to overcome him by appealing to ethical principles ; I, for my part, can see that such attempts are doomed to utter failure. When we remember that capitalism has snapped the iron chains of the oldest religions, it seems to me hardly likely that it will allow itself to be bound by the silken threads of the wisdom that hails from Weimar and Königsberg. So long as the giant continues to be all-powerful it is imperative to adopt such measures as will safeguard life and limb and goods and chattels. Place buckets of water in the shape of social legislation to protect the worker, appoint trusty men to carry them into practice, and you may extinguish the fire which is kindled in the peaceful abodes of our civilization.

But, then, it may be asked, will its raging last for ever ? Will it never be played out ? I believe it will. I believe that in the very nature of the capitalist spirit there are elements that are making for its break-up and decay. Cases of such decay we have already observed—in Germany and Italy in the 16th century, in Holland and France in the 17th, in England at the present time.* Doubtless special circumstances will partially account for the collapse in each case, but for the most part the result was brought about by the inherent tendencies in the capitalist spirit. As these influences were operative in the past, so they may be operative in the future. The spirit of enterprise (and with it naturally the capitalist spirit) dies when men sink into the comfortable ease of a life dependent on dividends ; or, on the other hand, when they are allured by the will-o'-the-wisps of society and fashion. The bourgeois waxes fat as his riches increase and as he accustoms himself to live on the interest of his capital, to be held in the vice of luxury, and to lead the life of a country gentleman. These

* [Cf. Mr. Edmund Holmes's *In Defence of What might be* (1914), chapter vi, " The Decadence of England."]

forces have been operative before; why should they cease to be active now?

Nor do these forces stand alone in our own day. In our own day capitalism must suffer wreck because of the increasingly bureaucratic character of all our undertakings. For that which is left after the dividend-receiver has had his share goes to the bureaucrat. It is clear enough that in a huge business run on a bureaucratic basis, where economic rationalism no less than the spirit of enterprise is a mechanical process, there is no room for the capitalist spirit.

But in all probability that spirit will be attacked from yet another quarter. As civilization increases the number of births decline, and before long the surplus of births over deaths vanishes away. Against such a tendency we seem powerless. No *lex Papia Poppæa*, no nationalist or religious revival, no problem plays will be of the slightest use in counteracting its results. As the population decreases capitalism will begin to lose strength. Was not its mighty progress in the 19th century due to the remarkable growth of the population?

And when the capitalist spirit has lost its power of expansion, what then? That does not concern us here. Possibly the blind giant may be condemned to draw the wagon of a democratic civilization; possibly it may be the Twilight of the Gods and the gold will have to be restored to the caverns of the Rhine. Who shall say?

NOTES AND REFERENCES

NOTES AND REFERENCES

INTRODUCTORY

LITTLE has been written on the subject of this book. Apart from the critical studies of the chapters of my *Modern Capitalism* which bear on the topics we may mention Max Weber's essays in *Archiv für Sozialwissenschaft und Sozialpolitik* (vol. 21) on " Die protestantische Ethik und der Geist des Kapitalismus." For the rest very miscellaneous sources have been drawn upon ; and their name is legion. For direct information as to the capitalist spirit we may find ample material in the personal utterances of men engaged in economic activities. Of course, this evidence must be carefully sifted ; and in many instances the direct opposite of what is stated may be concluded. Such direct evidence may be either occasional utterances, conversations, extracts from letters, and so on ; or autobiographies, wills, or reflections. But the indirect evidence is much more numerous. It may be classed under several heads :

(1) The actual achievements or modern business, which of necessity exemplify the capitalist spirit. Take such things as townplanning, organization of factories, transport facilities, technical aids of all sorts (railways, canals, waterworks, harbours), commercial organization (e.g. speed in calculations), insurance schemes, etc.

(2) Legal enactments and decisions—concerning competition, advertisements, price formation, interest.

(3) Moral maxims, whether of religious or secular origin. Here, too, may be included such things as social satires, party pamphlets, suggestions for reforms, and the like.

(4) Reflections of the age as seen in public opinion (say, the

attitude of people to certain callings ; the attitude of the nobility to trade), in literature, art, and science.

(5) The relationship of the social classes to one another—industrial peace or industrial war ; patriarchal interest of employer in employees, etc.

(6) Economic policy of a state—whether it favours free trade or protection, and so on.

The relative value of these sources must of course vary. The direct evidence is not abundant and thus not very fruitful of results. Nevertheless, there are cases where it is invaluable, particularly if you read between the lines. Especially does this hold good of memoirs and autobiographies of successful business men, in which the authors as a rule portray themselves as unselfish folk wholly occupied with the weal of the commonwealth, to whom money-getting is of comparatively little importance. (This last assertion may even hold good in some cases where the men concerned are steeped in wealth—say, Rockefeller, Carnegie, and others.) Some of the writers, however, are honest enough to lay bare their naked souls ; these obviously are the most useful authorities for our purpose. The autobiography of Strousberg [cf. pp. 175, 349] is a case in point. Another fact must not be overlooked. Most of the memoirs and autobiographies of this kind that we possess are of the men who stood head and shoulders above the crowd. Care is needed, therefore, in generalizing from them.

Of the remainder, the evidence numbered (1) above is most trustworthy : it never lies. That under (2) and (3) is also useful, but only when carefully sifted. Otherwise it is dangerous, so much so that some writers avoid it altogether.

CHAPTER I

1. St. Thomas, *Summa theolog.* IIa IIae, qu. 50, article 3.

2. St. Thomas, *Summa theolog.* IIa IIae, qu. 118, article 1.

3. Cf. my description of the seigniorial way of life in my *Luxus und Kapitalismus*, p. 102 ff.

4. Alberti, *Della famiglia*, p. 265.

5. Cf. Willy Boehm, *Friedrich Reisers Reformation des Kaisers*

Sigismund (1876), p. 218. " Es sind hantwerck darumb erdacht, das yederman sein täglich brot darmit gewin und soll niemant dem andern greiffen in sein hantwerck. damit schickt die welt ir notdurft und mag sich yederman erneren."

6. Keutgen, *Ämter und Zünfte* (1903), p. 84.

7. See, for example, B. C. Sattler, *Handelsrechnungen des deutschen Ordens* (1887), p. 8 ; or the Introduction to Kopp- mann's *Tölners Handlungsbuch* (xviii ff.) in the *Geschichtsquellen der Stadt Rostock*, I (1885) ; or the list of taxpayers of the City of Paris for 1292, published by Géraud (*Coll. des doc. inéd. S. I.*, vol. 8 (1837), where we read " La plupart des additions sont inexactes " (p. v).

8. This applies even to Pegolotti (14th century) and Uzzano (15th century).

9. H. Peetz, *Volkswissenschaftliche Studien* (1885), p. 186 ff.

10. A. Vierkandt, *Die Stetigkeit im Kulturwandel* (1908), p. 103 ff., a brilliant review of "Traditionalism."

11. F. Tönnies, *Gemeinschaft und Gesellschaft* (2nd ed., 1912), p. 112 ff.

12. A. Vierkandt [note 10], p. 105.

CHAPTER II

13. [For an English translation of the Edda, see *Corpus poeticum boreale*, by Vigfusson and F. York Powell, vol. 1, pp. 192 ff. Or, the translation by Miss Bray, issued by the Viking Club (Viking Club Publications, vol. 2).]

14. Gustav Freytag, *Bilder aus der deutschen Vergangenheit*, I, p. 184.

15. Luschin von Ebengreuth, *Allgemeine Münzkunde* (1904), p. 139.

15A. Lamprecht, *Deutsches Wirtschaftsleben*, vol. 2, p. 377.

16. Levasseur, *Histoire de l'industrie*, etc., vol. 1, p. 200.

17. Davidsohn, *Geschichte von Florenz*, vol. 1 (1896), p. 762.

18. Davilliers, *L'orfèvrerie et les arts décoratifs en Espagne*, quoted in Baudrillart, *Histoire du Luxe*, vol. 4, p. 217. Cf. also Soetbeer in the 57th Supplement of *Petermanns Mitteilungen*,

21.

19. Brückner, *Finanzgeschichtliche Studien,* p. 73; Schurtz, *Entstehungsgeschichte des Geldes* (1898), p. 120.

20. Amiet, "Die französische und lombardische Geldwucherer der Mittelalter" (*Jahrbuch für schweizerische Geschichte,* vol. I, p. 183).

21. Alberti, *Libri della famiglia,* p. 263.

22. Evidence on the point has been accumulated by E. Michael, *Geschichte des deutschen Volkes,* vol. I (1897), p. 139.

23.   " Regnat avaritia
                    regnant et avari

                  .   .   .

                  multum habet oneris
                  do, das, dedi, dare :
                  verbum hoc præ ceteris
                  norunt ignorare
                  divites, quos poteris
                  mari comparare."

Carmina Burana, No. lxvii, quoted by Michael [note 22], p. 142.

24. Michael [note 22], p. 142.

25. The text is quoted in C. Frey, *Loggia dei Lanzi.*

25A. *Regulo del governo di cura familiare,* p. 128, quoted in C. Guasti, *Ser Lapo Mazzei,* vol. I (1880), p. cxv.

26. These are a few instances from Alberti's pages. Some others may be found in *Della famiglia,* ed. G. Mancini (1908), pp. 36, 131, 132, 150, 208, 250, etc.

27. "El oro es excellentissimo, con el se hace tesoro y con el tesoro quien lo tiene, hace cuanto quiere en el mundo y llega que echa las animas al paraiso." Quoted in A. von Humboldt's *Examen critique de l'histoire de la Géographie du nouveau continent,* vol. 2 (1837), p. 40.

28. Cf. introduction to Vincent Tanara, *L'economia del cittadino in villa* (1648).

29. See, for example, Ulrich Gebhardt, *Von der Kunst reich zu werden,* Augsburg, 1656. The author despises gold, but his whole attitude (the very title of the book is significant) makes it appear that he was preaching to deaf ears, as he taught that the greatest wealth in the world was a kind heart and a sound mind.

CHAPTER III

30. Alberti, *Della famiglia*, p. 137.
31. V. Tanara [see note 28], p. 1.
32.   " Wiltu dich erneren
      du junger edelman,
      folg du miner lere
      sitz uff, drab zum ban !
      halt dich zu dem grünen wald
      wan der bur ins holz fert
      so renn in freislich an !
      derwüsch in bi dem kragen
      erfreuw das herze din
      nimm im was er habe
      span uss die pferdlin sin."

See W. Arnold, *Bibl. des Literarischen Vereins zu Stuttgart*, vol. 43 (1857), p. 101. For later periods (say 1400) see the Chronicle of Johannes Rothe of Creutzburg, edited by Karl Bartsch in *Mittelenglische Gedichte* (1860).

33. Uhland, *Alte hoch- und niederdeutsche Volkslieder*, vol. 1 (1844), p. 339.
34. H. Kapp, *Die Alchemie*, vol. 1 (1886), p. 12. A valuable supplement to this book will be found in Schmieder, *Geschichte der Alchymie* (1832). The author of this work still believes in alchemy, and thus gives us a glimpse into the soul of the adept.
35. " Es will fast jedermann ein Alchimiste heissen,
      Ein grober Idiot, der Jünger mit den Greisen,
      Ein Scherer, altes Weib, ein kurtzweiliger Rat,
      Der kahl geschorne Mönch, der Priester und Soldat."

See Kapp [note 34], vol. 1, p. 234, who quotes the *Examen alchemisticum* of Pantaleon.

36. Cf. also Paracelsus, *Cœlum philosophicum seu liber vexationum*, quoted by Kapp [note 34], vol. 1, p. 39.
37. See Louis Figuier, *L'alchimie et les alchimistes* (1860), p. 136.
38. Cf. H. von Sbrik, *Exporthandel Oesterreichs* (1907), p. 113.
39. In *Archiv für Sozialwissenschaft und soziale Politik*, vol. 34.

40. Ranke, *Fürsten und Völker von Südeuropa*, vol. 1 (1857), p. 410.

41. See G. Fagniez, *L'économie sociale de la France sous Henri IV* (1897), p. 33.

42. Charles Normand, *La bourgeoisie française au xvii siècle* (1908), p. 185. Beside the instances recorded in this valuable book, the following may be mentioned : In the 17th century there was the famous Theophraste Renaudot, "le fondateur du journalisme français, le cerveau le plus inventif peut-être de l'époque, dans lequel ont germé bon nombre d'idées utiles, à peine mêlées d'un grain d'utopie." Cf. G. d'Avenel, *Histoire économique*, vol. 1 (1894), p. 121. By his side may be placed Nicholas Blegny, who died in 1722. He has been described as " Apothecaire, écrivain, collectionneur et journaliste ; fondateur d'une société médicale, d'une maison de santé et d'un cours pour les garçons perruquiers ; premier chirurgien de la Reine et ' chirurgien ordinaire du corps de Monsieur ' ; chevalier d'industrie à l'occasion et finalement jeté en prison . . . auteur du ' Livre commode contenant les adresses de la ville de Paris, etc., par Abraham du Pradel, philosophe et mathematicien, Paris, 1692 ' " (new edition, 1878). Cf. E. Bonassé, *Dictionnaire des amateurs français au 17 siècle* (1884). [For an account of an English projector see Addison's *Spectator* (April 5, 1711).]

43. Cf. Mercier, *Tableau de Paris*, vol. 1, p. 222 (ch. 73).

44. In Adolf Beer, *Die Staatsschulden und die Ordnung des Staatshaushaltes unter Maria Theresia*, vol. 1 (1894), pp. 37–8.

45. The first lottery was instituted by the state in Florence in 1530 ; later developments of lottery came into existence in Holland in the 16th century, in Hamburg in 1610, in England in 1694, in Nuremberg in 1699. Cf. the article "Lotterie " in the *Handwörterbuch des Staatswissenschaften*. The interest in lotteries became intense towards the end of the 17th century. Cf. *Reflexions sur ce que l'on appelle bonheur et malheur en matière de Loteries*, Amsterdam, 1696.

46. I follow Max Wirth, *Geschichte der Handelskrisen* (1883).

47. W. Sombart, *The Jews and Modern Capitalism*, p. 88 [cf. for an evaluation of this book, "The Jews as an Economic Force," by M. Epstein, in *The Fortnightly Review*, April, 1914].

48. Defoe, *On Projects* (1697) [pp. 29, 30].

CHAPTER IV

48A. The problem treated in this chapter I first dealt with in an article on the subject in the *Archiv für Sozialwissenschaft und Sozialpolitik*, vol. 29 (1909). Cf. also H. Kurella, *Die Intellektuellen und die Gesellschaft* (1913).

49. The Greeks had a word to express the idea perfectly : χρηματίζειν. Cf. Plato, *Republic*, 434A.

CHAPTER V

49A. J. Burckhardt, *Kultur der Renaissance*, vol. 1 (3rd ed.), p. 23.

50. Carl Clausewitz, *Vom Kriege*, Bk. I, ch. 3. [There is now an English version of this book.]

51. Cf. J. Burckhardt [cf. note 49A], pp. 15, 16.

CHAPTER VI

52. Cf. also Lastig, " Beiträge zur Geschichte des Handelsrechts " in the *Zeitschrift für das gesammte Handelsrecht*, vol. 23, p. 152.

53. Clemens Sander, quoted in Ehrenberg's *Zeitalter der Fugger*, vol. 1 (1896), pp. 212–13.

54. C. Neuburg, *Goslars Bergbau* (1892), p. 191.

55. F. Dobel, " Der Fugger Bergbau und Handel in Ungarn " in the *Zeitschrift des historischen Vereins für Schwaben und Neuburg* (1907), p. 368.

56. H. von Sbrik [see note 38], p. 368.

57. P. Hitzinger, *Das Quecksilberbergewerk zu Idria* (1860), pp. 18, 24.

57A. U. Krafft, *Denkwürdigkeiten*, ed. Cohn (1862), p. 459.

58. K. Graf Sternberg, *Geschichte d. böhmischen Bergwerke*, vol. 1 (1836), p. 308.

59. G. R. Lewis, *The Stanneries* (1908).

60. H. Peetz [see note 9], p. 69.

61. H. Beck, *Geschichte des Eisens*, vol. 2, pp. 602 ff., 652.

62. Cf. Sternberg [see note 58], vol. 1, p. 389.

63. *Allgemeine Schatzkammer der Kaufmannschaft*, vol. 2 (1741), p. 734 f.

64. Cf. Savary's statement, " La plupart des personnes de qualité, de robe et autres donnant leur argent au négociants en gros pour le faire valoir ; ceux-ci vendent leur marchandise à crédit d'un an ou de quinze mois aux détaillants ; ils en tirent par ce moyen 10 % d'intérêt et profitent ainsi de 3 ou 4 %."

65. P. Kaeppelin, *La compagnie des Indes orientales* (1908), p. 6.

66. P. Kaeppelin [see note 65], p. 8. Cf. also Sternberg [see note 58], vol. 1, p. 2.

67. Cf. Sternberg [see note 58], vol. 1, p. 2.

68. Ed. Heyck, *Genua und seine Morium* (1886), p. 182.

69. W. Heyd, *Geschichte des Levantehandels im Mittelalter*, vol. 1 (1879), p. 255. For cases of piracy, cf. vol. 1, pp. 258, 263, 487, 489 ; vol. 2, p. 16. See also Tafel and Thomas, *Quellen zur oesterreichische Geschichte*, vol. 3, pp. 159–281.

69A. H. Pigeonneau, *Histoire du commerce de la France*, vol. 2 (1889), p. 170.

70. Published in Eugène Sue, *L'histoire de la marine française*, vol. 4 (1836), Bk. VII, ch. 1 and 2.

71. See *Histoire des Aventuriers*, by A. O. Oexmelin (J. Esquemeling), 1678. Cf. also P. Pyle, *The Buccaneers and Marooners of America*, 1891 ; Burney, *History of the Buccaneers of America*, latest edition, 1902 ; H. Handelmann, *Geschichte der Insel Haiti* (1856), p. 22. For a bibliography (not complete) of sea-robbery and piracy in the 16th and 17th centuries, see J. Pohler, *Bibliographia historico-militaris*, vol. 3 (1895), p. 737.

72. Froude, *History of England*, vol. 8 (1863), p. 451.

73. F. Hume Brown, *Scotland in the Time of Queen Mary* (1904), p. 72.

74. Gardiner, *Commonwealth*, vol. 1, p. 330, quoted in Cunningham's *Growth of English Industry and Commerce*, vol. 2 (1903), p. 188.

75. S. C. Hughson, *The Carolina Pirates and Colonial Commerce*, 1670–1740 (1894), one of the best books on the subject.

76. The most important documents illustrating the history of privateering in the North American colonies, including the very

valuable reports of the Earl of Bellamont to the Lords Commissioners of Trade, may be found in *Documents relating to the Colonial History of the State of New York*, vol. 4 (1854), pp. 306, 323, 447, 480, and 512. Cf. also Macaulay's *History of England*, vol. 10.

77. See, e.g., F. A. von Langegg, *El Dorado, Geschichte der Entdeckungenfahrten nach dem Goldlande El Dorado im xvi und xvii Jahrhundert*, 1888.

78. The philosopher's stone slowly began to be the accompaniment of the wished-for El Dorado. Cf., e.g., Laurentius Ventura in his *Aenigma della Pietra phisica* (1571) :—

> " Nell' India (parte più calda del mondo)
> Nasce pietra talhar ch'en se rinchiude
> Virtù infinite che vengon dal cielo."

Cf. C. G. von Murr, *Literarische Nachrichten zu der Geschichte des sogenannten Goldmachens* (1805), p. 40.

79. A good recent biography of Raleigh is that by Hugh de Sélincourt, *Great Raleigh* (1908).

80. Captain Francis Allen to Anthony Bacon, August 17, 1589, quoted by Douglas Campbell, *The Puritans in Holland, England, and America*, vol. 2 (1892), p. 120. [With regard to Drake, for a somewhat new aspect of his career see *New Light on Drake : a collection of documents relating to his circumnavigation*, translated and edited by Zelia Nuttall (The Hakluyt Society, 1914).

81. Benjamin of Tudela's travels. [There is an English translation of this interesting work by A. Asher, London, 1840.]

81A. Cf. G. Caro, *Sozial- und Wirtschaftsgeschichte der Juden*, vol. 1 (1908), p. 235.

82. See H. R. Fox Bourne, *English Merchants* (1886), for a study of English merchants in the early capitalist epoch.

83. F. A. von Langegg [see note 77]. Also Konrad Häbler, *Die überseeischen Unternehmungen der Welfer und ihrer Gesellschafter* (1903), and F. Eulenburg in the *Historische Zeitschrift* (1904), p. 104.

84. Ulrich Kraffts, *Merkwürdigkeiten*, ed. Cohn, 1862.

84A. H. Pigeonneau [see note 69A], vol. 2 (1889), p. 170.

85. Cf. Sieveking, *Genueser Finanzwesen*, vol. 1, p. 177 ; vol. 2, p. 99.

86. O. Burrish, *Batavia illustrata, or, A View of the Policy and Commerce of the United Provinces* (1728), p. 333.

87. Prince Neuwied, *Reise in Nordamerika*, vol. 1, pp. 351, 427, 552, 610 ; vol. 2, p. 71 ; quoted by Roscher, *Kolonien* (3rd ed., 1885), p. 267.

88. Heyd [note 69], vol. 2, p. 376.

89. Postlethwayt, *Dictionary of Commerce*, vol. 1, p. 241.

90. Report of the Lords Commissioners of Trade and Plantations, quoted by Anderson [note 132], vol. 3, p. 203. In Postlethwayt's *Dictionary*, vol. 1, p. 728, there is an account of the forts, munition, and men on the African coast.

91. Cunningham [see note 74], vol. 2, p. 70.

92. As is done for example in J. P. J. Dubois, *Vie des gouverneurs généraux avec l'abrégé des établissements hollandais aux Indes orientales* (1763).

93. Cf. E. Laspeyres, *Geschichte der volkswirtschaftlichen Anschauungen der Niederländer* (1863), p. 60.

94. Peter Mischler, *Das deutsche Eisenhüttengewerbe*, vol. 1 (1852), p. 201.

95. For instance see *Dictionnaire du Commerce*, under Société ; the *Introduction à la Correspondance administr. de Louis XIV*, vol 3, p. liv (by Depping) ; G. Martin, *La grande industrie sous Louis XV* (1900), p. 109 ; Postlethwayt, *Dictionary of Commerce*, vol. 2, p. 778 ; Anderson, *Origin of Commerce* [see note 132], vol. 2, p. 594 ; George Unwin, *Industrial Organization in the 16th and 17th Centuries* (1904), pp. 145, 165.

96. Cf. R. M. Garnier, *History of the English Landed Interest*, 2 vols, 1892, 2nd ed., 1908.

97. G. Knapp, *Die Bauernbefreiung*, 2 vols, 1887.

98. G. T. Lapsley in *English Historical Review*, vol. 14 (1899), p. 509.

99. Unwin [see note 95], p. 167.

100. Rymer, *Fœdera*, vol. 18, p. 870, quoted by Anderson [see note 132], vol. 2, p. 234.

101. Hugh de Sélincourt [see note 79], p. 89.

102. Anderson [see note 132], vol. 2, p. 594.

102A. Jars, *Voyages métallurgiques*, vol. 1 (1774), p. 190.

103. Cf. Claude Corbier, "Les forges à Guerigny" in *Bulletin de la Société nivernaise,* 1870.

104. G. Martin, *Louis XV,* p. 115.

105. Ibid. p. 110.

106. Ibid. p. 214.

107. Ibid. p. 115.

108. Cf. A. des Cilleuls, *La grande industrie* (1898), p. 59, and notes, 210.

109. Depping [see note 95], vol. 3, p. lx.

110. G. Martin, *Louis XIV* (1899), p. 318.

111. P. Hitzinger [see note 57], pp. 13, 14.

112. S. Worms, *Schwazer Bergbau* (1904), p. 37.

113. H. Beck, *Geschichte des Eisens,* vol. 2, p. 152.

114. Beck, vol. 2, p. 620.

115. Gustaf of Gejerstam, *Arbetarnes ställning vid fyra svenska grufoor.*

116. W. J. Ashley, *Woollen Industry,* p. 80 ; cf. Gibbins, *Industry of England* (1906 ed.), p. 147.

117. Rymer, *Fœdera,* 19, 35, quoted by Anderson [note 132], vol. 2, p. 335.

118. G. Martin, *Louis XV* (1900), p. 199.

119. A. de Calonne, *La vie agricole sous l'ancien régime en Picardie et en Artois* (1883), p. 111.

120. Cf. G. Martin, *Louis XV,* pp. 113, 214.

121. Cf. Karl Přibram, *Geschichte der oesterreichischen Gewerbepolitik,* vol. 1 (1907), p. 120.

122. T. Geering, " Entwicklung des Zeugdrucks im Abendlande seit dem 17ten Jahrhundert" in the *Vierteljahrschrift für Sozial- und Wirtschaftsgeschichte,* vol. 1, p. 409.

123. See the letters patent for 1577, 1603, 1615, 1655, 1727, and 1734 in A. des Cilleuls [see note 95], notes 17, 18, and 19.

124. For France, see P. Boissonade, *Organisation du Travail en Poitou,* vol. 1 (1900), p. 120. For Germany, *Allgemeine Schatzkammer der Kaufmannschaft,* vol. 3 (1742), p. 677. For England, Rymer, *Fœdera,* vol. 20, p. 191, quoted in Anderson [see note 132], vol. 2, p. 376.

125. The colonial systems in the Levant and in Central and South America I have described at length in my *Modern Capitalism,* vol. 1, p. 331.

126. J. C. Ballagh, *White Servitude in Virginia* (1895), p. 17 ;

E. J. McCormac, *White Servitude in Maryland* (1904), p. 11 ;
R. W. Jeffrey, *The History of the Thirteen Colonies of North America* (1908).

126A. T. Vogelstein, *Organisationsformen der Eisenindustrie und Textilindustrie in England und Amerika* (1910), p. 191.

127. *Lettres, etc., de Colbert*, par P. Clément, vol. 2, part 2, ccvii.

128. F. von Bezold, *Staat und Gesellschaft des Reformationszeitalters* (1908), p. 64.

129. Leipziger Sammlungen (ed. Zinken, 1745), vol. 9, p. 973, quoted by Schmoller in his *Jahrbuch*, vol. 15, p. 8.

130. Alfred Bosenik, *Über die Arbeitsleistung beim Steinkohlenbergbau in Preussen* (1906), p. 103.

131. See Levasseur [note 16], vol. 2, p. 246, for Colbert's work in founding the " Compagnie du Point de France."

132. A. Anderson [*An Historical and Chronological Deduction of the Origin of Commerce, from the Earliest Accounts*, 4 vols., 1787], vol. 3, p. 91.

133. Think of the " spirit " of the great speculator, and the mind immediately turns to the characterization of Saccard in Zola's *L'Argent*.

134. From the Clothworkers' Court Book, July 12, 34 Henry VIII, quoted by Unwin [see note 95], p. 57.

135. 3 & 4 Edward VI, c. 6, quoted by Unwin, p. 56.

136. Cf. Levasseur [see note 16], vol. 2, p. 163.

137. For Frankfort on the Main, see F. Bothe, *Beiträge zur Wirtschafts- und Sozialgeschichte der Reichstadt Frankfurt* (1906), p. 73 ; Kracauer, " Beiträge zur Geschichte der Frankfurter Juden im Dreisigjährigen Kriege " in *Zeitschrift für Geschichte der Juden in Deutschland*, vol. 3 (1889), p. 148. For London, see *History of the Trade in England* (1702), pp. 134, 164 ; C. Weiss, *Histoire des réfugiés protestants*, vol. 1 (1853), p. 337. For Bordeaux, P. Malvezin, *Les Juifs à Bordeaux* (1875), p. 196.

137A. Cf. W. Heyd [see note 69], vol. 2, pp. 295, 336, 477, 486. Cf. also the same writer's article, " Die italienischen Handelskompagnien auf Cypern " in *Zeitschrift für die gesammte Staatswissenschaften* (1865).

138. Cf. John Mackintosh, *History of Civilization in Scotland*, vol. 3 (1895), p. 300.

138A. Heinrich Heine in his *English Fragments* (1828), ch. iv.

139. " Un entrepreneur de fabrique qu'il connaisse ou qu'il ne connaisse pas le détail des opérations d'un grand objet, est celui qui les embrasse toutes, ainsi que les spéculations qui y ont rapport et qui a en sous ordre des contre-maîtres et des commis pour diriger les unes et les autres et les lui rapporter comme à un centre qui leur est commun. Ainsi l'homme qui est à la tête d'un établissement en grand, où l'on employe diverses sortes de matière ou d'un établissement où l'on modifie très diversement la même matière—cet homme est un entrepreneur. Si, au lieu de cela, il n'a, par exemple, à diriger qu'une manufacture de draps, de toiles, d'étoffes quelconques, dont les détails plus rapprochés, peuvent et doivent être sus et suivi imperturbablement par lui-même, cet homme est un fabricant : il a ou il n'a pas sous lui des contre-maîtres ; mais il est le premier contre-maître de sa fabrique." See article "Attelier" in the *Encyclop. méthodique manufact.*, vol. 1 (1785), p. 1.

139A. G. Schmoller, *Geschichte der deutschen Kleingewerbe* (1870), p. 580.

140. For Berlin, cf. O. Wiedfeldt, *Die Berliner Industrie* (1899), p. 79.

CHAPTER VII

141. See, for example, the so-called *Zibaldoni*, of which numerous instances are extant, as, e.g., the *Tesoro* of Brunetti Latini, the *Dittamondo* of Fazio degli Uberti, the *Zibaldone* of Giovanni Ruccellai. None of them has, to my knowledge, been edited. Extracts from the last named may be found in G. Marcotti's *Un mercante fiorentino e la sua famiglia nel secolo xv* (Florence, 1881). For a notice of this book see D'Ancona in the *Nuova Antologia* for July 15, 1881. These *Zibaldoni* were a sort of scrap book, in which their authors set down the important events of their land and family, extracts from their reading, their commercial experience and trade advice. The family books of Alberti are one of the principal sources of this kind ; an excellent edition of these is now available : Leon Battista Alberti, *I Libri della Famiglia*, editi da Girolamo Mancini, Florence, 1908. Agnolo Pandolfini's *Del governo della famiglia* (frequent editions since 1825), which was so highly

praised by Burckhardt [see note 49A], vol. 1, p. 164, is merely an almost verbal reproduction of Alberti.   Concerning the *Recordanze domestiche* of Luca di Matteo da Panzano (1406–61) there is some account (but not a good one) by Carlo Carnefechi, " Un fiorentino del secolo xv," in *Archivo storio italiano*, 5th series, vol. 4, p. 145.   Useful to a slight extent also is *Lettere di un notaro a un mercante del secolo xiv*, published by Cesare Guasti, under the title *Ser Lapo Mazzei*, 2 vols., Florence, 1880.

142. Alberti, *Della famiglia*, p. 142.   Pandolfini has almost the identical words.

143. Giovanni Ruccellai in his *Zibaldone* (1459), quoted in Marcotti [note 141], p. 106.

144. Ruccellai once more, in Marcotti, p. 112.

145. Alberti [note 142], p. 135.

146. Ibid. pp. 150–4.

147. Ibid. p. 154.

148. Ibid.

149. Ibid. pp. 198–9.

149A. Ibid. p. 163.

150. Ibid. p. 166.

151. Ibid. p. 45.

152. Ibid. pp. 121, 200.

153. Ibid. p. 200.

154. Ibid. p. 165.

155. Ibid. p. 137.

156. In a historical novel by Dimitry Sergew Mereschkowski, *Leonardo da Vinci*.   A German translation was published in 1912.

157. Cf. *Agricoltura tratta da diversi antichi et moderni scrittori. Da Sig. G. Alfonso d'Herrera . . . et tradotta di lingua spagnuola in italiana da Mambrino Roseo da Fabriano.   In Venetio, 1592.*

158. See the Italian translation of Etienne (1581), pp. 7, 10, 12, 14, 28, and ch. 6.

159. V. Tanara [note 31], pp. 2, 119, 202, 269.

160. *Le parfait négociant*, by Jacques Savary, 4th ed., vol. 1 (1697), p. 31.

161. *The Complete English Tradesman* (5th ed., 1745).

162. *Franklins Schatzkästlein*, ed. by von Bergk, vol. 1 (1839), p. 71.

163. *The Writings of Benjamin Franklin*, by Albert Henry Smyth, 1907, vol. 2, p. 370.

164. [Smyth, vol. 3, p. 408, " Preface to Poor Richard improved, 1758."]

165. " Poor Richard's Almanac," Smyth, vol. 3, pp. 413 and 417.

166. Smyth, vol. 2, p. 372.

167. Franklin's Autobiography, Smyth, vol. 1, p. 326.

168. Cf. *Le négociant patriote* (1779), p. 13.

169. Smyth, vol. 1, Introduction, p. 44.

170. Alberti, *Della famiglia*, pp. 133, 134.

171. Cf., e.g., Samuel Lamb in his memorandum against the foundation of a Bank in London (1659), in Lord Somers' Tracts. Cf. also the view of Owen Felltham in his *Observations* (1652) as to " the moderation and constancy " of the Dutch, and the greed of the English, who " would cheat all if it were in their power." Quoted by Douglas Campbell in his *Puritans*, vol. 2, p. 327. Compare furthermore Froude's *History of England*, vol. 12, p. 565, and F. A. Inderwick, *The Interregnum*, pp. 62, 79, 81.

172. Alberti [see note 170], pp. 139, 140.

173. Smyth, vol. 1, p. 307.

CHAPTER VIII

174. See, for example (Lucas de Burgo), *Summa de Arithmetica* (1494), ed. 1523, p. 198 [compare also Burke's famous dictum, in his *Reflexions on the French Revolution*, " The age of chivalry is gone, that of sophisters, economists, and calculators has succeeded "].

175. Some useful books of reference on the subject of the whole of Chapter VIII may be added. The *Liber Abaci* was published in 1857 by Buoncompagni. The system of double entry of Fra Luca is treated of by E. L. Jäger, *Lucas Pacioli und Simon Stevin* (1876). For a history of calculation consult any good history of mathematics. Furthermore, Hugo Grosse, *Historische Rechenbücher des 16 und 17 Jahrhunderts* (1901).

176. Alberti [note 170], pp. 191–2.

177. Smyth, vol. 1, p. 345.

178. Ludolf Schleicher, *Das merkantilische Hamburg* (1838), p. 75.

CHAPTER X

179. Burckhardt [note 49A], vol. 1, p. 78.

180. Ibid. vol. 2, pp. 107, 167.

181. For the sources see Burckhardt, vol. 2, p. 167.

182. Cf. also the " Proemio " in Crescenzi, *Dell' agricultura* (1605).

183. Cf. Buckle, *History of Civilization*, vol. 2, p. 67.

184. Sempere, *Monarchie Espagnole*, vol. 2, p. 50.

185. von Bezold [note 128], p. 45.

186. Ranke [note 40], vol. 1 (1857), p. 446.

187. Travellers of the 17th century all bear witness to the disappearance of the capitalist spirit from Spain in those days. Says a writer in 1699 : " Ils méprisent tellement le travail, que la plûpart des artisans sont étrangers." *Voyages faits en divers temps par M.M.*, Amsterdam, 1700, p. 80. An Englishman in 1693 reported : " They think it below the dignity of a Spaniard to labour and provide for the future," *Travels by a Gentleman*, London, 1702, p. 35. See also D'Aulnoy, *Relat. du Voyage d'Espagne*, Lyons (1693), vol. 2, pp. 369–70. All these authorities are quoted by Buckle [note 183], vol. 2, p. 64.

188. For Mexico (Spaniards) see A. von Humboldt, *Nouvelle Espagne*, vol. 4, p. 21. For Brazil (Portuguese), see von Eschwege, *Pluto brasiliensis* (1833), p. 251.

189. Montaigne, *Essays*, livre 1, ch. 30.

190. See P. Kaeppelin [note 65], p. 4.

191. P. Kaeppelin, pp. 4, 11, 16, 130.

192. *Le négociant patriote* (1779), p. 13.

193. Ibid. pp. 27, 228.

194. Cf. Pigeonneau [note 69A], vol. 2, pp. 175-6.

195. C. Normand [note 42], pp. 11, 42. See also Levasseur [note 16], vol. 2, p. 237, for the same point ; likewise Savary [note 160], vol. 2, p. 183. [That this French characteristic has in no wise disappeared in modern days is shown by Emile Faguet's book, *The Decay of Responsibility* (English version by Mrs. Putnam).]

196. Lassemas, *Traité du commerce de la vie du royal marchand* (1601), quoted by G. Fagniez [note 41], p. 253.

197. "Tout est perdu lorsque la profession lucrative du traitant parvient encore par ses richesses à être une profession honorée."

198. "Est stultissimum ac sordidissimum negotiatorum genus. . . ."

199. "Es ist vor allen ein überaus stinckende Sect der Kauffleut. . . ."

200. Otto Neurath, "Zur Anschauung der Antike über Handel, etc.," in *Jahrbücher für Nationalökonomie*, Series 34, p. 179.

201. Cf. my *Deutsche Volkswirtschaft im* 19*ᵗᵉⁿ Jahrhundert* (1913), pp. 100, 118.

202. All the following quotations are from Buckle [note 183], vol. 2, p. 160.

203. Such is the heading of a chapter in Schulze-Gaevernitz's valuable book, *Britischer Imperialismus und englischer Freihandel* (1906).

204. Ibid. p. 362.

205. Some of it will be found in T. Vogelstein [126A], p. 170.

CHAPTER XI

206. Alberti [note 170], p. 49.

207. Ibid. p. 139.

208. Ibid. p. 49.

209. *The Economy of Human Life* (1785), p. 338.

210. *The Way to Wealth* (edition by Dr. Bergk, 1838).

211. Ibid.

212. Alberti [note 170], p. 242.

213. *The Economy of Human Life*, p. 121.

[213A]. Smyth [note 163], vol. 1, p. 332.

[213B]. *The Complete English Tradesman*, part 2 (1727 ed.), pp. 97, 161 and 213.

214. G. Smith, *Diss. de privilegiis societatis Indiæ orientalis* (1786), quoted by Laspeyres [note 93], p. 91.

215. Laspeyres [note 93], p. 87.

216. Alberti [note 170], p. 165.

217. Cf. J. Godard, *L'ouvrier en soie*, vol. 1 (1899), pp. 38–9.

218. Cf. Fox Bourne [note 82], p. 394.

219. *The Jews and Modern Capitalism*, p. 122.

220. See *Allgemeine Schatzkammer der Kaufmannschaft* (1741), vol. 3, p. 148 ; vol. 4, p. 677 ; vol. 3, p. 1325 ; vol. 1, p. 1392.

221. W. Barrett, *The Old Merchants of New York City* (1863), pp. 22, 25.

222. *The Complete English Tradesman* (ed. 1727), part 2, p. 111.

223. Josiah Child, *A New Discourse of Trade* (4th ed.), p. 159.

224. See Unwin [note 95], p. 117.

225. See Levasseur [note 16], vol. 2, p. 257.

226. J. J. Becher, *Närrische Weisheit* (1686), p. 15.

226A. Cf. Carl Ergang, "Untersuchungen zum Maschinenproblem in der Volkswirtschaftlichen Lehre," in *Freiburger Volkswirtschaftliche Abhandlungen*, vol. 1, section 2 (1911), pp. 4 and 10.

227. Montesquieu, *Esprit des Lois*, bk. 23, ch. 15.

228. Postlethwayt [note 89], vol. 2, p. 121.

CHAPTER XII

229. Walter Rathenau, *Reflexionen* (1908), p. 81.

230. Ibid. p. 82.

231. See my essay in *Archiv für Soziale Wissenschaft*, vol. 29, p. 700, where I have elaborated this subject.

232. Andrew Carnegie's *Autobiography*.

233. Report of the Indiana Commission (1900), p. 795.

234. *Dr. Strousberg und sein Wirken.* By himself (1876), p. 397.

235. L. Jolles, "Eine wirtschaftliche Personlichkeit" in *Der Tag*, No. 215 of 1909.

236. W. Rathenau [note 229], p. 99.

237. John R. Rockefeller's *Memoirs*.

CHAPTER XIII

238. Ludwig Feuchtwanger, "Die ethischen Grundlagen der Nationalökonomie," in Schmoller's *Jahrbuch*, vol. 37 (1913), p. 961.

239. See F. Rochfahl, "Kalvinismus und Kapitalismus" in *Internationales Wochenschrift* (1909), p. 1293.

240. Cf. for instance Rathenau [note 229], p. 92.

CHAPTER XIV

241. Consult the *Handwörterbuch der Philosophie*, by Dr. Rudolf Eisler (1913), for "natural gifts." Also H. Kurella [note 48A].

242. Werner Siemens, *Lebenserinnerungen*, p. 296.

243. Cicero, *Brutus*, p. 257.

244. Xenophon, *Œconomicus*, chaps. 2, 9, and 12.

245. Columella, *De re rustica*, lib. xi. ch. 1.

CHAPTER XV

246. Cf. H. E. Ziegler, *Die Naturwissenschaft und die sozial-demokratische Theorie* (1893), p. 251.

247. For the ethnography of Scotland, see W. F. Skene, *Celtic Scotland*, 3 vols. (1876–80) ; John Mackintosh, *History of Civilization in Scotland*, 4 vols. (1892).

248. A. W. Wiston-Glynn, *John Law of Lauriston* (1907), p. 3.

249. For a good account of the ethnology of the Iberian Peninsula see H. Schurtz, "Die Pyrrhenäen-Halbinsel," in Helmholts' *Weltgeschichte*, vol. 4.

250. Cf. J. Jung in Helmholts, vol. 4, p. 366.

251. Cicero, *De officiis*, I, c. 42. Cf. Otto Neurath [note 200], p. 577.

252. G. Toniolo, *Dei remoti fattori della potenza economica di Firenze* (1882), pp. 12, 46.

253. For the Etruscans, see Müller-Deecke, *Die Etrusker*, 2 vols. (1877). Cf. also Pauli, "Die Urvölker der Apenninhalbinsel" in Helmholts [note 249], vol. 4 ; also H. Genthe, *Über den etruskischen Tauschhandel nach den Norden* (1874).

254. Müller-Deecke, ibid. vol. 2, p. 325.

255. Livy, v. 1.

256. Davidsohn [note 17], vol. 1, p. 39.

257. Skene [note 247], vol. 1, pp. 145, 191, 231.

258. J. Klumker, *Der friesische Tuchhandel zur Zeit Karls des Grossen* (Doctorate dissertation, University of Leipzig).

259. T. Hume Brown, *Scotland in the Time of Queen Mary* (1904), p. 182.

259A. Cf. Luigi Passerini, *Gli Alberti de Firenze. Genealogia, storia e documenti*, 2 vols., 1869.

CHAPTER XVI

260. Alberti, pp. 164, 198, 264 *et passim.*

261. Cf. N. Tamassia, *La famiglia italiana net sc. xv e xvi* (1910), p. 40.

262. Marcotti [note 141], p. 106.

263. Ibid. p. 46.

264. Xenophon, *Œconomicus*, ch. 11.

265. Ibid.

266. Max Weber, *Römische Agrargeschichte* (1891), p. 225.

267. Cf. Columella [note 245], lib. i. ch. 1.

268. Ibid. lib. xi. ch. 1.

269. " Divitiæ grandes homini sunt vivere parce."

CHAPTER XVII

270. Alberti [note 141], p. 54.

271. Ibid. p. 122.

272. Cf. Charles Dejob, *La foi religieuse en Italie au xiv siècle* (1906).

273. Cf. G. Toniolo, *Dei remoti fattori della potenza economica di Firenze* (1882).

274. Cf., for instance, O. Hartwig, *Quellen und Forchungen zur älteren Geschichte von Florenz*, vol. 1 (1875), p. 93.

275. Charles de Ribbe, *Les familles et la société en France avant la Révolution d'après des documents originaux*, 2nd ed., 2 vols., Paris (1874). The book contains numerous extracts from the *Livres de raison* of the 15th to the 18th centuries.

276. W. Sombart, *The Jews and Modern Capitalism*, p. 191 ff.

CHAPTER XVIII

277. Cf. Jacob Strieder, " Kirche, Staat und Frühkapitalismus" in the *Hertling Festschrift* (1913). See also, for further references, Sombart's *Der Moderne Kapitalismus*, vol. 1 (1902).

278. Our principal source is to be found in the writings of St. Thomas himself. The citations in the following notes are from the Jubilee edition of the work, *S. Thomæ Aquinatis Summa theologica*, Rome (1886). Even more important are the writings of the later Schoolmen, notably the *Summa theologica* of St. Antonine of Florence, of which I have used the Florentine edition of 1741, *S. Antonini . . . summa moralis, cura Th. Mariæ Mammachi et Dionysii Remedelli* (the best edition is that of Verona of 1741). Beside these two authorities the following should likewise be consulted : *Bernhardini Senensis Opera omnia*, 5 vols., Paris (1636) ; *Chrys. Javellus, Philosophia œconomica divina atque christiana*, Venice (1540). As for modern works, the following may be mentioned : W. Endemann, *Studien in der romanisch-kanonischen Wirtschafts- und Rechtslehre*, 2 vols. (1874–83) ; Funk, " Über die ökonomischen Anschauungen der mittelalterlichen Theologen," in the *Zeitschrift für die gesammten Staatswissenschaften*, vol. 25 (1869). A good piece of work, unfortunately left unfinished, is M. Maurenbrecher's Leipzig doctorate dissertation, *Thomas von Aquinos Stellung zum Wirtschaftsleben seiner Zeit*. Antonine of Florence has been carefully studied by Carl Ilgner in his book, *Die volkswirtschaftlichen Anschauungen Antonins von Florenz* (1904). Another piece of work worth mentioning in this connection is Franz Keller's *Unternehmung und Mehrwert. Eine sozial-ethische Studie zur Geschäftsmoral* (1912). (This forms the twelfth volume of the *Schriften der Görres-Gesellschaft, Sektion für Rechts- und Staatswissenschaften*.) Finally, Ernst Troeltsch will be found suggestive in his *Die Soziallehren der christlichen Kirchen und Gruppen* (1912).

[For a good account in English of the canonist doctrines, see Professor Ashley's *Economic History*, vol. 1, part 1, ch. 3, and part 2, ch. 6.]

279. St. Thomas, *Summa* [note 278], II^a II^{ae}, qu. 153, a. 2 and 3.

280. "Virtus consistet in medio rei vel rationis." Cf. Antonine, *Summa moralis* [note 278], II, 9, cap. 3 and 4.

281. St. Thomas [note 278], II^a II^{ae}, qu. 155, a. 1.

282. Ibid. qu. 98, a. 5.

283. Antonine, *Summa moralis* [note 278], II, 9.

284. The Canonist doctrines stand most stringently for the Jewish teaching that sexual intercourse should be only for the purpose of propagation. Cf. St. Thomas [note 278], II^a II^{ae}, qu. 153, a. 2 and 3.

285. St. Antonine [note 278], II, 6, 8, § 1.

286. Ibid. IV, 5, 17, § 4.

287. St. Thomas [note 278], qu. 129, a. 4.

288. St. Antonine, IV, 5, 17, § 1.

289. Ibid. II, 6, 8, § 1.

290. Cf. also St. Thomas, qu. 117, 118, and 119.

291. St. Antonine, II, 6, 8, § 1.

292. Ibid.

293. Ibid.

294. Ibid. II, 9, 2, § 2.

295. Ibid.

296. Ibid. II, 1, 16, § 2. Cf. also the whole of chap. 17, the superscription of which is " De variis fraudibus, quæ committitur in negotiando."

297. Alberti [note 141], p. 134.

298. St. Thomas [note 278], qu. 49, 53, 123.

299. Cf. Part II, 9 of *Summa moralis* [note 278].

300. St. Thomas [note 278], qu. 53, a. b.

301. Cf. Ilgner [note 278], p. 151.

302. St. Antonine [note 278], IV, 2, 3.

303. Ibid. II, 11, § 1.

304. Ibid. I, 7, 3, § 2.

305. Ibid. II, 1, 11, § 1.

306. Cf. the commentary of Cardinal Cajetan to St. Thomas [note 278], qu. 118, a. 1.

307. St. Antonine [note 278], II, 1, 16, § 2.

308. Bernhardini Senensis [note 278], 3, 311. Cf. F. Keller [note 278], pp. 35, 78.

309. St. Thomas [note 278], qu. 78, a. 2.

310. St. Antonine [note 278], III, 8, 4, § 2.

311. Ibid. II, 1, 6, § 16.   Cf. Bernhardini Senensis, Sermo 42, ch. 2 [note 278].

312. Bernhardini Senensis [note 278], 34, ch. 3.

313. "Dans pecuniam . . . artefici ad materias emendas et ea eis artificiata faciendum." St. Antonine [note 278], II, 1, 5, 37.

314. Ibid. II, 1, 5, 46.

315. "Modo societatis." Ibid. II, 1, 5, 37.

316. Ibid. II, 1, 6, § 15, § 29. Cf. Bernhardini Senensis, Sermo 42, ch. 2.

317. St. Antonine, II, vol. 1, ch. 5, § 34.

318. Ibid. II, 1, 5, § 37.

319. Ibid.

320. Ibid. II, 1, 6, §§ 16 and 36; also II, 1, 16, § 2.

321. "Sunt nobiles qui nolunt laborare ; et ne pecunia eis deficiat paulatim consumendo, tradunt eam mercatori vel trapezitae, intendentes principaliter aliquid annuatim recipere ad discretionem eorum salvo tamen capitali : tamen clare usura est."

322. St. Antonine, II, 1, 2, § 6

CHAPTER XIX

323. Baxter, *Christian Directory*, vol. 1 (1678), pp. 218, 220, part 2, ch. 28.

324. Ibid. vol. 1, pp. 219, 229.

325. Hutcheson, *Exposition of the Book of Job*, p. 296; Binning, *Sermons*, vol. 3, p. 359, quoted in Buckle [note 183], vol. 2, p. 388; Cockburn, *Jacob's Vow, or Man's Felicity and Duty*; Boston, *Human Nature in its Fourfold State*, p. 300.

326. Abernethy, *Physick for the Soul*, p. 488, quoted by Buckle [note 183], p. 387; Hutcheson [note 325], p. 387.

327. Baxter [note 323], vol. 1, pp. 237, 245.

328. Burnet's *History of His Own Time*, vol. 1, p. 108; Mackintosh [note 138], vol. 3, p. 269.

329. Baxter [note 323], vol. 1, p. 229.

330. Isaac Borrow, *Of Industry*, p. 104.

331. Ibid. p. 3.

332. Ibid. p. 78.

333. Ibid. p. 62.

334. Ibid. p. 94. Cf. A. C. Applegarth, *Quakers in Pennsylvania* (1892), p. 10, and William Penn, *Fruits of Solitude* (1697).

335. Selections from the Records of the Kirk-Sessions of Aberdeen, p. 32, quoted in Mackintosh [note 138], vol. 3, p. 265.

336. *Le négociant patriote*, p. 240.

337. See Buckle [note 183], vol. 2, p. 381.

338. Applegarth [note 334], pp. 10, 16, 26.

339. St. Thomas [note 278], qu. 134, a. 1.

340. Cf. the destruction of images in the parish church of Perth on May 11, 1559, after Knox had stirred up the multitude. The *First Book of Discipline*, by the Scotch Reformer, condemns all idolatry. See John Knox, *Works*, vol. 2, p. 183; vol. 1, pp. 320, 361.

341. St. Thomas [note 278], qu. 135, 1.

342. Isaac Borrow [note 330], p. 66. Cf. also Baxter's *Directory*, vol. 1, pp. 108, 214, 378.

343. Borrow [note 330], pp. 50, 51.

344. Baxter [note 323], vol. 4, p. 104.

CHAPTER XXI

345. Max Weber, "Protestantische Ethik," in the *Archiv für die gesammte Staatswissenschaften*, vol. 25, p. 35.

346. Cf. his reply to H. Karl Fischer's criticisms, in the same journal, vol. 25, p. 246.

CHAPTER XXII

347. W. Sombart, *Krieg und Kapitalismus* (1913), p. 7.

348. For instances see note 347 in the last-named book.

349. Cf. Schmoller in his *Jahrbuch*, vol. 15, p. 8.

350. Cf. Levasseur [note 16], vol. 2, p. 256.

351. Cf. Sélincourt [note 79], p. 259.

352. Cf. Unwin [note 95], p. 168.

353. Cf. Levasseur [note 16], vol. 2, p. 37.

354. Cf. W. Sombart, *Die deutsche Volkswirtschaft im 19ten Jahrhundert* (3rd ed., 1913), p. 118.

355. Alberti [note 141], pp. 36, 37.

356. Cf. Sombart [note 354], p. 110 and [note 347], p. 28.

357. Dr. Shadwell in *The Times*, quoted by Schulze-Gaevernitz [note 203], p. 121.

358. J. Burckhardt [note 49A], vol. 1, p. 69.

359. W. Petty, *Several Essays in Political Arithmetic* (1699), p. 185.

360. *Discourse of the Religion of England,* 1667, quoted by H. Hallam, *Constitutional History,* vol. 3 (1827), p. 451.

361. *État de la France . . .* Par le Comte de Boulainvilliers, 6 vols., 1737. Cf. also Ch. Bénoit, *Histoire de l'édit de Nantes,* 5 vols., 1693.

362. Cf. Ranke, *Französische Geschichte,* vol. 3, p. 456.

CHAPTER XXIII

363. For the influence of aliens in England see W. Cunningham, *Alien Immigrants to England* (1897). For Russia, see Ernst Freiherr von d. Brüggen, *Wie Russland europäisch wurde. Studien zur Kulturgeschichte* (1885).

364. Broglio d'Ajano, *Die Venetianer Seidenindustrie* (1895), p. 24.

365. Sieveking, " Genueser Seidenindustrie " in Schmoller's *Jahrbuch,* vol. 21, p. 102.

366. A. Alidolfi, *Instruttione delle cose notabili di Bologna* (1621), p. 37. Cf. also, W. Sombart, *Luxus und Kapitalismus,* p. 180.

367. E. Parifet, *Histoire de la Fabrique lyonnaise* (1901), pp. 29, 30. Cf. Sombart [note 366], p. 179.

368. T. Geering, *Basels Industrie,* p. 471.

369. Bujatti, *Geschichte der Seidenindustrie Österreiches* (1893), p. 16.

370. For further details see, for England, Cunningham [note 363], Price, *The English Patents of Monopoly* (1906), pp. 55, 82. For Holland, O. Pringsheim, *Beiträge,* p. 31. For France, Levasseur [note 16] contains a mass of material. See, too, B. P. Boissonade, " L'industrie du Papier en Charente " in the *Bibliothèque du Pays Poitevin,* No. 9 (1899), p. 8. For Germany, G. Schanz, *Zur Geschichte der Kolonisation und Industrie in Franken* (1884); E. Gothein, *Wirtschaftsgeschichte des Schwarzwalds,* vol. 1 (1896); C. Frahne, *Textilindustrie im Wirtschaftsleben Schlesien's* (1905), p. 90. For Austria, Sbrik [note 56], p. 3. For Sweden, L. Beck, *Geschichte des Eisens,* vol. 2, pp. 900, 1290. For Russia, A. Brückner, *Peter der Grosse* (1879); F.

Matthæi, *Die Industrie Russlands in ihrer bisherigen Entwicklung,* vol. 1 (1871).

371. For further details see W. Sombart, *The Jews and Modern Capitalism.* Cf. also W. W. Kaplun-Kogan, *Die Wanderbewegungen der Juden* (1912). [See also, *Jewish Immigration to the United States,* by Samuel Joseph (Columbia University Studies in Political Science), 1913, and *Jewish Life in Modern Times,* by Israel Cohen (1914), Book I, ch. 1.]

372. Books about Protestant emigrants and immigrants are very numerous. I may mention the following as being among the best : C. Weiss, *Histoire des réfugiés protestants de France depuis la révocation de l'édit de Nantes jusqu'à nos jours,* 2 vols. (1853), which is the classical book on the subject ; W. E. I. Berg, *De Réfugiés in de Nederlanden na de herroeping ven het edict van Nantes,* 2 vols., 1845 ; J. S. Burn, *History of the French, Walloon, Dutch, and other Foreign Protestant Refugees settled in England, from Henry VIII to the Revocation of the Edict of Nantes, with notices of their trade and commerce, copious extracts from the registers, lists of the early settlers, etc.* (1846) ; Cunningham [note 363] ; Erman and Reclam, *Mémoires pour servir à l'histoire de réfugiés,* 9 vols. (1782–99) ; Charles Baird, *History of the Huguenot Emigration to America,* 2 vols. (1885).

373. Weiss [note 372], vol. 1, p. 104.

374. J. Sembrzycki, " Die Schotten und Engländer in Ostpreussen," in *Altpreussische Monatschrift,* vol. 29 (1892), p. 228.

375. See Moritz Jaffe, *Die Stadt Posen unter preuss. Herrschaft,* p. 14. Also T. A. Fisher, *The Scots in Germany,* and the same writer's *Scots in Eastern and Western Prussia.* See also E. Siegel, *Geschichte des Posamentiergewerbes* (1892), p. 42.

376. Paul Schulze, " Die Seidenindustrie," in *Handbuch der Wirtschaftskunde Deutschlands,* vol. 3 (1904), p. 658. Cf. Berg [note 372], vol. 1, p. 285.

377. Weiss [note 372], vol. 1, p. 225.

378. Ibid. vol. 1, p. 138.

379. O. Wiedfeldt, *Statistische Studien zur Entwicklungsgeschichte der Berliner Industrie* (1898), p. 209.

380. Ibid. p. 386.

381. In Erman and Reclam [note 372], vols. 5 and 6, there is a complete list of the industries established by Frenchmen

382. *Verzeichnis der Vorsteher und sämtlicher Mitglieder der*

teutsch und französisch vereinigten Kaufmannschaft der Tuch- und Seidenhandlung hiesiger Residenzien nach alphabetischer Ordnung zum Anfang des Jahres 1808 von den Ältesten aus den Gildebüchern angefertigt und zu haben bei der Witwe Arendt im Börsenhause.

383. Bayle, *Dict. hist. et crit.*, in article "Kuchlin."

384. Berg [note 372], vol. 1, p. 167.

385. Ibid. vol. 1, p. 218 ; Weiss [note 372], vol. 2, p. 18.

386. See also Ricard, *Le négoce d'Amsterdam* (1723), p. 6. This book came under my notice after the publication of my book on the Jews and modern capitalism. Ricard relates that the Stock Exchange, although it had 4,500 members, was generally full, save only on Saturdays, "when the Jews were not present."

387. J. N. de Stoppelaar, *Balthasar de Moucheron* (1901), quoted by S. van Brakel, *De hollandsche Handelscompagnie en der zevenentiende eeuv* (1908), p. 4.

388. Leti, *Teatro belgico*, 2, p. 148, quoted by Berg [note 372], vol. 1, p. 212.

389. See Weiss [note 372], vol. 2, pp. 135–6.

390. Ibid. vol. 2, p. 135.

391. Berg [note 372], vol. 1, p. 169.

392. O. Pringsheim, *Beiträge*, p. 32.

393. W. Cunningham, *Alien Immigrants to England*, p. 69.

394. See Douglas Campbell, *The Puritans*, vol. 1, p. 269.

395. Cf. Weiss [note 372], vol. 1, p. 132.

396. For fuller details see J. S. Burn [note 372], p. 254 ; Cunningham [note 393], pp. 178, 212, 235, 263 ; Campbell [note 394], vol. 1, p. 489, and Lecky, *History of the Eighteenth Century*, vol. 1, p. 205.

397. The figures are taken from the article "Auswanderung" (by E. von Philippovich) in the *Handwörterbuch der Staatswissenschaften*, vol. 1, p. 283.

398. E.g. Tocqueville, Chevalier, F. Löher, to name but three. Roscher utilized these reports in his splendid chapter on the "Geistigen Character des Koloniallebens" in his book on Colonies (1st ed., 1848 ; 3rd ed., 1885).

399. Th. Vogelstein [note 126A], p. 177.

400. F. Ratzel, *Vereinigte Staaten*, vol. 2, p. 579.

CHAPTER XXIV

401. Petrarca, *Epist. de reb. famil.*, lib. xx, letter 1. [The original Latin is a beautiful piece of writing, well worthy, as Sombart says, of being read more than once.]

402. *Mémoires de Colbert au roi*, 1670. *Lettres*, ed. Clement, vol. 7, p. 323.

403. K. Häbler, *Die Fuggersche Handlung*, p. 56.

404. Levasseur [note 16], vol. 2, p. 546.

405. Cf. P. Kaeppelin [note 65], p. 201.

406. Quoted by Ranke [note 362], vol. 4, p. 322.

407. Ibid.

408. Berg [note 372], vol. 1, p. 218; Le Moine de l'Espine, *Le négoce d'Amsterdam* (1710), p. 39.

409. Mariet, a wine merchant of Paris, got away with 600,000 florins; Gaylen, a bookseller of Lyons, with a million, and his brother with 100,000. The majority of the rich merchants came to Holland from Normandy, Brittany, Poitou, and Guienne, often enough in their own ships. See Berg [note 372], vol. 1, p. 218; Weiss [note 372], vol. 2, p. 18.

410. Cf. S. van Brakel, *Die Hollandsche Handelscompagnie*, p. xiv.

411. Levasseur [note 16], vol. 2, p. 293.

412. Onslow Burrish [note 86], p. 353.

413. See Weiss [note 372], vol. 1, p. 132, and Berg [note 372], vol. 1, p. 219.

414. W. Sombart, *The Jews and Modern Capitalism*, pp. 55, 87.

415. According to Erasmus Philips, *State of the Nation* (quoted by James, *Worsted Manufacture*, 1857, p. 207), English exports between 1702 and 1712 were of the average annual value of £2,881,357; according to Woods, *Survey of Trade*, it was £2,389,872 in the years 1707–10, and £2,103,148 in the years 1713 and 1714. See Anderson [note 132], vol. 3, pp. 41, 63.

416. O. Burrish [note 86], part 2, section 9.

417. Hayne's *Great Britain's Glory* (1715), p. 15, quoted by James [note 415]. Cf. also Cunningham [note 74], vol. 2, p. 196.

418. Postlethwayt, *Dictionary of Commerce*, article " Assiento."

419. See Adam Smith, *Wealth of Nations*, book iv, ch. 6.

420. Cf. Bento Carqueja, *O capitalismo moderno e as suas origens em Portugal* (1908), p. 132.

421. Cf. James [note 415], p. 184. See also Postlethwayt [note 418], article "Brazil."

422. Bento Carqueja [note 420], p. 125.

423. v. Eschwege [note 188], p. 284.

CHAPTER XXV

424. Cf. W. Sombart [note 354], ch. 8.

425. Vierkandt [note 10], p. 109.

426. For a detailed study of the point see W. Sombart [note 354], p. 136.

427. L. Muratori, *SS. rer. ital.*, vol. 12, p. 1011 (for Milan); vol. 18, p. 172 (for Bologna, 1356).

428. L. Darmstaedter and R. du Bois-Reymond, *Vier tausend Jahre Pionierarbeit in den exacten Wissenschaften* (1904), p. 24.

429. W. Sombart [note 354], p. 139.

CHAPTER XXVI

430. W. Sombart, *The Jews and Modern Capitalism*, p. 170.

431. Alberti [note 141], p. 256.

432. G. Freytag [note 14], vol. 2, p. 228.

433. Davidsohn [note 17], vol. 1, p. 601.

434. Mrs. Richard Green, *Town Life in the Fifteenth Century* (1894), vol. 1, p. 152; vol. 2, p. 156.

435. P. Hume Brown [note 73], p. 163.

436. Max Scheler, *Über Ressentiment und moralisches Werturteil* (1912), a brilliant essay.

CHAPTER XXVII

437. *Année sociologique*, vol. 6, p. 483.

438. See Sombart's Essay, " Der kapitalistische Unternehmer,"

in *Archiv für Sozialwissenschaft und soziale Politik*, vol. 29, p. 698.

439. Alberti [note 141], p. 137.
440. A. Carnegie in his *Autobiography*.
441. Dr. Strousberg [note 234], p. 396.
442. Hume's Essays, vol. 2, p. 57.